THIRD EDITION

# Media, Crime, and Criminal Justice

## IMAGES, REALITIES, AND POLICIES

**RAY SURETTE**

*University of Central Florida*

THOMSON ™

WADSWORTH

Australia • Brazil • Canada • Mexico • Singapore
Spain • United Kingdom • United States

# THOMSON

## WADSWORTH

*Media, Crime, and Criminal Justice:*
*Images, Realities, and Policies,* **Third Edition**
*Ray Surette*

Senior Criminal Justice Editor:
  Carolyn Henderson Meier
Assistant Editor: Jana Davis
Editorial Assistant: Rebecca Johnson
Technology Project Manager: Susan DeVanna
Marketing Manager: Terra Schultz
Marketing Assistant: Jaren Boland
Marketing Communications Manager: Linda Yip
Project Manager, Editorial Production:
  Jennie Redwitz
Creative Director: Rob Hugel
Art Director: Vernon Boes
Print Buyer: Doreen Suruki

Permissions Editor: Kiely Sisk
Production Service: Mona Tiwary, ITC
Photo Researcher: Stephen Forsling
Copy Editor: Kay Mikel
Illustrator: International Typesetting and
  Composition
Cover Designer: Yvo Riezebos
Cover Image: © Louie Psihoyos/Corbis
Compositor: International Typesetting and
  Composition
Text and Cover Printer: Transcontinental/
  Louiseville

**Thomson Higher Education**
**10 Davis Drive**
**Belmont, CA 94002-3098**
**USA**

For more information about our products,
contact us at:
**Thomson Learning Academic Resource**
**Center 1-800-423-0563**
For permission to use material from this text
or product, submit a request online at
**http://www.thomsonrights.com**.
Any additional questions about permissions
can be submittted by e-mail to
**thomsonrights@thomson.com**.

Printed in Canada
1 2 3 4 5 6 7 10 09 08 07 06

Library of Congress Control Number: 2005938044

Student Edition: ISBN 0-534-55147-5

*To my family: Susan, Jennifer, Paul, and Timothy—thank you*

# *About the Author*

**Ray Surette** has a doctorate in criminology from Florida State University and is a Professor of Criminal Justice and Legal Studies at the University of Central Florida. His crime and media research interests revolve around the media's effects on perceptions of crime and justice and media-generated crime and criminal justice policies. He has published numerous articles and books on media, crime, and criminal justice topics and is an internationally recognized scholar in the area. He has published two other books that also explore the relationship between media and crime: *The Media and Criminal Justice Policy* and *Justice and the Media: Issues and Research*. He has published research on the growth and development of public information officers in criminal justice agencies, crime-and-justice infotainment programming, copycat crime among incarcerated juveniles, the effects of massive news coverage of celebrity trials on similarly charged noncovered trials and on police recruits, and the effect of news coverage of corrections on municipal jail population trends. He is currently working on a book on copycat crime as well as studying the use of computer-aided camera surveillance systems in public spaces and the associated media portrait and public acceptance of these systems; media-oriented terrorist events; and media use, fear of crime, and criminal justice policy support.

# Brief Contents

# Contents

## Chapter 8

## *The Media and Criminal Justice Policy*       *201*

## Chapter 9

## *Media and Crime and Justice in the Twenty-First Century*       *224*

# Foreword

Everyone who studies crime and justice shares a sense of frustration about the way media depictions dominate the common viewpoint on crime and criminal justice, often in ways that distort reality. The television show *CSI*, for example, is great entertainment but hardly fits the way 99 percent of crimes are solved. So-called real police stories follow some officers as they go about their duties, but even though the film is real, the portrait of police work that results is distorted by the focus on chase scenes and angry encounters. *Judge Judy* bears little resemblance to actual judges in demeanor or behavior. *The Practice* always presents cases with some sort of twist, but such cases are the exception rather than the rule. The nightly news covers crime with an eye to generating high ratings, not great insight. American culture has an affinity for crime as a source of stimulation and even entertainment, but the result is that what we think we know about crime and justice from the way our media portray it often corresponds poorly to the everyday reality of crime and justice.

For those who are professionals in the business of criminal justice—those who wish to reform or improve justice practices and crime prevention effectiveness—the media portrayals are often an impediment. It is not so much that the media get it wrong as that they focus on aspects of crime and justice that are, in the scheme of things, not so important. Of course we all want to apprehend serial killers and stop predatory sex offenders, but they are uncommon in the life of the justice system. The more pressing themes of improving the effectiveness of treatment programs, youth prevention systems, crime control strategies, and so forth can get lost in the way the media focus on images of crime that are much more engrossing to the everyday citizen.

It is, therefore, with extraordinary pleasure that I welcome the third edition of Ray Surette's *Media, Crime, and Criminal Justice* to the *Wadsworth Contemporary Issues in Crime and Justice Series*. Created to provide detailed and effective exposure of important or emerging issues and problems that ordinarily receive insufficient attention in traditional textbooks, the series also provokes thought and changes perceptions by challenging us to become more sophisticated consumers of crime-and-justice knowledge. Its titles seek to expose myths about crime and justice, deepen understandings of the nature of crime and the processes of justice, and inspire new perspectives on these topics.

For those who seek a book that will make you an informed student of crime-and-justice policy and practice, you could not do better than the one you are now holding. Professor Surette is an astute student of popular culture, the social power of symbols, and the effect of media on public imagination. In this book he provides a detailed examination of the ways that media coverage affects our popular understanding of justice. The results are sometimes subtle and sometimes blatant. For example, the way the nightly news covers crime creates a subtle bias on the part of the public that our cities are dangerous and that the justice system is incapable of protecting innocents. By contrast, the way punishment is covered creates a much less subtle bias that our system of justice is lenient. Both of these biases are partly right, but mostly wrong. And the reality—much more complex than the public perception—is often not widely understood.

Surette writes about every aspect of crime and justice. The book opens with a thorough and authoritative description of the way our "realities" about crime and justice are constructed from social sources of knowledge. It is this fact that makes the media portrayal of crime and justice so important, because media are among the most powerful sources of social information. The book then considers in turn the three main agencies of criminal justice: the police, the courts, and corrections, with a chapter devoted to each topic. The final chapters consider the broader problem of crime prevention and criminal justice policy in the context of a media-dominated social construction of crime.

In the end, this is a book that helps us to rethink crime by offering a critical perspective on how we go about understanding it. Crime is not popular culture, and criminal justice is not entertainment. On the contrary, crime is a crucial social problem rooted in related social problems such as inequality and poverty. Criminal justice is a key function of the state that is less powerful with regard to our safety than we might like but more important to our everyday rights than we would ordinarily think.

This is an important book, a book that carves out new areas for thinking and challenges the popular mind-set about crime and justice. I commend it to you.

**Todd R. Clear**
*Series Editor*

# Preface

The third edition of *Media, Crime, and Criminal Justice* is written expressly for collegiate undergraduate criminal justice, students. It is my belief that to understand contemporary crime and justice students have to understand the role the media play in the life cycle of criminal justice issues and policies. Coming of age in a media culture where crime-and-justice content is pervasive, undergraduates need and are attracted to courses that help them understand the media ocean they live in. They also bring a priceless enthusiasm and interest in the subject, and this fully revised third edition taps into that enthusiasm. This book also helps students to become critical media consumers and insightful observers of the ever-evolving relationship between media, crime, and justice. Students who have not considered the linkages between the media, crime, and justice will find the discussions enlightening and will never again sit through a crime show or newscast without a thoughtful reaction and recognition of the underlying processes that generate the crime-and-justice media they receive.

The book organizes a large amount of research, concerns, and criminal justice policy efforts from far-flung disciplines. Knowledge is drawn from criminal justice, criminology, sociology, political science, law, public administration, journalism, medicine, psychology, and communication research. Sources include traditional academic and professional journals as well as numerous popular culture media such as magazines, newspapers, music, videogames, films, and the Internet. As an undergraduate introductory text, the third edition serves as an entrée to research questions and social concerns relevant to crime and justice without the weight of extensive graduate-level discussions of statistics and research designs. The discussions provide a basic understanding of the theoretical ideas and concepts that frame the research, the major findings that have been generally accepted by researchers in the field, the issues that are still under debate, and the questions that have yet to be addressed.

The media are especially important in the construction of crime-and-justice reality, and an important goal of this edition is to help students to be critical media consumers and insightful observers of the evolving relationship between the media, crime, and justice. Massively covered criminal trials, advances in media technology, new types of media content—and new ways of delivering the content—continually increase the impact of media on crime and justice. In addition, social concern that media violence causes social violence, parallel efforts to use the media to reduce crime and violence, and the development of an intrusive, intensive media-driven culture work to feed public and academic interest. However, most people interact with the media as passive consumers. They are conditioned to receive media knowledge without considering where this information comes from, what effect it has on their attitudes and perceptions, or how it affects society. This book encourages readers to ask questions about the media, such as why certain images of crime are linked together in newscasts, why one crime story is placed on the front page and another on page eleven, and why some explanations of crime and some criminal justice policies are emphasized over others.

The third edition will serve as the main text in a media, crime, and justice course and as a supplementary work in courses where the instructor wishes to feature connections between media, crime, and justice. It is a particularly useful supplementary text for introduction to criminal justice, introduction to law enforcement, criminal justice policy, victimization, and crime prevention courses. The text can be used by students with or without substantial backgrounds in communications, journalism, criminal justice, law, and the additional disciplines that make up this inherently interdisciplinary subject.

## NEW FOR THE THIRD EDITION

In the second edition of *Media, Crime, and Criminal Justice,* material was organized along media lines with entire chapters devoted to the content of crime and justice in news and entertainment media. In the third edition, material is reorganized with the perspective of the undergraduate criminal justice student in mind. The presentation follows criminal justice system dimensions, and new chapters are devoted to media and crime, media and crime fighting, media and corrections, and media and the judicial system. Organized into nine chapters, the book now follows the content and influence of the media from the committing of crime through the sequential components of the criminal justice system as typically covered in undergraduate criminal justice courses.

Within this new organization, the connection between media and criminal justice policy is emphasized. Pervasive media images of predatory criminals work as steering currents on criminal justice policy, and each chapter includes a discussion of how media renditions affect a particular area of criminal justice policy. Recognition of this policy linkage is vital because the media determine in important ways what behaviors we criminalize, how we approach crime control, how we handle criminal cases, how we sentence convicted offenders, and what correctional conditions and programs we create. In addition, the media's portraits of crime and justice not only influence the activities of the entire criminal justice system but sway the public's beliefs about, expectations of, and demands placed on the system.

In a very real way the media construct our crime and justice policy. To help students understand how this happens, the book employs the theoretical perspective of social constructionism. Chapter 2 introduces the basic ideas and elements of social constructionism and applies this theory to media, crime, and justice. Chapters 3 through 6 cover the basic elements of crime and criminal justice. Public interest is most acute at the beginning of the crime process and wanes as one moves through the criminal justice system. The order of these chapters reflects that interest, with crime and criminality addressed in Chapter 3, law enforcement in Chapter 4, the courts in Chapter 5, and corrections in Chapter 6. Chapter 7 focuses on crime control and issues related to increased surveillance and public acceptance of this in the post-9/11 world. Chapter 8 deals with media influence on criminal justice policy, and Chapter 9 looks ahead to two opposing but equally troubling futures based either on a free-wheeling infotainment model or a heavily restricted model of media and crime-and-justice issues. Additional changes found in the third edition include the following:

- **Chapter 1: Predators, Pictures, and Policy** This chapter serves solely as an introduction to the media, crime, and justice relationship and provides historical and conceptual overviews. Discussions of infotainment, reality television, the blurring of fact and fiction, and crime and justice as a mediated experience are included.
- **Chapter 2: Social Constructionism** This new chapter is dedicated to explaining the ideas of social constructionism. The chapter provides applications of social constructionism to the media, crime, and justice area within discussions of the media's role in the social construction of road rage, killer drunks, and the Rodney King arrest.
- **Chapter 3: Crime and Criminality** Another new chapter, it covers the "criminological theory" that one finds in the media. The chapter discusses how crime, criminals, and explanations of criminality are

portrayed and how these media portraits can be criminogenic and related to criminal behavior. Copycat crime and media-oriented terrorism are discussed in detail.

- **Chapter 4: Crime Fighters** This chapter focuses on the media portrait of crime fighting. It represents a new approach to this issue and compares professional sworn law enforcement officers with civilian crime fighters as they are mutually constructed in the media. Material on the unique nature of the portrait of policing found in the infotainment media is also included.

- **Chapter 5: The Courts** This chapter covers the judicial system as currently portrayed in the media, focusing on the media co-optation of the courts as infotainment vehicles within massively covered "media trials" (the O. J. Simpson murder trial being a well-known example). In addition, discussions of long-standing issues such as pretrial publicity, courtroom control of news media, reporter access to proceedings and offenders, and new discussions on the images of courtrooms and male and female attorneys are included.

- **Chapter 6: Corrections** This new chapter covers the media portrait of correctional institutions, prisoners, and correctional officers. The chapter reviews the limited sources of knowledge the public has regarding corrections and the implications of this limitation on the social construction of corrections and correctional policy. The stereo-types of prisoners, correctional officers, and correctional institutions found in the media are discussed.

- **Chapter 7: Crime Control** This chapter discusses how criminal justice practitioners increasingly use the media and media technology to reduce crime, gather information, patrol communities, deter offenders, and process cases. Expanded and reorganized sections on Madison Avenue–style anticrime advertisements and the judicial use of cameras and videotapes in court proceedings are included. In addition, the recent explosion of camera-based public surveillance systems is discussed in depth.

- **Chapter 8: The Media and Criminal Justice Policy** This chapter provides an overview of the media content of crime and justice and its explicit connections to criminal justice policy. The chapter details three tenets of crime-and-justice media that have direct implications for criminal justice policy and discusses the media's relationship to the general public's beliefs and attitudes about crime and justice.

- **Chapter 9: Media and Crime and Justice in the Twenty-First Century** This new concluding chapter distills the main points and forecasts what readers might expect to find over the next decades using scenarios of two opposing but equally troublesome futures. In scenario one, totally free-wheeling, interactive, infotainment media dominate in a society having little social control on the media. In scenario two, strict social control on the media exists with rigid restrictions on crime-and-justice content along with extensive media-based anticrime and public surveillance efforts. The lessons of each scenario and the coming age of "criminal justice pixel policy" are discussed.

Reflecting the third edition reorganization, additional pedagogical features include the following:

- Classic media examples and a collection of lighter sidebar material frame discussions and highlight connections between what students are reading in the text and what they are seeing, hearing, and reading in their daily lives.
- Chapter objectives are outlined at the beginning of each chapter.
- Discussion questions, in-class activities, out-of-class assignments, and suggested readings can be found at the end of each chapter.
- Numerous tables, figures, and photos illustrate theoretical ideas and research findings.
- Key terms are set off in boldface type in the text, and a full glossary has been included at the end of the book.
- An updated bibliography and substantive end-of-chapter notes are also featured.

## ACKNOWLEDGMENTS

I would first like to thank the individuals at Thomson Wadsworth who contributed to the development and production of this book. Sabra Horne, Shelley Murphy, and Jay Whitney provided encouragement and support in the early development of the project and were especially helpful in conceptualizing the transition from the second to the third edition. Elise Smith kept the developmental process moving and alive. I worked closely with Carolyn Henderson Meier throughout the final publication stages, and this book would not exist without her efforts, suggestions, and insights as editor. Rebecca Johnson diligently prepared the manuscript for production. Kay Mikel provided excellent editing. Stephen Forsling acquired the photographs, Kiely Sisk assisted in obtaining permissions, and ITC created the artwork and graphics. All of them exhibit an attention to detail that I lack, and I thank all of them for their patience and professionalism.

Also deserving of thanks are the many reviewers who, over the years, have offered their insights into the present and previous editions of the book. They include:

David Altheide, Arizona State University
Randolph William Boucott, Northeastern Illinois University
William Farrell, University of Michigan, Flint
Michael Hallett, University of North Florida
Byron Johnson, Morehead State University
Richard Kania, University of North Carolina, Pembroke
Raymond Kessler, Sul Ross State University
Lynette Lee-Sammons, California State University, Sacramento
Lucien Lombardo, Old Dominion University
Joan Luxenburg, University of Central Oklahoma
Joan McCord, Temple University
Marianne O. Nielsen, Northern Arizona University
Caryl Segal, University of Texas at Arlington
Rick Sheffield, Kenyon College

Thanks are also due to Roy Roberg, the former editor of the *Wadsworth Contemporary Issues in Crime and Justice Series*, for his contributions to the first edition. I extend my sincere appreciation to them all; the final work has been much improved and strengthened by their suggestions regarding organization, materials, and knowledge.

Finally, my family deserves special thanks. My wife Susan—the love of my life—and my three children, Jennifer, Paul, and Timothy, provide constant love and understanding. Without them, my personal reality would certainly be empty and uninspired.

# PREDATORS, PICTURES, AND POLICY

CHAPTER OBJECTIVES

After reading Chapter 1, you should have an appreciation of the relationship of media to crime and criminal justice and media's importance for criminal justice policy. You should also have an overview of the history of crime-and-justice media and understand basic differences between the types of media and types of media content important for the media portraits of crime and justice commonly found today.

## MEDIA AND CRIMINAL JUSTICE: A FORCED MARRIAGE

Why should one study crime, justice, and the media? There is one very good reason and many secondary ones. Before we explore those reasons, try a quick experiment. Pick up today's newspaper and look at the local television schedule. Note the number of shows that deal with committing, solving, or fighting crime. Next turn to the movie listings and do the same. Flip through the newspaper, look especially at the local news section, and count the number of crime-and-justice stories. Do the same with the evening's televised local and national news programs. If you subscribe to any magazines, check their contents for articles that are crime or justice related. If you're reading a novel, is a crime or a criminal an important element of the story? Write down the names of five people who received a lot of publicity within the past two years. How many of the five were connected to a crime, investigation, or trial? Finally, note what people talked about at work or school yesterday and today. How often are crimes and justice issues discussed?

I'm willing to bet that much of your television and movies, your written and TV news, your pleasure reading, and your conversations involve crime-and-justice issues. From the fictional to the factual, crimes, criminals, investigations, and trials course through our media. At the most basic level, crime, justice, and the media have to be studied together because in twenty-first-century America they are inseparable, wedded to each other in a forced marriage. They cohabit in an often raucous, sometimes riotous, but ultimately unavoidable relationship.

How did the marriage come about? Crime and justice has always provided a substantial portion of the media's raw material. Criminal trials and heinous crimes, along with their victims, investigators, judges, attorneys, and citizens, provide the popular crime-and-justice stories, which are packaged, molded, and marketed. In tandem, the images, ideas, and narratives that dominate the media influence how people think about crime and justice. The behaviors we think should be criminalized, who we feel should be punished, what the punishments should be, and how we think the police, judges, attorneys, correctional officers, criminals, and victims should act are all influenced by the media portraits of crime and justice. Compounding these influences, the technological ability of media to gather, recycle, and disseminate information has never been faster or broader, and mass media has never been more diverse. More crime-and-justice media content is available to more people via more avenues and in more formats today than ever before. A flood of technologies—from CDs, to cable television and satellite networks, to VCRs, to the Internet, to electronic games, to virtual reality devices—create a fast-paced media inspired and dominated by entertainment values and visual images.[1] This new high-speed media world raises concerns when the media's pace and values are applied to society. It is a special concern in the area of crime and justice.

However, the fact that a contentious relationship exists between media and criminal justice is not the most important reason to study crime and the media. The most important effect of this marriage is on criminal justice policy. The media have had important effects on criminal justice policy in America for a long time. For example, the book *Uncle Tom's Cabin* had an effect on slave laws in the mid-1800s, the film *I Am a Fugitive from a Chain Gang* affected U.S. correctional practices in the 1930s, and more recent movies and books like *The Silence of the Lambs* influenced policies aimed at a "rampant" serial killer threat. All of these attest to the ability of media to drive criminal justice policy.

Today that ability has risen to new heights. We live in an era of **pixel policy** where media renditions of reality frequently drive crime-and-justice practices at blinding speed.[2] The media and criminal justice policy link is easily seen in the contemporary craze for **memorial criminal**

**justice policies**, which are named for individuals, usually victims. Hence, today we have "Megan's Law" and "Amber Alerts" due to massive publicity of a heinous crime and its innocent victim. Even when not named after an individual, much of our criminal justice policy exists because of the impact of high-profile crimes being co-opted as symbols for specific policy campaigns. The "Three Strikes and You're Out" legislation and the co-optation of the kidnapping and murder of twelve-year-old Polly Klaas in California in the late 1990s is a classic example of this pixel policy process.[3] Today no politician can be "soft" on crime, and we even expect the president to hold a position on local crime policy. It was not that long ago that it would have been inappropriate for the White House to have a national crime policy. Crime was seen as a local issue and a realm for state level policy at most. But in today's media environment, the president and Congress are expected to forward policy for local street crime, neighborhood school violence, municipal police needs, and lower court criminal trials.

That local criminal justice issues are seen as needing national policy responses is due to the national character of the media–criminal justice marriage. Current criminal justice policy has been described as just another commodity governed by what is newsworthy and salable via the media—what fits the needs of the media and voters.[4] Thus contemporary media cover local crime through a national lens. In addition to raising selected local crimes to national prominence, local crime is portrayed in the media as being beyond the ability and resources of local criminal justice. The solutions to crime painted as sensible are given a punitive federal orientation. "What must the nation do about crime?" is the question of the day rather than "What does my community need to do about crime?" The most important reason for examining the often unhappy media–criminal justice marriage is that it ultimately determines how we react to crime and how we spend our tax dollars.

Although most important in terms of actual social impact, the media–criminal justice policy connection is not seen by the public as the most significant media effect on crime and justice. The public worries most about a set of concerns more visible in the media. These concerns—media-oriented terrorist events, copycat crime, coverage of media trials, and media-generated social violence—provide secondary reasons for studying the media, crime, and justice. These are all significant issues, which will be discussed in depth, but the media's ultimate impact is on how we spend our taxes, what and who we criminalize, and how we deal with offenders. The criminal justice policies we support and pursue due to the media ultimately affect these secondary worrisome issues as well.

# THE BLURRING OF FACT AND FICTION

What is the state of the media–criminal justice marriage today? First, everyone appears to be wedded to the media in some fashion. Whether measured in terms of hours of television viewed, movie attendance, music purchases, or the popularity of video games and the Internet, the social experience and impact of media are enormous. Today, virtually everyone is an audience member of some form of media. In a basic way, media provide the broadly shared, common knowledge in our society independent of occupation, education, and social status. The knowledge acquired via mass media is generally perceived as less important and more transient, but also as more fun and enjoyable. When compared to religious information or institutional histories, which can extend for centuries, media-generated knowledge has a shorter life span, usually not exceeding a generation. Indeed, generations are often defined and can be distinguished by the media that is current during their youth. This is particularly true for popular music. Denoting the shorter temporal knowledge cycle, media knowledge and products can be observed to mature, age, and die. They find their way to the mass media kidneys (for example, game shows and late night cable talk shows for once popular celebrities) and are eventually excreted as historical footnotes of popular culture.

With technological progress and the broadening influence of media, concerns began to grow among researchers, academics, social observers, and a number of government and public individuals. In addition to worries about possible direct criminogenic effects such as copycat crime and media-oriented terrorism, concern rose when it was realized that the extracts of reality the media create and market, whether in entertainment or news, influence the public's view of reality.[5] Even nonentertainment media snapshots of reality found in the news present a specific, narrow slice of the world that has been chosen, reshaped, and marketed to the public.[6] Although the bulk of media content, even the content purported to be real, is usually recognized by the public as unrealistic and heavily edited, continued exposure to media content ultimately influences one's view of reality, and this influence increases in areas where alternate sources of information are less available. Like candy to cavities, a diet heavy on media will rot your perception of reality.

Within this media-generated perception of crime-and-justice reality, a core set of images, headed by the image of a predatory violent stranger, is identified and exploited by both the media and criminal justice policy makers.[7] The contemporary media serve as an ever-quickening and expanding knowledge circulatory system; quickly moving ideas, images, and information. An important recent development is the **looping** of media content. Looping results when events and information are repeatedly cycled and recycled through the media into the culture to reemerge in new contexts in differing media.[8] For example, a police car chase video cycles from courtroom evidence to local news footage, to infotainment program content, to a clip inserted in a comedy movie, to varied and sundry Internet websites. This continuous looping and reformatting of content results in the blurring of fact and fiction. People come to believe fictional events are real, that real events didn't happen, and hybrid—part real, part fiction—events flourish. Such effects are particularly common in the crime-and-justice arena. Thus many believe Hannibal Lector is a real serial killer and Jack the Ripper is fictional, and real events such as the Kennedy assassination become hopelessly confounded in a blur of factual and fictional portrayals. In an odd way, people no longer trust the news (which is supposed to be true) but seem to be more willing to believe entertainment and infotainment media (which don't try very hard to be truthful). Today many do not believe the news reports regarding the conclusions of the Warren Commission Report on the Kennedy assassination but do believe the Oliver Stone movie about it.[9]

In the end, the direction of influence between crime and justice on one side and media on the other is a two-way street—the mass media influence crime and justice, and crime-and-justice events become grist for the media. In addition to the myriad entertainment products that deal in crime and justice, the media and media technology are simultaneously perceived as both a major cause of crime and violence and a powerful potential solution to crime. While blaming the media for many social ills, we also look to the media to help reduce violence and drug use, deter crime, and bolster the image of the criminal justice system. In law enforcement we look to the media to aid in criminal investigations, manhunts, and street and vehicle patrols. In the courts we look for assistance in processing criminal cases, reducing case backlogs, conducting trials, presenting testimony and evidence, and deciding guilt. In corrections, we look to media images for our perception of correctional institutions, programs and personnel, and to enhance security and surveillance. The media–criminal justice marriage is truly a love-hate relationship, and as far as criminal justice policy is concerned, it is the most important relationship that exists. To understand both the historical development and the future of crime and justice in America, one must take into account the influences of the media and understand how crime-and-justice events become popular media products. Gaining that understanding is the basic goal of this book.

# A Brief History of Crime-and-Justice Media

A necessary step in exploring the relationship between the media and crime and justice is to first look at the basic structure of the media in America. For a discussion of crime and justice, the media can be thought of as roughly structured along two dimensions: types of media and types of content. Four types of media are found in the United States: print, sound, visual, and new media. As shown in Table 1.1, each media type has enjoyed dominance during a historic period. Of course, all types are still found today, and the new media often combine print, sound, and visuals in new ways. Table 1.1 also reflects the historic trend in the development of media to include more information, which is more easily accessed, and which makes the mediated experience more and more similar to actual experience. Each media type's relationship to crime and justice can be understood through a brief history.

## Print Media

Print was the first medium to generate a mass market, usually dated as beginning in the 1830s with the emergence of the U.S. penny press newspapers—daily newspapers that were popular in major Eastern cities. One of the first such newspapers, the *New York Sun,* began to include a daily police-court news column in 1833 and experienced a notable circulation boost.[10] Other penny dailies followed suit, and human interest crime stories quickly became a staple of these inexpensive and popular newspapers. Class oriented, these early papers portrayed crime as the result of class inequities and often discussed justice as a process manipulated by the rich and prominent. They frequently contained due process arguments and advocated due process reforms while presenting individual crimes as examples of larger social and political failings needing correction.[11] Helped by the success of the penny press, which spurred an increased literacy rate, a market for weekly crime magazines exemplified by the *National Police Gazette* soon followed. By the twentieth century, magazines focusing on crime, sex scandals, corruption, sports, glamour, and show business all flourished.[12] Providing an early model for contemporary news and modern trash-TV programs, mass marketing and consumption of crime infotainment was born.

***Detective and Crime Thrillers***   The two most popular print-based crime genres to emerge in nineteenth-century print media were detective and crime thriller magazines and "dime" novels. Both were escapist literature,

| TABLE 1.1 | Crime-and-Justice Media History | |
|---|---|---|

*Sound Media Dominate*

| Antiquity | Theater, folktales, and myths | Limited access and distribution to local audiences; urban legends are a current example. |
|---|---|---|
| 1200–1500s | Ballads | Hip-hop music provides contemporary examples. |

*Print Media Dominate*

| 1400–1700s | Pamphlets and broadsheets | Gallows sermons were a popular criminal justice example. |
|---|---|---|
| 1830s | Penny press | First mass-marketed media. |
| 1880s | Dime novels | Detective and crime novels marketed to audience segments. |
| 1890s | Yellow journalism | First mass infotainment media. |

*Visual Media Dominate*

| 1910s | Film introduced | First homogenized audience. |
|---|---|---|
| 1920s | Commercial radio networks | Modern programming and economic structure established; first in-home delivery. |
| 1930s | Film dominates | Social concerns; first serious research and censorship. |
| 1930–1940s | Comic books peak | Public crusades against them as corruptors of youth. |
| 1950s | Television | Mass visual, electronic, live, in-home delivery; origin of pixel media. |
| 1970s | Cable television | Narrowcasting and audience fragmentation across all media. |

*New Media Arrive*

| 1980s | Videocassette recorders | Unedited home access to films. |
|---|---|---|
| | Electronic games | First interactive media. |
| 1990s | Computer games and Internet | Digital reality and worldwide access. |
| 2000 to present | Virtual reality devices | Media and computer-augmented experiences; pixel policy era. |

and by the latter half of the nineteenth century they described crime as originating in individual personality or moral weakness rather than being due to broader social forces. By downplaying wider social and structural explanations of crime found in the earlier penny press newspapers, these novels helped reinforce the existing social order—the status quo. In addition, the "heroic" detectives in these works closely resembled the criminals they apprehended—they were calculating and often were odd loners.[13] Detective and crime thrillers of the late nineteenth century thus mark the beginning of a more violent popular media that was less critical of social conditions and contributed to the construction of a social reality where crime is predatory and rooted in individual failure more than in social ills. The portraits of crime and justice produced during this time are surprisingly similar to those found today; both present images that reinforce the status quo, promote the impression that competent, often heroic individuals are pursuing and capturing criminals, and encourage the belief that criminals can be readily recognized and crime ultimately curtailed through aggressive law enforcement efforts.

*Comic Books*    Marketed to both children and adults, one of the more socially influential print media to develop in the twentieth century was the comic book. From their beginning, comic books featured crime-fighting policemen, private detectives, and costumed superheroes. Combining pop art with printed texts, comic books have constructed some of the more sophisticated images and analyses of crime and justice found in the media.[14] Evolving out of the newspaper-based comic strips of the 1890s and combined with the twentieth-century pulp magazine market, comic books first appeared in the 1930s. In addition to fictional comic stories, reality-crime comics appeared in 1942, featuring stories about actual criminals and their crimes. These criminal-point-of-view comics became the most popular comic book genre between 1947 and 1954.[15] Similar to contemporary popular music and video games, comic books regularly underwent periods of public concern and attack, the strongest coming in the late 1940s and early 1950s. The outcry and criticisms resulted in a self-adopted industry code that banned torture, sadism, and detailed descriptions of crimes. Comic books enjoyed great popularity, particularly with young males into the 1980s, because they filled a media void. Comics could present criminals, heroes, and crime-fighting action beyond the sound limits imposed by radio and the technologically limited special effects of film and television. Today comic books have declined in popularity as electronic video games have gained in popularity. But comic books persist as part of the **multimedia web**, and their crime-and-justice portrayals still prosper via licensing deals that span films, toys, food, cartoons, and prime time television shows.

The primary difference between contemporary print media in its varied forms and contemporary electronic media is not found in their constructed images of crime and justice but in access to and social penetration of their content. From the late nineteenth-century media dominated by print to the contemporary media dominated by electronically delivered visual images, the constructed messages of crime and justice have remained relatively constant, but the social impact has

As this 1954 comic book cover illustrates, a morbid interest in heinous crimes and their exploitation can be found in many time periods and many types of media.

changed. To access print media, the consumer needs to be literate, gain access to the materials, and make a clear decision to use or not use them. Exposure to their content has therefore always been less "mass" and more selective. Exposure to the modern, electronically dominated mass media images and messages, on the other hand, is difficult to avoid. The first medium to have an omnipresent capability was audio, and it was distributed via radio broadcast networks.

## Sound Media

First delivered and mass-marketed via radio networks, pure audio media have evolved from vinyl records to 8-track tapes, to compact discs, to MPI files, and other digital forms. Sound media are obviously neither print nor visual, but they bridge the two by delivering information in a linear fashion akin to print while evoking mental images and emotions analogous to visuals. In the 1920s, radio networks dominated as the home entertainment and information medium.[16] Despite coexisting with film, radio portrayals of criminality were different. The primary difference being, of course, that violence could only be heard, not seen, on radio. Their impact should not be underestimated however. As Orson Welles discovered after his 1938 *War of the Worlds* radio broadcast caused social panic, for some, "hearing is believing."

Together with films, radio imagery established the cultural framework that television would subsequently exploit. Exemplified by coverage of the *Hindenburg* explosion and disaster, the Lindbergh baby kidnapping trial, and the Scopes "monkey" evolution trial, radio established itself as the first live, on-the-scene news reporting medium. The current television news format of thirty- to sixty-second news spots presented within established categories (the world, the nation, sports, weather, economics, crime, and so forth) originated with radio programming. Within these news categories, the industry use of "news themes" was created in which coverage of a particular type of crime would prevail. The news would give a type of crime saturation coverage for a short time and then turn to something new. Together with the producers of the film industry's newsreels, which brought weekly visual coverage of news to the public, radio producers created the style that television would embellish: short-term, visceral, emotional news coverage of discrete "events."

On the entertainment side, radio drama, particularly at its height during the 1930s and 1940s, included a substantial and popular—though never a dominant—proportion of crime-fighting, detective, and suspense programming.[17] During this time, a number of classic programs such as *The Shadow*, *Sherlock Holmes*, and *True Detective* could be heard. Other "Radio Noir" programs, as they came to be termed, gave the culture a host of private detectives including Nick Carter and Philip Marlowe, wise-cracking tough-guys who disdained the police. Radio crime programming also included hardened federal agents and reality programming. One popular early show,

*Gang Busters*, which began in 1935, is the forerunner of current crime stoppers and *Most Wanted* style programming. The best known of the early radio cop shows was *Dragnet*, which made a successful transition to television in the 1950s and established the format for the 1950s television docudramas based on police procedures and investigations.

The suspense programming found in radio also foretold the more graphic visual effects found in today's media. Unrestrained by concerns about offensive pictures, radio was able to conjure up mental images via sound effects that could not be shown in films of the time. These grisly sound effects preceded today's graphic visual special effects—sizzling bacon for an electric chair execution, Life-Savers crushed between teeth for bones being snapped, chopped cabbages for heads being severed, and wet noodles squished with a bathroom plunger for the eating of human flesh. Collectively, radio crime-and-justice programming provided the models for modern day crime-and-justice reality programming, the contemporary stereotypes of criminals and criminal justice, the heavy emphasis on law enforcement activities over other segments of the criminal justice system, and the exploitation of sensational heinous crimes. All aspects of contemporary crime-and-justice media that are so berated today are traceable to early radio. Not surprisingly, television programmers borrowed heavily from this tested and popular set of narratives and themes in developing their crime programming in the 1950s.

## *Visual Media*

*Film*   It was films at the beginning of the twentieth century that first provided the media with the ability to blanket all of society. The movie industry nationalized media content by making its content available to every social, economic, and intellectual stratum. Initially silent and inexpensive, the movies did not even require a common language as radio programming did. The images were universally available and widely consumed, and film rapidly came to reflect and shape American culture. By 1917 the U.S. motion picture industry was established as the premier commercial entertainment form in the world. By the 1930s some 80 million people per week in a U.S. population of 122 million (or two of every three Americans) attended a movie.[18] With their immense popularity, the movies were the first modern mass media, and their emergence heralded the creation of a twentieth-century mass culture that crossed geographic, economic, and ethnic lines. As both a social event and a source of social information, movies were the first medium able to bypass the traditional socializing agents of church, school, family, and community and directly reach individuals with information and images.

Though not every movie, television show, or radio program produced during a particular time frame portrayed the same crime-and-justice theme, dominant themes have been identified with certain periods.[19] Beginning with films and carried on in radio dramas, the first media criminals were descendants of Western outlaws, but unlike the "bandit heroes" and other gang members of Western dime novels, early film criminals were usually portrayed as urban citizens. Most of these early twentieth-century portraits depicted ruthless crooks engaged in corrupt business practices in the pursuit of wealth, a motif that has remained popular to this day. Also common in film plots between 1910 and 1920 were nostalgic portrayals of a simple youthful criminality, reflecting street gang experiences among working-class immigrants. Such films reflected the social impact of large immigrations into the United States during the early part of the twentieth century. From the 1920s to the 1950s, the media criminal slowly evolved from an early-twentieth-century immigrant into a sullen returning World War I veteran, again transformed in the 1930s into a high-rolling bootlegger and Depression-era gunman, and finally into a modern corporate or syndicate executive-gangster. In the 1940s, depictions of violence, terrorism, and murder also became more graphic as gangsters, policemen, and detectives (many now with weapon fetishes) became more violent and less distinguishable from one another.[20] Following World War II, the new visual medium of television came on the scene and combined characteristics of both film and radio to quickly become the dominant medium.

*Television*    Introduced between 1948 and 1951, home television soon replaced radio as the prime home entertainment medium, forcing the movie industry to restructure and driving radio dramas into history.[21] Television was not just radio and newspapers with pictures, it was an entirely new medium that fundamentally influenced the shape and content of all media and in doing so helped create a new and different society. The social impact of television has been compared to the medieval Christian church's influence on European culture.[22] Television's growth and public acceptance was phenomenal, and the existing business models for commercial radio facilitated television's rapid emergence. CBS and NBC already existed as radio networks, and broadcasting was already accepted as a for-profit business venture. Because the nature and needs of the market dominated programming decisions from the beginning, television programming has always aimed at attracting and holding the largest possible audience. Borrowing its basic themes and programming ideas from film, radio, and stage, and reformatting them in broadly palatable, noncontroversial products, television quickly came to be described as a vast wasteland of recycled, mediocre programs.

Despite the critics, Americans embraced television. In 1977 the number of television sets to Americans reached a one to one ratio and has never declined.[23] Although computer, videogame, and DVD screens now compete for viewer attention, into the 1990s television viewing ranked as the third most time-consuming activity (after sleep, work, or school) for Americans. If you are a typical American, for every ten years of your life you will spend one solid year (8,760 hours) looking at a television screen.[24]

In creating content, television executives found a gold mine in crime programming. Although television was modeled after radio, crime was never a dominant part of radio programming (ranging from 4 percent in 1932 to a peak of 14 percent in 1948), but crime and justice was a substantial portion of programming and a social concern from television's inception.[25] Crime shows became a staple of prime time television entertainment in the late 1950s. Prompted by the success of adult Westerns and later by a program called *The Untouchables*, crime shows accounted for around one-third of all prime time shows from 1959 to 1961.[26] This trend leveled off during the 1960s but began to increase again during the early 1970s until it reached a peak in 1975, when almost 40 percent of the three then dominant networks' (ABC, CBS, and NBC) prime time schedules contained shows focusing on crime and law enforcement.[27]

While the major television networks periodically de-emphasize crime programming, the total amount of crime-and-justice programming available via television is greater than ever with crime themes found across all types of programming. Special programming such as movies shown on television, miniseries, program promotions, syndicated programs, and local, satellite, and cable network programming all contain significant proportions of crime-related content.[28] Collectively, these varied sources of new and recycled content make crime and violence the most common content found on television. Today the main difference between the visual media of film and television is that violent crime on television is shown in much the same manner as sex. The television audience is taken to the point at which a sex act or a murder is about to occur and then the scene is either heavily edited or cut away from. Films show both more graphically, the violence usually more graphically than the sex.[29] And, of course, those with VCRs, DVD players, satellite access, or cable today can easily access graphic depictions of both.

## New Media

In addition to the traditional print, sound, and visual media, we have available today a set of new media exemplified by the Internet and video games. What differentiates new media from traditional media are three

The newest addition to crime and media concerns is the interactive nature of realistic virtual reality video games. In these games players participate in violent acts and are rewarded for them within the game.

characteristics that together make these media less focused on large, passive, heterogeneous audiences. First, they target small homogenous audiences that have a special interest in a narrow type of content. This characteristic was first developed in the traditional media of radio where you find jazz, classical, and classic rock stations and in print media where you find specialized magazines like *Tattoo Art* and *True Detective*. Described as **narrowcasting** as opposed to broadcasting in the television industry, the key is that these new media do not try to attract everyone but instead target a small but loyal audience that shares an interest in a subject and content. The effect of this approach is readily apparent on the Internet where one can find a large number of highly focused, narrow content dedicated websites. A subject search of the best known serial killers, for example, will produce a number of such dedicated sites.

The second characteristic is the **on-demand** nature of the new media, which means that the delivery of content is controlled and determined to a much greater degree by the consumer. First available for music via phonographs and records, the invention of the VCR was the major technological breakthrough that allowed consumers of visual media content to determine the time and place of consumption. Today a number of commercial products allow selective use of television shows, movies, music, and games. Thus people with a special interest in shows about criminal forensics can have those programs automatically recorded for subsequent viewing at their discretion. Except perhaps for live events that one wants to experience in real time, little media content must be consumed at a particular time and in a particular place today.

The third characteristic that is most unique to the new media is that of **interactivity**. The new media allow the consumer to be an active participant in the development of the content. Interactivity is most apparent in the realm of video games where the electronic content is immediately determined by the button pressing of the players.[30] Whether a character is killed or spared, a crime solved or not, a criminal killed or escaped is not predetermined by a story author but is postdetermined by gamers. In addition, chat rooms, blogs, and Internet vote sites all allow web surfers to create and influence the news content they will consume.

The significance of these three characteristics is that the new media moves the audience from passive media customers to active media coproducers. Combined with computers to generate virtual realities, new media experiences are the closest to actual experienced reality available. For crime and justice, this means that media consumers can experience committing a murder rather than just observing one, help to catch an offender rather than just watch over the shoulder of a crime fighter, and determine guilt or innocence of the defendant rather than just follow a trial.

## TYPES OF CONTENT

In addition to the different types of media, four basic types of content appear throughout the media. Figure 1.1 portrays the basic media content areas: advertising, news, entertainment, and infotainment. As shown, today advertising content overlays and infiltrates all other content and infotainment has emerged to create a niche between news and entertainment. Traditionally, news, entertainment, and advertising were sufficient to define the media content landscape, but today infotainment is a significant addition. With content looping, the movement of information and images into and between the four media content areas today can be rapid and multidirectional, and the boundaries between media areas are porous and increasingly blurred. The explosion of infotainment media vehicles means that one can be hard pressed to decide which of the four content categories some recent media products fit into.

### News

News in the media is that portion that is marketed as true, current, and objective information about the significant events of the world. Although it has markedly expanded in the number of media outlets and its

FIGURE **1.1**
**Types of Media Content**

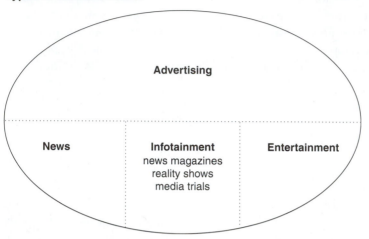

definition of significant events, contemporary news is best exemplified by local television news programming. Herbert Gans identifies two news categories: routine news and disorder news. Crime news falls under news about disorder, and crimes are usually presented as threats to social and moral order. Crime news has been subsequently termed "social control" news, and crime events are often reported with accompanying information about law enforcement efforts and new expanded social control policies such as curfews and dress codes.[31] A crime news story normally unfolds in three ordered segments.[32] It begins with an anchorperson's announcement that a crime has occurred. The viewer is then transported to the scene of the crime for a firsthand look. Finally, the focus shifts to the identity and apprehension of the offender and related efforts of law enforcement officials. In addition to these three elements, today, crime news is action-packed drama narrated by superstar journalists.[33] It is show business. Daily television newscasts have gone from the hard-news format of the mid-twentieth-century broadcasts to a much softer format that constructs stories to fill entertainment functions, and crime is the most prominently featured subject.[34] Contemporary news is essentially voyeurism. In crime-and-justice news, you are usually informed about real events and real people, but these events are often rare and distant. They display the lives of people caught up in extreme circumstances, involving bizarre crimes, spectacular trials, and extraordinary situations. News provides filtered, molded snippets of the abnormal criminal events of the world for voyeuristic consumption.

Crime-and-justice news today is an escape from the normal via a construction of the unusual.

## Entertainment

Entertainment is escapism. It involves all of the media content that is not forwarded as reflecting any specific reality or real event. Entertainment content is popular because it takes people to places that do not exist and provides a pleasurable escape from reality. It entertains and transports. It provides a view of something that cannot be otherwise seen and describes experiences that will not be personally experienced. Entertainment offers brief visits to constructed fabricated worlds to experience events that do not happen. In the entertainment world of crime and justice, you will see impossible crimes, fights, and adventures by people with abilities that no humans possess. The entertainment products of the media are best thought of as play, and crime-and-justice content has been estimated to account for about one-fourth of all output.[35]

## Advertising

Advertising is work. It is the lifeblood of the mass media. Advertising can be conceived as all of the media content purposely geared to persuade monetary decisions. Traditionally distinct from other content, the boundary between advertising and the rest of mass media has dissolved. One now commonly sees product placements in films, stories produced by corporate public relations offices in the news, and infomercials disguised as talk and news shows. The sole media realm found to be relatively free of crime and violence, advertising has become a pervasive, multiavenue, continuous media campaign interwoven into and throughout other media content. News, entertainment, and advertising are still what most people think of when they consider the broad categories of mass media content, but a fourth content type, infotainment, which crosses all of the traditional media boundary lines, has emerged as a significant area for contemporary crime and justice.

## Infotainment

The most important change in contemporary crime-and-justice media is the explosion of infotainment products. **Infotainment** can be defined as the marketing of edited, highly formatted information about the world in disguised entertainment media vehicles. The feel with infotainment media is that you are learning the real facts about the world; the reality is that you're getting a highly stylized rendition of a narrow, edited slice of the world.

A. The Store Door the Prisoners first knocked at.——B. The Gate they entered through to the Dwelling.——C. The Door they entered at, and where LABEE stood on the Watch—— D. A Cave, at the side of the house for storing of provision, milk, &c. for family use.

# THE ONLY COPY

OF THE

## Life, and the Testimony

### That Convicted

# Michl. Monroe

## alias James Wellington.

AT A COURT OF OYER AND TERMINER,
Held at Chester, Pennsylvania, on the 20th of October 1824.

## For the Murder of Wm. Bonsall,

AT HIS DWELLING ON THE DARBY ROAD.
On the Night of the 22d of May, last.
Containing the Testimony of MARY WARNER, PHŒBE BONSALL,
DR. MORRIS C. SHALCROSS, &c. before the Court.
Together with a List of the Jury.
*This is the Only Original Copy.——All others are Spurious.*

Philadelphia: Printed and for Sale at 38 Chesnut St.

Harvard Law Library, Special Collections

Note the focus in this nineteenth-century news pamphlet on a violent, predatory crime and criminal, the symbolic hanging, and the visual rendition of the crime scene with its promise of one-of-a-kind details— all precursors to elements found in contemporary crime-and-justice media content.

In that infotainment combines aspects of news, entertainment, and advertising under a single umbrella, its emergence makes it less sensible to discuss the three traditional media components separately. News, entertainment, and advertising are no longer unique media spheres due to infotainment's influences.[36]

Crime perfectly fits infotainment demands for content about real events that can be delivered in an entertaining fashion, and infotainment content based on crime and justice has existed for centuries. Crime pamphlets and gallows sermons are two early examples, but infotainment has always played a minor role in the media's crime-and-justice content. Why did infotainment explode in the late twentieth century? The basic answer to this question is that as the media, led by television, became more visual, intrusive, and technologically capable, the viewing audience simultaneously became more voyeuristic and entertainment conscious.[37] The ability of satellites to instantaneously beam information around the world has allowed the public to watch riots, wars, and other events as they happen, heightening the dramatic, unedited entertainment value of what previously would have been reported as after-the-fact news events, or not reported at all. For example, with the use of news helicopters, it is now common for local television stations to follow high-speed car chases and broadcast them live. Irrespective of its social importance, a visual event that might not have been mentioned in the news a decade or two ago can be a contemporary lead news story as a result of simply having been videotaped. Along the same lines, the growth of surveillance cameras provides the footage for a bevy of television programs that rely on showing crimes as they happened. By providing a large inexpensive pool of visual events to market, such technological improvements have allowed for much of the infotainment programming that exists today. However, while improved technology increased the potential amount of infotainment, it does not explain its actual quantity.

The quantity of infotainment programming is tied to the second reason that news and entertainment has blurred. With expanded hours and new networks competing for narrowing audience shares, many more hours of programming were needed and networks had greater difficulty attracting and holding an audience.[38] The addition of entertainment elements to news content was embraced as a solution.[39] Beginning in the late 1980s, modern crime-related infotainment programs began to appear on television, and the line between crime-and-justice news and entertainment quickly dissolved.[40] Today a clear demarcation between news and entertainment in the media no longer exists, and consumers are hard pressed to differentiate crime-and-justice news from crime-and-justice entertainment. This blurring is particularly apparent in traditional news content as even the most serious and violent crimes are often given an entertaining slant. We still look to news to

Dramatic pictures provided by police car and helicopter pursuits often result in less important crimes being shown to national audiences.

provide a reliable record of what's real, but today's gyrating stew of journalism, entertainment, and infotainment makes establishing what is real regarding crime and justice a haphazard process.

Reality crime-and-justice programs were the first pseudo–news programming in the crime-and-justice infotainment genre. These programs have never been hugely popular (*COPS* enjoying the highest ratings), but they continue to have substantial audiences and are extremely profitable. Today's large amount of contemporary infotainment media is made feasible by the development of the media's technological capabilities, coupled to the need for more programming, and encouraged by its profit possibilities. Led by television, print and radio followed suit, and today all media produce substantial amounts of infotainment content across a broad spectrum of junk shows such as celebrity sports, lifestyles, interview, game, and pseudoscience shows. Among these, some of the more successful are found within the host of crime-and-justice infotainment vehicles.

As a result, the crime-and-justice media landscape is populated with varied and numerous infotainment products that did not exist a decade ago. Within this media crime-and-justice infotainment world, the crime control model triumphs. Employing real crimes, reenactments, and documentary-like formatting, the realism in which these shows cloak themselves encourages their acceptance as accurate pictures of the world.[41] However, contrary to their image of reality, these programs are clearly structured along entertainment lines. They commonly employ the oldest entertainment crime story structure known: *"crime → chase → capture."*[42] Their acceptance and impact as true renditions of reality is underscored by viewers' attempts to get the police to arrest the actors who portray suspects in the reenactments. Three types of crime-and-justice infotainment are common: newsmagazines, reality-based crime shows, and media trials. Collectively they dominate the contemporary mass media crime-and-justice infotainment market.

*Newsmagazines*    Newsmagazines extend the application of the entertainment values found in lesser degrees in much of the daily news content. Daily newscasts, because of time and format constraints, cannot afford to spend too much time on any one story before having to move on to the next. They therefore cannot fully develop an entertainment context. However, newsmagazines can devote more minutes to the most interesting (that is, the most sensational, violent, dramatic, or scandalous) stories. Within these electronic magazine programs, an event can be fully constructed as an entertainment vehicle with stereotypic story lines, plots, characters, victims, villains, and dramatic endings.[43] At one end within this genre are programs that are electronic versions of the supermarket tabloid newspapers. These include trash-TV talk shows emphasizing confrontation and sexual deviance and tabloid news shows emphasizing bizarre, violent crimes. At the higher end are the weekly newsmagazine shows such as *60 Minutes* and *20/20*.

Other than matters of taste, what makes programs at both ends of the spectrum worrisome is that by presenting expanded, apparently in-depth stories they convey the impression that an issue is being discussed from multiple sides and that a full contextual review of a topic is being provided. However, as in regular news, in newsmagazine programming high-profile, sensationalist crimes and criminals are emphasized, with a focus on individual, random, stranger-on-stranger acts of violence. Television news-magazines also reflect the process of **commodification**, the packaging and marketing of crime information for popular consumption. They continue the broader popular media's painting of crimes and criminals with portraits that are nearly always simplistic and individualistic.

*Reality-Based Crime Shows*   As news drifts more toward entertainment, entertainment programmers looked to traditional news formats to design talk shows and documentaries that would be accepted as credible and realistic by their audiences. In doing so, they have produced some of the more popular television programming thus far in the twenty-first century, and virtually all aspects of life have been presented as a reality program at one time or another. Reality-based crime shows that entertain by sensa-tionalizing real stories about crime and justice are of particular interest. These shows typically employ dramatizations of actual crimes interspersed with police narrative and interviews or actual video footage that features police officers investigating crimes, questioning suspects, and making arrests.[44]

Concerns with these programs arise directly from their claim to be presenting reality—that they are objective purveyors of true stories about crime and justice. Despite their use of the trappings of traditional news and journalism, crime reality shows are thinly disguised entertainment, and the reality that they construct is not pretty. They mix reconstructions, actors, and interviews and employ camera angles, music, lighting, and sets to enhance their dramatic and entertainment elements. Viewers are further encouraged to accept the content as straightforward through the use of self-labeled "correspondents" and "reporters." Law and order, social control, and the point of view of law enforcement officials dominate with stereotyped portraits of crimes, criminals, and victims. The crime-and-justice world found in reality-based crime shows appears as a violent, crime-prone underclass held in check by the police.

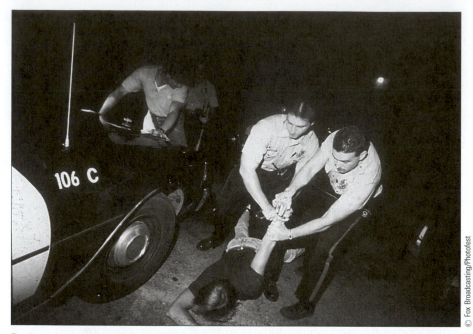

Reality crime shows give the impression that they deliver accurate, unadulterated information about crime and justice. They actually deliver a highly edited and formatted package of entertainment presented as crime-and-justice knowledge.

*Media Trials*     Society has long been intrigued by the inner workings of the criminal justice system. Prior to cameras being allowed into America's courtrooms in the late 1970s, the most realistic-looking views of judicial proceedings came from courtroom television dramas such as *Perry Mason* and classic films like *To Kill a Mockingbird*. Today the drama is often "real," or at least not based on fictional cases. Cameras have moved into courtrooms to cover deliberations, to record the emotional responses of participants, and to conduct interviews with family members. Some made-for-TV courtroom shows are more akin to game shows than to judicial proceedings. The media hijacking and dramatization of actual criminal cases has generated the **media trial**—the co-optation of ongoing cases by the media, which are developed and marketed with entertainment style storylines.

A media trial can be defined as a regional or national crime or justice event in which the media co-opt the criminal justice system as a source of drama, entertainment, and profit.[45] Media trials are distinguished from typical news coverage by the massive and intensive coverage that begins either with the discovery of the crime or the arrest of the accused. In a media trial, the media cover all aspects of a case, often highlighting extralegal facts. Judges, lawyers, police, witnesses, jurors, and defendants are interviewed, photographed, and frequently raised to celebrity status. Personalities, personal relationships, physical appearances, and idiosyncrasies are commented on regardless of legal relevance. Coverage is live whenever possible, pictures are preferred over text, and text is characterized by conjecture and sensationalism. A media trial is, in effect, a dramatic miniseries developed around a real criminal case. The murder trial of O. J. Simpson represents a well-known addition to a long series of high-interest, massively publicized, media co-opted judicial events.[46] The history of these media trials reveals that they occur with regularity. In the twentieth century more than two dozen trials were declared the "trial of the century" by the press.[47] Proto media trials can even be found in the late nineteenth century, the best known being the 1893 Lizzie Borden ax murder trial. Over the course of the twentieth century, interest in these trials by the media, the public, and the marketplace grew steadily. Following their period of intense public and media scrutiny, the trials pass into popular folklore and relative obscurity. Recognition of names such as Fatty Arbuckle, Sacco and Vanzetti, Bruno Hauptmann, the Rosenbergs, Patty Hearst, and others have faded after onetime mesmerizing public interest and media attention.

In the coverage and marketing of these trials, the trials become palettes for the social construction of the criminal justice system. They provide concise and simplistic explanations of crime within the authoritative and dramatic vehicle of a "real" trial. In practice, crime in these productions is nearly universally attributed to individual characteristics and failings rather than to social conditions. Media trials represent the final step in a long process of merging news and entertainment—a process that now often results in extensive multimedia and commercial exploitation. That the source of media trials is the judicial system eases the merger, for media trials allow the media industry to attract and entertain a large general audience while maintaining its public image as an objective and neutral reporter of news. The end result is that in media trials the merging of information and entertainment is fully achieved.

## CRIME AND JUSTICE AS A MEDIATED EXPERIENCE

Each step in the evolution of types of media and their content brings the **mediated experience**—the comparative experience that an individual has when he or she experiences an event via the media versus actually personally experiencing an event—a bit closer to the actual experience. More than ever before, an individual today can experience crime and criminal justice through the media and come away with the sensation of actual experience. Media presentations are evolving toward a media reality that is ever closer to an actual real-world experience and, thus, is more popular and more profitable. Radio provided sound, live coverage, and home delivery. Films provided continuous viewing and eventually sound and were therefore closer to actual experience than either print or radio. Television provided a combination of image, sound, live coverage, and home delivery, a mediated experience that was both similar to actual experience and easy to access.

Recent media technological developments have evolved to create new media vehicles that increase access and choice in media consumption and move the media-created realities ever closer to experienced reality. Video and cable networks have immensely increased the choices people have regarding what media content they expose themselves to, and the World Wide Web has increased global choice and access. Introduction of electronic interactive games and computer-generated images have moved the mediated experience via virtual and augmented reality to be closer to a real-world experience while simultaneously shifting the audience from passive observers of events to electronic participants.

This evolution of the media has had a significant impact on the criminal justice system; today mediated crime-and-justice experience and knowledge dominates real-world crime-and-justice experience and knowledge. For most of us, experiencing crime and justice via the media is preferable to experiencing crime-and-justice events directly. Few seek out the experience of being a crime victim, but many enjoy seeing crimes committed in the media. The mediated experience—where one is warm, dry, safe, and able to see and hear from multiple points of view with the capacity to pause and replay the experience—is also preferable to actual experience for many other criminal justice events such as working a street patrol, attending a criminal trial, or serving a prison sentence.

Despite media impressions to the contrary, most Americans have extremely limited direct experience with crime and the criminal justice system. Receiving a traffic ticket remains the most common mode of formal contact between citizens and law enforcement. Of those victimized by crime, having something stolen is far more common than any sort of violent victimization, and writing bad checks remains the most common criminal felony offense. Violent victimization also tends to be concentrated in lower class social groups. Thus, for most Americans the mediated experience is the main source of their crime-and-justice experience and knowledge.

The cumulative result of this ongoing media evolution is that today we live in a multimedia web where content, particularly images, appear ubiquitously throughout the media landscape in a vast unavoidable morass of mediated information, events, personalities, and products.[48] Caught in the mutations, the nature of contemporary crime and justice has changed. We live in a pixel culture with crime-and-justice pixel policies. What we believe about crime and justice and what we think ought to be done about crime and justice is based on a view of reality that has been filtered and refiltered through the electronic, visually dominated, multimedia web. Thus a crime will appear on the news, its reenactment in film and television programming, its 911 dispatch tape in a pop song as background, and its participants interviewed in print and on radio and television talk shows and their experiences chronicled in books. In such ways mediated experiences become more socially significant and influential than actual experiences.

In some instances the mediated event blots out the actual event so that what people believe happened based on widespread media renditions supplants what actually happened. The facts of an event such as the videotaped beating of Rodney King become irrelevant in the face of the mediated rendition of the event. This trend toward media portrayal over reality is particularly powerful in crime and justice where pop news, entertainment, and advertising combine with the pervasive infotainment content found in newsmagazines, reality-based shows, and media trials to construct our mediated crime-and-justice reality. And from this mediated reality we create our crime-and-justice policies.

In sum, five realities of twenty-first-century media are important for crime and justice:

1.  Our mass media is an electronic, visually dominated media. Print and audio are secondary in social impact. Content is fluid and moves quickly from medium to medium. Images have more value than other media content, and multimedia renditions of events are the norm. The evolution of the media has been toward the goal of making mediated experience indistinguishable from actual experience.
2.  The current marketing structure of the media is geared toward narrowcasting, or targeting smaller, more cohesive audiences than were previously the focus. However, content is constantly reformatted, reused, and looped to ultimately reach multiple and varied markets.
3.  The media must be understood as a collection of for-profit businesses. Each media business must make money to survive, and the primary purpose of media is not to entertain or inform an audience but to deliver an audience to an advertiser. From a media business perspective, advertising is the most important content. From the consumer and social impact side, the most important content is often infotainment.
4.  Media businesses exist within a highly competitive environment. Most new media ventures fail, and the life spans of media outlets and

products are brief. Content must be marketable and must quickly attract an audience.

5. The U.S. media resides in a nonpaternalistic relationship with the government. The government is not prone to directly involve itself in determining content (though the government does enjoy holding periodic hearings about content). Generally, except for some broad parameters, the media determines both content and marketing. The government role in the mass media is largely as a hands-off regulator, issuing licenses and controlling access to broadcast frequencies.

What these media realities collectively mean is that the U.S. mass media is driven by market considerations. The media environment is best understood as a multimedia web existing in a freewheeling marketplace. Within this market, content appears and reappears in varied and dispersed contexts, and images have the greatest value. Crime and criminal justice content has become a particularly valuable media commodity. The real world of criminal justice has reacted to this media commodification process, and the two sides have entered a twenty-first-century ballet in which each leads the other, spinning off criminal justice policies as they dance. In this dance, two views of the media's impact on justice coexist. In one popular perspective, the media are criticized as criminogenic and as undermining the values of law and order. In the second perspective, popular among academics, the media are criticized as purveyors of fear, moral panics, factual distortions, and supporters of the status quo.[49] Being many things with diverse content, contemporary media of course does both.

In that the criminal justice system is a process that runs from criminality through law enforcement, courts, and corrections to criminal justice policies, the balance of this book explores this media–criminal justice relationship within a systems perspective. Media constructions of crime, law enforcement, the judicial system, and corrections as currently portrayed in the mass media are presented first, followed by chapters dedicated to media's relationship to crime control and policy formation.

## DISCUSSION QUESTIONS

1. Thinking back to your childhood, what changes can you note in the way crime and justice is portrayed in the media today? Are they positive or negative changes in your view?

2. Do you feel that the media today more often promote crime control or due process goals?

# In-Class Activities

1. Compile a list of events that have been looped in the media. Note how many are originally real versus fictional events and how the original event has been altered and used in new media contexts.
2. Come up with a list of criminal justice memorial policies and note the characteristics of the persons and events they memorialize and the policies they established. Discuss what the characteristics of the crimes and victims say about criminality and crime in America and what the resulting policies suggest as a general philosophy of criminal justice.
3. List some common social experiences such as attending a concert, a football game, or meeting new people and ask how many prefer the mediated experience over the real-world experience and why. Discuss the advantages and disadvantages of mediated experiences over real ones.

# Assignment

Keep a media diary for one week, noting how much and what types of media you consume. Discuss in class individual differences in preferences for different types of media. For example, do criminal justice majors watch more crime-and-justice programming than prelaw students? Do female students prefer different media than males? Do some individuals avoid certain types of media or media content?

# Suggested Readings

Frankie Bailey and Donna Hale. 1998. *Popular Culture, Crime and Justice*. Belmont, CA: Wadsworth.

Yvonne Jewkes. 2004. *Media and Crime*. London, UK: Sage.

Joshua Meyrowitz. 1985. *No Sense of Place*. Oxford, UK: Oxford University Press.

# Notes

1. Altheide, *Creating Fear*, 128.
2. Leishman and Mason, *Policing and the Media*, 144. Don Oberdorfer historically places the transition to pixel policy within the coverage of the Vietnam War: "The electronics revolution, which took the battlefield into the American living room via satellite, increased the power and velocity of fragments of experience, with no

increase in the power or velocity of reasoned judgment. Instant analysis was often faulty analysis" (Oberdorfer, *TET!*, 322).

3.   Shichor and Sechrest, *Three Strikes and You're Out*.

4.   Mathiesen, "Television, Public Space and Prison Population"; Curran, "Communications, Power and Social Order."

5.   Surette, "Some Unpopular Thoughts about Popular Culture."

6.   Adoni and Mane, "Media and the Social Construction of Reality."

7.   This focus on violent predatory crime is tied to a historical interest in crime and justice as theater. Crime and justice has been a source for story lines since antiquity, and the media construct crime as predatory and as a frightening (and hence entertaining) phenomenon caused by individually based deficiencies (Ball, *The Promise of American Law*).

8.   Manning, "Media Loops."

9.   Langer, "Legacy of Suspicion."

10.  Gordon and Heath, "The News Business, Crime, and Fear," 227.

11.  Papke, *Framing the Criminal*, 35.

12.  Gorn, "The Wicked World."

13.  Stark, *Glued to the Set*, 237.

14.  For an overview see Nyberg, "Comic Books and Juvenile Delinquency."

15.  Ibid., 61.

16.  DeFleur and Ball-Rokeach, *Theories of Mass Communication*, 84; Cheatwood, "Early Images of Crime and Criminal Justice."

17.  Cheatwood, "Early Images of Crime and Criminal Justice."

18.  Armour, *Film*, xxi.

19.  Leitch and Grant, *Crime Films*.

20.  Allen, Livingstone, and Reiner, "True Lies"; Broe, "Class, Crime, and Film Noir," 22; Reiner, Livingstone, and Allen, "No More Happy Endings?", 115–118.

21.  See Leishman and Mason, *Policing and the Media*, chapter 4 for a history of police shows on British television.

22.  Curran, "Communications, Power and Social Order," 210.

23.  Stevens and Garcia, *Communication History*, 143.

24.  For example, in 1990 the Subcommittee on the Constitution stated: "The typical American child is exposed to an average of 27 hours of TV each week—as much as 11 hours per day for some children. That child will watch 8,000 murders and more than 100,000 acts of violence before finishing elementary school. By the age of 18, that same teenager will have witnessed 200,000 acts of violence on TV including 40,000 murders" (cited in Perlmutter, *Policing the Media*, 33).

25.  Commenting in *The New York Times Magazine* (November 28, 1954, 56) television producer Gilber Seldes states: "Television finds itself on the defensive, facing investigations and threats. Most of these arise from the part of the program schedule usually held as the industry's worst—its endless stream of crime shows, many of them available to children."

26.  Dominick, "Crime and Law Enforcement in the Mass Media."

27.  Lichter, Lichter, and Rothman describe early crime-and-justice television content as seeming to require "two shootouts with police, a beating, and a cold-blooded murder" (*Prime Time*, 282).

28.  Cole, *The UCLA Television Violence Monitoring Report*; Gunter, Harrison, and Wykes, *Violence on Television*.

29.  Todd, "The History of Crime Films."

30.  Gunter, *The Effects of Video Games on Children*.

31.  Thompson, Young, and Burns, "Representing Gangs in the News," 427; see also Dowler, "Comparing American and Canadian Local Television Crime Stories," 589–590.

32.  Gilliam and Iyengar, "Prime Suspects," 561. Yvonne Jewkes discusses twelve news values operating in the twenty-first century that result in crime news focusing on violent rare crimes (*Media and Crime*, 40–60). Robert Reiner summarizes the differences between crime news and crime as the overreporting of serious crime, especially murder and other violent crimes; the concentration on crimes that are solved; and coverage of offenders and victims who are disproportionately older and from a higher social class than their counterparts in reality (*The Politics of the Police*, 141).

33.  For a recent history of crime news, see Reiner, Livingstone, and Allen, "From Law and Order to Lynch Mobs," who note an increase in news reports of crimes involving celebrities (both as victims and offenders) or drugs and portray crime as an imminent risk.

34.  Altheide and Snow, *Media Worlds in the Postjournalism Era*; Graber, "The Infotainment Quotient"; Surette and Otto, "A Test of a Crime and Justice Infotainment Measure."

35.  Reiner, "Media Made Criminality," 389.

36.  Although the extension of its impact is recent, infotainment has existed in some form since at least the seventeenth century. In the mid-1600s, for example, newspaper weeklies carried details of the more interesting crimes along with moral exhortations to their readers to avoid crime, sin, and evil. Early folk music in the form of crime ballads also established crimes and criminals as accepted sources of social entertainment and narrative. Hanging, public floggings, branding, and other punishments of the time were as much popular entertainment as criminal justice events.

37.  Surette and Otto, "A Test of a Crime and Justice Infotainment Measure."

38.  The growth of infotainment in television news has been traced to the year 1963 when network television news expanded from 15 to 30 minutes. Doris Graber quotes a memo from Reuven Frank, executive producer for *NBC Nightly News*: "Every news story should, without any sacrifice of probity or responsibility, display the attributes of fiction, of drama. It should have structure and conflict, problem and denouncement, rising action and falling action, a beginning, a middle, and an end. These are not only the essentials of drama; they are the essentials of narrative" ("The Infotainment Quotient," 483).

39.  Brants and Neijens, "The Infotainment of Politics," 150; Graber, "The Infotainment Quotient."

40.  Cavender and Fishman, "Television Reality Crime Programs."

41.  Fishman and Cavender, *Entertaining Crime.*

42.  Cavender, "In the Shadow of Shadow."

43.  Tunnel, "Reflections on Crime, Criminals, and Control."

44.  Cavender, "In Search of Community on Reality TV"; Oliver, "Portrayals of Crime, Race, and Aggression."

45.  Surette, "Media Trials."

46.  See Chiasson, *The Press on Trial.*

47.  Wasserman, "No Big Deal."

48.  Manning, "Media Loops."

49.  Reiner, "Media Made Criminality," labels the two competing views as subversive and hegemonic.

# SOCIAL CONSTRUCTIONISM

## CHAPTER OBJECTIVES

After reading Chapter 2, you will have a theoretical foundation for exploring the realm of media, crime, and justice. You will learn the primary concepts of social constructionism and their applications to crime and justice and be able to use social constructionism for understanding developments in criminal justice policy.

## THE SOCIAL CONSTRUCTION OF CRIME AND JUSTICE

In his 1922 book, *Public Opinion,* Walter Lippmann remarked: "For the most part we do not first see, and then define. We define first and then see.... We pick out what our culture has already defined for us, and we tend to perceive that which we have picked out in the form stereotyped for us by our culture."[1]

By pointing out that society sees reality largely as society has constructed and agreed to see it, Lippmann insightfully described the core idea of social constructionism.[2] Under social constructionism, people create reality—the world they believe exists—based on their personal experience and from knowledge gained through social interactions.[3] The process is the same for everyone although the end result, your personal idea of reality, can contain highly individualistic elements. Understanding the social construction of reality process and the concepts of social constructionism will help you understand the impact of the media on crime and justice.

The traditional Western viewpoint is that reality and knowledge of the world are independent of human processes and grounded totally in autonomous, freestanding events. Social constructionism sees reality in a very different light. **Social constructionism** views knowledge as

**31**

something that is socially created by people. Beginning from the premise that accepted knowledge about the world need not mirror an objective reality, social constructionism focuses on human relationships and the way relationships affect how people perceive reality. Social constructionism emphasizes studying the shared meanings that people hold—the ideas, interpretations, and knowledge that groups of people agree to hold in common.[4] In the social constructionist view, shared meanings are invariably the result of active, cooperative social relationships and may or may not be tethered to objectively measured conditions in the world.[5] In social constructionism people tacitly agree to see the world in a specific way.

Therefore, in social constructionism, the degree to which a given constructed reality prevails is not directly dependent on its objective empirical validity but is instead strongly influenced by shifting cultural trends and social forces. The world may be in one state, but people can believe it is in another state and act accordingly. In fact, social conditions may be seen as major social problems at one time and then subside, without the physical situations they concern having undergone any real change. Regarding crime, for example, not only can social behaviors be criminalized or decriminalized independent of changes in victimization or offense rates, in social constructionism such mismatches are expected.

## THE SOURCES OF SOCIAL KNOWLEDGE

Social constructionists seek to understand the process through which agreement is constructed and the forces and conditions that influence when an accepted construction changes; that is, when a society's agreement about its reality alters. Within the social construction perspective, perceptions of social conditions change as social knowledge about those conditions change. People acquire social knowledge from four sources: personal experiences, significant others (peers, family, and friends; also called conversational reality), other social groups and institutions (schools, unions, churches, government agencies), and the media. The social construction of reality theory recognizes three kinds of reality: experienced reality, symbolic reality, and socially constructed reality. In addition to personal experience, we also learn about and define reality from the experiences of others, and to a considerable extent, from the portrayals found in the media. Because media are such an integral part of our reality, we have good reason to examine the messages they convey.

## Experienced Reality

The first source of knowledge, **experienced reality**, is one's directly experienced world—all the events that have happened to you. Knowledge gained from experienced reality is relatively limited but has a powerful influence on an individual's constructed reality. For example, in a survey of citizens in Los Angeles, California, researchers found that nearly twice as many citizens credited direct and conversational reality sources of knowledge as more important than media sources in forming their views of the police.[6] Along the same lines, personal victimization is the most powerful source for defining one's view of how serious a particular crime is. However, even in the fixated-with-crime society found in the United States, personal victimization remains comparatively rare. Serious victimization tends to be concentrated in high-risk groups of citizens comprised mostly of lower income and minority persons. Irrespective of the impression one might get in the media, crime-and-justice experienced reality is not widespread. What is widespread is access to symbolic reality.

## Symbolic Reality

The next three sources of knowledge—other people, institutions, and the media—share their knowledge symbolically and collectively form one's symbolic reality. All the events you did not witness but believe occurred, all the facts about the world you did not personally collect but believe to be true, all the things you believe to exist but have not seen, make up your **symbolic reality**. The difference between experienced and symbolic reality can be illustrated with a few questions: Do you believe the moon exists? Why? Because you can see it directly. You have experienced reality knowledge of its existence. Do you believe the moon has an atmosphere? Why not? Because you have been told it has no air, you've read it has no air, and you have seen pictures of men in space suits on the moon.[7] You have based your belief about the moon's atmosphere on symbolic reality knowledge. Both experienced and symbolic knowledge can shape our view of reality. Now let's apply these ideas to crime. How many serial killers have you personally met? For most of us the answer is none. Yet if asked to list some common characteristics of serial killers, you would likely be able to offer an answer you believe to be correct. Your response would be based totally on symbolic reality knowledge.

In fact, most of what we believe about the world comes from symbolic reality. In large, advanced, industrialized societies like the United States, media dominate our formation of symbolic reality, overwhelming our limited experienced reality knowledge and symbolic reality information we receive from other people and institutions. It is because so much of our social knowledge is gained symbolically from the media that there is concern over media's content. Media are centrally situated in the distribution of knowledge, and what we see as crime and justice is largely defined, described, and delimited by media content.

## Socially Constructed Reality

The knowledge individuals gain from their experienced and symbolic reality is ultimately mixed together, and from this mix we each construct our own "world." The resulting **socially constructed reality** is perceived as the "real" world by each individual—what we individually believe the world to be like. This subjective reality differs to some degree between individuals because their experienced realities differ and what they incorporate from their symbolic realities varies. However, individuals with access to similar knowledge and who frequently interact with one another tend to negotiate and construct similar social realities. The pun "Reality is a collective hunch" is a humorous but apt summary of this social construction process. The end result is a socially constructed subjective reality that directs social behavior. People behave according to how they believe the world is. Significant for crime and justice, the media comprise the most important element in defining reality for most people.[8]

## The Social Construction Process and the Media

The role of the media in the social construction process is diagrammed in Figure 2.1, which presents four stages of social constructionism. In Stage 1, we have the actual physical world we live in. In this stage, events such as crimes or terrorist acts occur and are noted by individuals and organizations. The physical world and its properties and conditions provide the boundaries that the following stages must normally work within. Competing constructions cannot maintain credibility if they obviously run counter to the physical reality of the world. For example, a mayor of a city might wish to forward a social construction of her community as peaceful and safe. However, if there is rioting in the streets, her social construction would not be competitive for long.

In Stage 2, competing constructions first offer differing descriptions of what the physical world is like—what the physical conditions and facts of the world are. Frequently these descriptions are of social conditions that have been identified as social problems, such as drugs or crime. Hence, a social construction of the crime issue might include statistics and stories to support the construction that crime is out of control. Second, constructions also usually offer differing explanations of why the physical world is

FIGURE **2.1**
**The Stages of Social Construction**

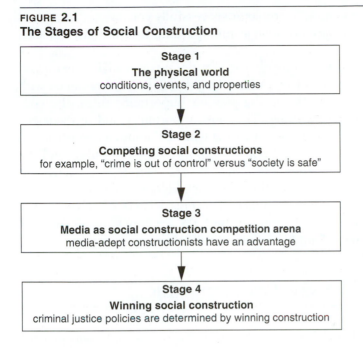

> **Stage 1**
> **The physical world**
> conditions, events, and properties

> **Stage 2**
> **Competing social constructions**
> for example, "crime is out of control" versus "society is safe"

> **Stage 3**
> **Media as social construction competition arena**
> media-adept constructionists have an advantage

> **Stage 4**
> **Winning social construction**
> criminal justice policies are determined by winning construction

as it is purported to be. The constructions will forward various histories and theories to map out how and why their description of the physical world happened. Therefore, statements like "crime is out of control because the criminal justice system is too lenient" might be part of a construction. Finally, based on their descriptions of the world and their explanations of why it so exists, these competing constructions often argue for a set of public and individual policies that should be supported and pursued. "In order to get crime under control, we must impose longer prison sentences" is an example of one such policy position.

In Stage 3, the media help filter out competing constructions. This is where the media play their most powerful role. Persons forwarding constructions compete for media attention, and the media tend to favor positions that are dramatic, are sponsored by powerful groups, and are related to preestablished cultural themes. In this way, media act as filters, making it difficult for those outside the mainstream to access the media and promote their constructions. By giving some constructions more credibility and coverage than others, the media make it hard for other constructions to gain legitimacy. Construction advocates who are not adept with the media are effectively shut out of the social construction competition. In effect, they never get on the playing field. For example, disorganized, poor, crime-ridden neighborhoods frequently find it difficult to get their other community problems successfully constructed as serious social problems. They are not seen as unimportant; they are just not seen at all.

Stage 4 represents the emergence of a dominant social construction of the world. Because most of us have very little direct experience with crime-and-justice reality, the media play an important role in the construction that eventually prevails. The most important result of the social reality construction competition is that the winning dominant construction directs public policy. The social policies supported by the public and the solutions forwarded by the policy makers are tied to the successful construction. For crime and justice, this socially constructed reality will define the conditions, trends, and factors accepted as causes of crime, the behaviors that are seen as criminal, and the criminal justice policies accepted as reasonable and likely to be successful.

## The Concepts of Social Constructionism

The perspective of social constructionism involves a set of concepts that further detail how the social construction competition works. Basic to the social construction process are claims makers, who compete with one another and argue for the social acceptance of their specific constructions of reality.

### Claims Makers and Claims

**Claims makers** are the promoters, activists, professional experts, and spokespersons involved in forwarding specific claims about a social condition.[9] As long ago as 1916, Ivy L. Lee, a founding member of the American public relations movement, noted:

> It is not the facts alone that strike the public mind, but the way in which they take place and in which they are published that kindle imaginations. The effort to state an absolute fact is simply an attempt to give you my interpretation.[10]

Hence, claims makers do more than just draw attention to particular social conditions; they shape our sense of what the conditions mean and what the social problem is. Every social condition can be constructed in many different ways. For example, crime can be constructed as a social, individual, racial, sexual, economic, criminal justice, or technological problem, and each construction implies different policy courses and solutions.

FIGURE **2.2**
**Examples of Factual and Interpretative Claims**

| Crime is out of control... | because of the lax sentencing of criminal judges. |
| --- | --- |
| *Factual claim* | *Interpretative claim that offers an explanation of why crime is out of control* |

| Cocaine is a dangerous drug... | whose use and sale must be criminalized. |
| --- | --- |
| *Factual claim* | *Interpretative claim with associated policy* |

These solutions are imbedded in the claims made by the competing claims makers.

Claims can be thought of as coming in two basic flavors: factual and interpretative (see Figure 2.2).[11] **Factual claims** are statements that purport to describe the world. These are statements about what happened and are promoted as objective "facts" about the world. For example, "crime is out of control" is a claim about the physical condition of crime in society. Factual claims are also made to categorize or type an event. A statement along the lines of "This murder is an example of the rage that is common on our highways" would be a factual claim forwarded to categorize a murder as fitting into a specific type of killing—in this case, road rage. Factual claims are the descriptions, typifications, and assertions regarding the extent and nature of conditions in the physical world.

**Interpretative claims** are statements that focus on the meanings of events. They do one of two things: either they offer an explanation of why a set of factual claims is as described, or they offer a course of action—a public policy—that needs to be followed to address the conditions or events described in the factual claims. Together, factual and interpretative claims target the beliefs and attitudes that people hold about the world: what they think the conditions of the world are, what they feel are the causes of those conditions, and what they think the solutions are.

One strategy involving claims often used to get a social construction accepted by the public is called **linkage**. Linkage involves the association of the subject of the social construction effort with other previously constructed issues (see Box 2.1). For example, drugs are often linked to other social problems such as crime. The strategy of linkage would be to

## 2.1   *Linking Satanic Cults to Serial Homicide*

Phillip Jenkins provides an example of an attempt to link satanic cults to serial murder in the 1980s:

> Estimates about the numbers of victims varied greatly, but one commonly cited figure suggested that some fifty thousand ritualistic sacrifices occurred each year. In 1988, for example, the American Focus on Satanic Crime (a work especially targeted at law enforcement professionals) suggested that Satanists are connected with "the murders of unbaptized infants, child sexual abuse in day-care, rape, ritual abuse of children, drug trafficking, arson, pornography, kidnapping, vandalism, church desecration, corpse theft, sexual trafficking of children and the heinous mutilation, dismemberment and sacrifices of humans and animals. [They are] responsible for the deaths of more than 60,000 Americans each year, including missing and runaway youth."

---

*Source:* Phillip Jenkins, *Using Murder* (New York: Aldine de Gruyter, 1994, 197), quoting Alan Peterson, "The American Focus on Satanic Crime," foreword.

argue that a drug must be criminalized or other types of crime will increase. The linkage of crime to danger and calamity is also employed in the social construction process, and crime-and-justice issues are often linked to the endangerment of health, welfare, families, and communities.[12] The acceptance of a claim of linkage between one social phenomenon and another issue that is already seen as harmful raises the concern and public importance of the linked issue.[13] Hence, the social importance of drug abuse is heightened when drugs are linked to crime, and the same linkage makes other correlates of crime, such as poverty, appear less important.

Claims makers hope to have their claims accepted as the dominant social construction of reality. For a construction to be successful, its claims must be accepted. If the dominant social construction becomes "crime is out of control," then those who have made that claim have been successful. When the president states that the culture of violence in our schools must be addressed, he is forwarding a claim about the world that also suggests a response to the claimed condition of the world. New laws and policies directed against the "culture of school violence" would indicate the success of the president's construction of a new social problem. To further enhance their likelihood of success, claims makers also frequently make use of preestablished constructions, or frames, to advance their claims.

## Frames

In the social construction of the crime-and-justice arena, prepackaged constructions, or **frames**, include factual and interpretative claims and associated policies. A frame is a fully developed social construction template that allows its users to categorize, label, and deal with a wide range of world events. Frames simplify one's dealing with the world by organizing experiences and events into groups and guiding what are seen as the appropriate policies and actions. Regarding crime and justice, preexisting frames make the processing, labeling, and understanding of crimes easier for the person holding that frame's view of reality. If a crime can be quickly placed into a preestablished frame, it will be seen as another example of a particular type of crime needing a particular type of response. A senseless murder, for example, might become "another predator killing that resulted from a lenient criminal justice system." Such crimes can be cognitively dealt with and quickly tied to a policy position. You do not have to spend a lot of time understanding a crime or a criminal that has been fitted into a crime-and-justice frame. The cause of the crime, explanations for why it occurred, and what needs to be done are already built into the frame. Certain U.S. crime-and-justice frames have deep historical roots. Criminologist Theodore Sasson describes five crime-and-justice frames that compete today in the United States.[14] All five frames offer explanations of crime, point to specific causes, and come with accompanying policies. These frames are summarized in Table 2.1.

***Faulty Criminal Justice System Frame***    The first frame holds that crime results from a lack of "law and order." People commit crimes because they know they can get away with them because the police are handcuffed by liberal judges. The prisons are revolving doors. The only way to ensure public safety is to increase the swiftness, certainty, and severity of punishment. Loopholes and technicalities that impede the apprehension and imprisonment of offenders must be eliminated, and funding for police, courts, and prisons must be increased. The faulty system frame is symbolically represented by the convicted, repeat rapist or by the image of inmates passing through a revolving door on a prison.

***Blocked Opportunities Frame***    This frame depicts crime as a consequence of inequality and discrimination, especially in unemployment, poverty, and education. People commit crimes when they discover that the legitimate means for attaining material success are blocked. Unemployment, ignorance, disease, filth, poor housing, congestion, and discrimination all contribute to a crime wave that is seen as sweeping our nation.[15] "If you're going to create a sink-or-swim society, you have to expect people to thrash before

| TABLE 2.1 | Crime-and-Justice Frames | | |
|---|---|---|---|
| **Frame** | **Cause** | **Policy** | **Symbols** |
| Faulty system | Crime stems from criminal justice leniency and inefficiency | The criminal justice system needs to "get tough." | O. J. Simpson "Handcuffed police" "Revolving door justice" |
| Blocked opportunities | Crime stems from poverty and inequality | The government must address the "root causes" of crime by creating jobs and reducing poverty. | "Flipping burgers" at McDonald's; Dead-end, low-paying jobs |
| Social breakdown | Crime stems from family and community breakdown | Citizens should band together to re-create traditional communities. | "Take back the streets" "Family values" |
| Racist system | The criminal justice system operates in a racist fashion | African Americans should band together to demand justice. | Rodney King; O. J. Simpson; "Profiling" |
| Violent media | Crime stems from violence in the mass media | The government should regulate violent imagery in the media. | "Life imitates art" Copycat crimes |

they go down" is an example of a claim associated with the blocked opportunity frame.[16] To reduce crime, government must ameliorate the social conditions that cause it. Hence, blocked opportunities are symbolically portrayed through references to dead-end jobs held by inner-city youth, such as flipping burgers at McDonald's.

*Social Breakdown Frame*   This frame depicts crime as a consequence of family and community disintegration, skyrocketing rates of divorce, and out-of-wedlock births. Social breakdown has both conservative and liberal versions. The conservative version attributes family and community breakdown to "permissiveness," which is exemplified by the protest movements of the 1960s and 1970s and government-sponsored welfare. The liberal version attributes family and community breakdown to unemployment, racial discrimination, and the loss of jobs and income. An example of a social breakdown claim was made by then President Bill Clinton: "In America's toughest neighborhoods, meanest streets, and poorest rural areas, we have seen a stunning breakdown of community, family and work at the heart and soul of civilized society. This has created a vast vacuum into which violence, drugs and gangs have moved."[17]

*Racist System Frame*   The racist system frame focuses on the criminal justice system rather than on crime. This frame depicts the courts and police as racist agents of oppression. In this frame, police resources are seen as dedicated more to the protection of white neighborhoods than to reducing crime in minority communities. Black offenders are more likely than whites who commit comparable offenses to be arrested, convicted, and sentenced to prison, and the death penalty is administered in a racist fashion. In radical versions of this frame, the basic purpose of the criminal justice system is to suppress a potentially rebellious underclass. An example of this claim was offered by then Undersecretary of State Nicholas B. Katzenbach: "We have in these United States lived under a dual system of justice, one for the white, one for the black."[18] The racist system frame is symbolized by the beating of motorist Rodney King and the trial of O. J. Simpson.

*Violent Media Frame*    It is not surprising in a culture swamped in media that a frame reflecting concerns about the media exists. The media violence frame depicts crime and social violence as a consequence of violence on television, in the movies, and in popular music. It is argued that violence in the mass media undermines respect for life. To reduce violence in society, this frame directs us to first reduce it in the mass media. It is forwarded by claims such as the following: "By the time the average child reaches age 18, he will have witnessed some 18,000 murders and countless highly detailed incidents of robbery, arson, bombings, shooting, beatings, forgery, smuggling and torture."[19] The media violence frame is symbolically referenced by allusions to violent visual media, videogames, and musical lyrics. Theodore Sasson notes that despite being perceived as the least important general explanation of crime and violence, media violence is seen as at least a partial explanation of violent crime by nearly all Americans. Violent media is not seen as the most important source of our cultural violence, but there is a broad consensus that the media substantially contribute to violent crime.

*How Frames Influence Crime-and-Justice Policy*    All five frames are supported by some portion of the public, and the frames are not mutually exclusive. People often simultaneously support more than one frame, applying one frame to one set of crimes and criminals and another frame to other events. Crime-and-justice claims makers can guarantee a level of support if they can fit their competing social construction within one of these frames. Analogous to a political candidate running as a Republican or a Democrat, and thereby being assured of the votes of loyal party members, these five established frames are resources that can be tapped by criminal justice claims makers to forward individual claims and policies. By fitting their claims and desired policies within one of these preexisting frames, they tap into a pool of public support. Many crime-and-justice events can be differently constructed using different frames. For example, in Table 2.1, O. J. Simpson's trial is symbolic for two frames: Those who thought him guilty of murder see his acquittal as evidence that the criminal justice system is faulty and must be tougher; those who saw him as innocent see his arrest and prosecution as an example of a racist criminal justice system. The 1999 Columbine High School shootings were used as support for the social breakdown frame, with the shooters portrayed as coming from dysfunctional families; the media violence frame, with the shooters portrayed as under the spell of violent videogames; and the faulty system frame, with the system blamed for not recognizing dangerous youth and preventing their acquisition of weapons.

The five frames jockey with one another for influence over how criminality is understood in society, which criminal justice policies enjoy public support, and how new crimes and criminals are conceived. The process through which crime-and-justice frames fall in and out of favor is closely tied to the social construction competition that is constantly being conducted in the media. In addition to being part of their own frame, by focusing on certain types of crimes or giving access to specific frame-promoting claims makers, the media can boost frames ahead of one another. As will be discussed in later chapters, although all five frames get some media play, recent crime-and-justice content and portraits tend to favor the faulty system and social breakdown frames over the other three. In addition to these fully constructed frames, less comprehensive social construction tools, known as narratives, are available to claims makers.

## Narratives

Narratives are particularly popular and useful in the social construction of crime-and-justice reality. Not to be confused with genres or standard story lines, and unlike frames, which are fully developed crime-and-justice con-structions, **narratives** are less encompassing, preestablished social con-structions found throughout crime-and-justice media.[20] Narratives are crime-and-justice mini-portraits that the public already recognizes. Nar-ratives are not broad explanations of crime and do not include wide-scale public policy directions like frames; instead narratives outline the recur-ring crime-and-justice types and situations that regularly appear in the media.[21] The "naïve innocent" who stumbles into victimization is one recur-ring crime narrative. The "masculine, heroic crime-fighter" who cannot be swayed by corruption or hardship is another. The most popular, longest running criminal narrative is the "innately evil predatory criminal" most recently highlighted in serial killer movies. Table 2.2 describes some

| TABLE 2.2 | Examples of Common Crime-and-Justice Narratives | |
|---|---|---|
| **Narrative** | **Costume** | **Characteristics** |
| The PI | Cheap suit and car | Loner, cynical, shrewd, shady but dogged |
| The rogue cop | Plainclothes disguise, often has special hi-tech equipment | Maverick, smart, irreverent, violent but effective |
| The sadistic guard | Unkempt uniform | Low intelligence, violent, racist, sexist, perverted, enjoys cruelty and inflicting pain and humiliation |
| The corrupt lawyer | Expensive suit and office | Smart, greedy, manipulative, dishonest, smooth talker and liar, able to twist words, logic, and morality |
| The greedy businessman | Very expensive office and home, trophy wife | Very smart, decisive, and polished, unquenchable sometimes psychotic need for power and wealth |

additional common narrative portraits of the criminal justice system found across the media. Narratives can be utilized to quickly establish the characteristics of a criminal, a victim, or a crime-fighter and as supportive examples for larger crime-and-justice frames. In practice, narratives are frequently linked to the faulty system frame by inferring a simplified single-cause explanation of crime and shared common elements of random, predatory violence and innocent victims.[22]

The existing cultural stock of narratives that can be drawn upon also influence what is said and not said about crime. They provide ready-made story lines to apply to current crime-and-justice events and thereby give a sense of predictability and understanding to even the most senseless criminality. As socially shared symbols of crime and justice, their use reduces the need to explain cause and effect, and accompanying crime-and-justice interpretative claims can remain unstated yet implicitly accepted. The evil predatory criminal narrative, for example, offers an explanation of the most heinous crimes. In the same way that a wolf by its nature preys on others, a violent crime needs no further explanation than to evoke the descriptor "evil predator." In the same vein that you don't need an explanation for why a wolf attacks sheep, but would need one to explain a wolf that did not, the predatory criminal narrative supplies an explanation for why criminals attack the law-abiding. Without having to expressly spell it out, the predator criminal narrative explains that it's just the innate nature of criminals; it's what they do and what they are. In the crime-and-justice social construction competitive process, narratives are often applied to specific criminal events, which are then attached to larger constructions and forwarded as examples of what is wrong in society. In crime-and-justice social constructionism, these special focus events are called symbolic crimes, and they play an important social construction role.

## Symbolic Crimes

**Symbolic crimes** are crimes and other criminal justice events that are selected and highlighted by claims makers as perfect examples of why this particular crime-and-justice construction should be accepted. The beating of Rodney King, the kidnapping and murder of Polly Klaas (see Box 2.2), the murder trial of O. J. Simpson, the Columbine school shootings, and the World Trade Center bombings are well-known symbolic crimes. Symbolic crimes are trumpeted to convince people of the existence of a pressing crime-and-justice problem and a desperately needed criminal justice policy. They are taken up by claims makers and forwarded as either "the types of crimes we can expect to happen more often because we have allowed a set of conditions to fester" or as "an example of what a new criminal justice policy will correct if we implement it." Frequently, a symbolic crime is used for both—to show what happens because of, in their view, obviously erroneous past practices and conditions, and as evidence to argue for specific policy changes.

To fulfill their persuasive social construction function, symbolic crimes are often the worst, most grievous examples that can be found. The formula for using symbolic crimes in crime-and-justice social construction is as follows:

**Step 1.** Find the worst crime you can—the most innocent victim (child victims are often used) or most heinous criminal (animalistic predatory serial killers are popular).
**Step 2.** Add and link your construction to your symbolic crime (for example, to raise the issue of pornography, after a child murder claim that "this child would be alive today if the suspect did not have access to pornography."
**Step 3.** Success equals an increased importance of your issue and public acceptance of your construction (social acceptance of media with sexual content declines as more people see this sort of media as having serious, sometimes deadly consequences).

Thus, if you wish to forward capital punishment as a necessary social policy, as a claims maker you would seek out a symbolic crime committed by someone who had murdered previously, avoided execution, was released into society, and killed again. If you are opposed to capital punishment, you would look for a case where an innocent individual was wrongly executed as your symbol of the wrong that results from a policy of capital punishment.

## 2.2  A Symbolic Crime: Polly Klaas's Kidnapping and Murder

In October 1993, 12-year-old Polly Klaas was abducted from her bedroom slumber party in Petaluma, California, and a criminal justice policy,
Three Strikes and You're Out, took off in California and across the
nation. The essence of Three Strikes laws is a mandatory long-term
prison sentence for anyone found guilty of a third felony conviction—
their "third strike." For Three Strikes advocates, Polly Klaas's murder
became the symbolic crime that produced the media heat and provided
the lifting power for a new, previously unpopular criminal justice policy.
Two days after the abduction, the television show *America's Most
Wanted* ran a segment about the case, and actress Winona Ryder put up

The kidnapping and murder of Polly Klaas became the symbolic crime for
claims makers advocating "Three Strikes and You're Out" legislation.

*A Symbolic Crime: Polly Klaas's Kidnapping and Murder (continued)*

a $200,000 reward. A benefit concert was held on October 25 with well-known pop culture singers and comedians. Two months later Polly's body was found. Richard Davis, a previously convicted sexual offender, confessed to both the kidnapping and murder of Polly Klaas, and following his trial he was sentenced to death. With the kidnapping and murder of Polly Klaas, the "Three Strikes and You're Out" claims makers had a powerful symbolic crime that they were able to employ to construct the crime problem as being generated by predatory violent recidivists who are repeatedly released by a faulty, overly lenient criminal justice system. To prevent future heinous crimes like the murder of Polly, the proposed correction was a new criminal justice policy, Three Strikes and You're Out (discussed in greater detail in Chapter 8).

---

As the social construction process is distilled into a single, concrete, emotion-laden dramatic event that can be easily portrayed by the media, quickly interpreted by the public, and is difficult for opponents to argue against, an effective symbolic crime can be the difference between winning and losing a social construction competition. When claims makers win a social construction competition, they gain another benefit—they gain ownership of social problems and issues.

## Ownership

**Ownership** is the identification of a particular social condition with a particular set of claims makers who come to dominate the social construction of that issue. Claims makers own an issue when they are sought out by the media and others for information regarding the problem and for opinions regarding the reasonableness of competing social constructions and policies associated with the issue. Some groups by virtue of their superior power, finances, status, organization, technology, or media access have more ability to make their constructions appear legitimate—to make their version of reality stick—and to take effective ownership of an issue. Because of their media access and control of crime data, law enforcement agencies have proprietary ownership of crime. When a new type of crime is constructed, law enforcement usually has the first call regarding how that crime will be constructed and related policy choices debated. Box 2.3 describes the application of

## 2.3   Ownership, the Media, and Criminal Justice

Phillip Jenkins relates how ownership of "serial murder" by the FBI resulted in substantial tangible benefits for the agency: "The dominance of the FBI's experts can be observed throughout the process of construction. They successfully presented themselves as the best (or only) authorities on the topic, and they assisted journalists and writers who reciprocated with favorable depictions of the agency. The federal officials stood to gain substantially . . . because establishing the reality of a problem provided added justification for their BSU (Behavioral Science Unit), a new and unorthodox unit seeking to validate its skills in areas such as profiling and crime scene analysis. Once it was established that the FBI could and should have jurisdiction over this type of crime, it was not difficult to seek similar involvement in other offenses that could plausibly be mapped together with serial homicide."

Additional implications of ownership are described by Suzanne Hatty: "We live in a knowledge society comprised of 'authorized knowers,' [Certified experts] and individuals not associated with the State or its agencies. Within the system of knowledge production, the version of reality of the authorized knower is privileged [and] individuals not certified as experts have limited means by which to challenge the legitimacy of the [claims] issued by the 'authorized knowers.' Within the arena of crime and deviance, the police are the dominant group. By virtue of their proximity to crime, the police are seen to possess first-hand knowledge not available to others. Further, the police define the categories of behavior understood as criminal and through their collection of statistical data and their unique access to acts of disorder; they maintain control over discussions about crime in society. The police are assisted by journalism. The partnership between police and journalists ensures that the police continue to shape the problem of crime, and that the news media continue to present the public with visual images of deviance. This mutually-beneficial arrangement promotes the legitimacy of both the police and the media as credible sources of expert knowledge [about crime] in society."

---

*Sources:* Phillip Jenkins, *Using Murder* (New York: Aldine de Gruyter, 1994), 213; Suzanne Hatty, "Police, Crime and the Media: An Australian Tale," *International Journal of the Sociology of Law* (vol. 19, 1991), 171–172.

the social constructionism concept of ownership to the relationship of the media and criminal justice and provides a specific example of the FBI and serial murder.

## THE SOCIAL CONSTRUCTION PROCESS IN ACTION

To fully demonstrate the social construction process as it is applied to crime and justice, three examples of recent criminal justice social constructions are provided.

### Social Construction of Road Rage

In this example, a new crime was constructed by the media. The media do not usually take on this role as much as they act as a filter and playing field among various claims makers, but an example of a media-created crime can be seen in the construction of highway shootings. Joel Best analyzed the imagery concerning highway violence from several major newspapers and television stations. He found that after an initial story dealing with highway violence appeared, the media began linking a number of different types of highway incidents together as a new type of crime today known as "road rage." Best summarizes:

> In short, the media described freeway shootings as a growing problem, characterized by random violence and widespread fear. Without official statistics or public opinion polls bearing on the topic, reporters relied on interviews with their sources to support these claims. Thus, the eleven network news stories used thirty-eight clips from interviews: eleven with law enforcement officials promising to take action or advising caution; thirteen victims describing their experiences; ten person-in the-street interviews revealing public concern; and four experts offering explanations.[23]

Best found that the media sought not only to describe but to explain and interpret the problem. The media would say, for example, that highway congestion coupled with the anonymity of the car could trigger these violent outrages in people. The media also offered competing interpretative claims for the problem of highway violence. Some interpreted it as a faulty system frame problem and that more law enforcement was the solution to the problem. Others saw it as a traffic problem. Freeway violence would be lessened if the roads were not so congested. Other claims were that freeway violence was a gun access problem, or a lack of courtesy problem (fitting the social breakdown frame). Best concludes that in this case the media was the primary claims maker in the construction of

Socially constructed by the news media, today "road rage" is recognized as a new type of crime.

road rage, taking on this role in part because of a slow news period. Needing a new crime, the news media went out and constructed one.

## Reconstruction of Driving Under the Influence

Media can also influence the crime construction process by raising the perception of a crime's seriousness. An example of this type of influence can be seen in the public's evolving beliefs about drinking and driving. Driving under the influence has been legally defined as a crime for a long time. However, until recently there was not broad, consistent public support for its prosecution. Not surprisingly, enforcement was lax and haphazard. Prior to the 1980s, DUI was socially constructed primarily as an individual rehabilitation problem. News accounts told of how lawmakers wanted to lessen the penalties for DUI. During this period, lawmakers rationalized that the current penalties were too harsh and that the imposition of stiff penalties such as license revocation would interfere with the offender's ability to work. The media used nonpejorative words like *errant* to describe the actions of those convicted of DUI.

Beginning in the 1980s, new claims makers such as MADD (Mothers Against Drunk Driving) attacked this dominant social construction of the drunk driver.[24] Whereas drunk drivers had been seen as troubled individuals, when socially reconstructed, they became individuals who cause trouble. MADD could not have done this without waging a successful media-based social construction campaign that, in turn, affected how this crime was seen by the public.

Since the 1980s, DUI has been constructed as a much more serious crime. The drunk driver is now characterized as a "killer drunk" and one of society's pressing problems. There was clearly a shift in the media's construction of drinking and driving and subsequently how society reacted to drinking and driving. No longer viewed as an individual problem needing treatment, DUI offenders were now constructed as a menace to society, and support grew for much stricter DUI laws and their enforcement and prosecution. DUI was successfully reconstructed and is now seen by most people as a serious crime deserving harsh punishment.

## Competing Constructions of the Arrest of Rodney King

One infamous example of social constructionism in crime and justice is the arrest and beating of Rodney King, caught on videotape on the night of March 3, 1991. After a high-speed car chase, Mr. King was arrested and violently subdued by members of the Los Angeles Police Department. This event provides an example of the social construction competition process in which different constructed realities strove to become the dominant view. Even though the arrest was videotaped and many factual claims about the event were unquestioned, such as how many times Mr. King was struck, a competition regarding cause and interpretation of the beating—the constructed interpretation of the event—developed.

Three different constructions of the cause and meaning of the event competed, with each construction suggesting widely different policies. In Construction A, King resisted arrest and the beating was justified by King's prior actions. The law enforcement policy implications from this construction are minimal. The police were justified; therefore, the police officers were not acting inappropriately, and no changes are required.

In Construction B, the beating was unjustified but was an isolated incident of unwarranted police violence carried out by a few rogue police officers. The officers were not acting appropriately but were also not typical or representative of L.A. police officers. This version implies the policy response of firing the bad apples and reprimanding the officers involved in misrepresenting the incident. Targeted internal individual discipline is all that is needed.

In Construction C, the beating is unjustified and seen as an example of an endemic problem of unwarranted and consistent police violence toward minorities. Fitted within the racist system frame, the officers are seen as

A frame from the citizen videotape showing a Los Angeles police officer striking Rodney King. The disagreement over what the footage meant resulted in three different social constructions of the Rodney King beating vying for public acceptance.

acting as many L.A. officers would have acted, and the beating reflects an organizational tolerance of excessive violence toward minorities. The policy changes required from this construction involve drastic change in the L.A. police culture. It indicates the need to revamp the administration and training of the department and make extensive organizational changes.

In the end Construction C and its interpretation won the construction competition. The L.A. police chief eventually resigned, and a new, black chief was hired. The Rodney King beating displays how even for events in which factual claims are not disputed, vigorous competition among interpretative claims related to those facts can still occur.

## SOCIAL CONSTRUCTIONISM AND CRIMINAL JUSTICE POLICY

As stated earlier, the ultimate social importance of social constructionism is found in its implication for criminal justice public policy. For it is with our crime-and-justice policy decisions that we decide how we are going to collectively respond to crime, deal with offenders, and spend our taxes. Figure 2.3 lays out the relationship between the media, social

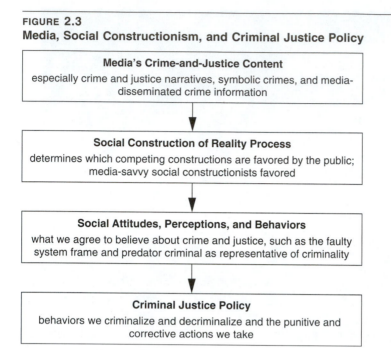

**FIGURE 2.3**
**Media, Social Constructionism, and Criminal Justice Policy**

**Media's Crime-and-Justice Content**
especially crime and justice narratives, symbolic crimes, and media-disseminated crime information

**Social Construction of Reality Process**
determines which competing constructions are favored by the public; media-savvy social constructionists favored

**Social Attitudes, Perceptions, and Behaviors**
what we agree to believe about crime and justice, such as the faulty system frame and predator criminal as representative of criminality

**Criminal Justice Policy**
behaviors we criminalize and decriminalize and the punitive and corrective actions we take

constructionism, and criminal justice policy. As shown, the relationship between the media and their crime-and-justice content influences the social construction of crime-and-justice reality by supplying the narratives, symbolic crimes, and basic information needed to create factual and interpretative claims. The media further provide the arena for the crime-and-justice social construction competition to be held, thereby favoring media-savvy claims makers. This in turn encourages a particular set of social attitudes and perceptions about crime and justice; predatory criminality and an overly lenient justice system are recent popular examples. The final and most important influence in this relationship chain is on criminal justice policies. How policies are presented and perceived determines whether they are supported or opposed.

In the end, media emerge as one of three engines of social construction of reality. As diagrammed in Figure 2.4, our most influential social construction engine is composed of personal experience and information received directly from people close to us, our **conversational reality**. Together these two components provide the foundation of our personal socially constructed reality. When we have applicable experiences or direct access to people we personally know who have had applicable experiences, we trust that knowledge above all other. The media,

**FIGURE 2.4**
**The Engines of Social Construction**

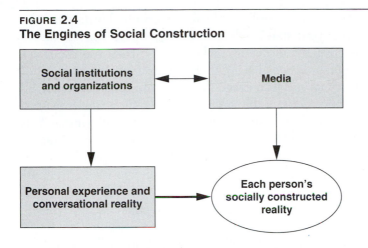

comprised of news, entertainment, advertising, and increasingly infotainment, creates a more pervasive, broadly distributed information engine in
the social construction process. The media establish and maintain powerful frames for perceiving the broader, distant world while controlling the
distribution of widely shared social knowledge—or knowledge not gained
directly or from our conversational reality. The content of this socially
shared knowledge at any particular time is largely determined by the
gyrations of the media. The third social construction engine is knowledge
supplied by the various institutions, organizations, and agencies that collect
and disseminate statistics, information, and claims about the world. Annual
FBI and Department of Justice reports about crime in America are
examples. The institutions of the third engine have a dependent relationship with the media. Little knowledge can be disseminated directly from
these institutions and organizations to individuals, so agencies and institutions of the third engine must utilize the media for effective distribution of
their factual and interpretive claims. The media, in turn, utilize these
organizations for newsworthy and interesting credible claims makers,
claims, and marketable infotainment.

The most important insight to be gained from a social constructionism perspective is the recognition of the social construction competition
that is constantly being waged. Social construction of crime-and-justice
reality is constant, and recognizing the claims makers, claims, and
strategies involved helps in following the competition. All views of
reality are constructed, and being aware of this aids in deciding which
of the competing crime-and-justice constructions you embrace. The social
construction process is not inherently pernicious or evil, but we must

recognize the process to thoughtfully evaluate the criminal justice policies that result. The adage "your stand is determined by where you sit" directs us to consider the positions of claims makers—who they represent and what they stand to gain or lose by having their claims accepted or rejected. Ultimately, the prize from social construction is not the construction of any particular crime-and-justice issue but influence over the social construction process. Access to the media and the social reality media construct are the grand goal. If you can influence a reality-defining engine in a society, you can create the social reality of that society for many people. Therefore, winning one social construction contest puts you on the inside track for winning future contests in the same manner that successfully constructing a new type of crime in the present makes it easier to construct new ones in the future. If one construction of social reality gains permanent control of the media social construction engine, other constructions will no longer be competitive. If punitive criminal justice policy and predatory criminality totally dominate media content, entire frames and alternate ideas about crime and justice will disappear from serious public consideration. With these concepts and concerns in mind, we turn to the social construction of criminals, crime, and justice in the media, beginning in Chapter 3 with crimes and criminals.

## DISCUSSION QUESTIONS

1. What were your expectations of college when you were in high school? What were your sources of information about college life? Why was the information the media supplied important, or was it? Was the constructed reality you had of college in high school similar to the reality you found?
2. Discuss which of Sasson's five frames you feel do the best in the media.

## IN-CLASS ACTIVITIES

1. Show an excerpt from a local or national newscast and identify as many social construction concepts as possible (claims makers, frames, narratives, symbolic crimes, linkage, and ownership).
2. View the movie *The Rodney King Incident: Race and Justice in America* (1998) by Michael Pack Films for the Humanities and Sciences (www.films.com) and identify and discuss the social

construction process, claims makers, claims, the use of the King arrest as a symbolic crime, and the social and policy impacts of its social construction.

# ASSIGNMENT

Deconstruct a local newspaper or newsmagazine story about crime and identify the claims makers and the factual and interpretative claims. Note if any symbolic crimes or crime-and-justice narratives are employed. Was linkage utilized, and which of the five common crime frames did the story best support?

# SUGGESTED READINGS

Gregg Barak. 1995. *Media, Process, and the Social Construction of Crime*. New York: Garland.

Joel Best. 1995. *Images of Issues*. New York: Aldine de Gruyter.

Kenneth Gergen. 1999. *An Invitation to Social Construction*. Thousand Oaks, CA: Sage.

Gary Potter and Victor Kappeler. 1998. *Constructing Crime*. Prospects Heights, IL: Waveland.

Malcolm Spector and John Kitsuse. 1987. *Constructing Social Problems*. New York: Aldine de Gruyter.

# NOTES

1.  Lippmann, *Public Opinion*, 54.
2.  The ideas included within a social construction of reality fall under the broad umbrella of the sociology of knowledge tradition.
3.  Gergen, "Social Constructionist Inquiry."
4.  Lindlof, "Media Audiences as Interpretive Communities."
5.  Spector and Kitsuse, *Constructing Social Problems*, 6.
6.  Maxson, Hennigan, and Sloane, *Factors that Influence Public Opinion of the Police*, 10.
7.  I have assumed that you are not one of the few astronauts who have been to the moon and have experienced reality to draw upon for these questions.
8.  Adoni and Mane, "Media and the Social Construction of Reality."
9.  Best, *Images of Issues*, 327.

10.   As quoted in Sherwin, *When Law Goes Pop,* 142.

11.   Joel Best describes a claim as an argument with four elements: that some condition exists, that it is troubling and ought to be addressed, that it has specific characteristics such as being common or increasing, has known causes or serious consequences or is a particular type of problem, and that a particular action should be taken to deal with it ("The Diffusion of Social Problems").

12.   Thompson, Young, and Burns, "Representing Gangs in the News," 427–428.

13.   Ferrel, "Criminalizing Popular Culture."

14.   Sasson, *Crime Talk,* 13–17. See also Reiner, *The Politics of the Police,* 139.

15.   Sasson, *Crime Talk,* 14.

16.   David Bruck as cited in Sasson, *Crime Talk,* 15.

17.   As cited in Sasson, *Crime Talk,* 15.

18.   As cited in Sasson, *Crime Talk,* 16.

19.   Sasson, *Crime Talk,* 16, quoting Thomas Elmendorf's testimony before the House Subcommittee on Communication.

20.   In the broader research world, media narratives share many characteristics with "scripts" as developed by cognitive psychologists (see Schank and Abelson, *Scripts, Plans, Goals, and Understanding*). They also are related to the concepts of "motif" and "rhetorical idioms," both of which refer to recurring rhetorical elements and speech used to describe and culturally anchor social problems. Unlike narratives, these are brief common catch-phrases and metaphors used to describe crime. Examples include these phrases: epidemic, menace, scourge, crisis, blight, casualties, tip of the iceberg, war on drugs, crime, gangs, or terrorism (Ibarra and Kitsuse, "Vernacular Constituents of Moral Discourse," 47). See also Best and Hutchinson, "The Gang Initiation Rite as a Motif in Contemporary Crime Discourse," 384.

21.   Examples of popular crime-and-justice narratives are offered by Rafter (*Shots in the Mirror,* 141–146): (1) Mystery and detective narratives: basic pattern is of the search, most P.I. and cop films fall into this category; (2) Thrillers: unexpected violence, nail-biters, regular episodic scares; (3) Capers: complicated audacious heist, planning, organization and member recruitment, and execution; (4) Justice violated/justice restored: many prison films, false accusations and unjust punishments; (5) Disguised westerns: heroic outsider reluctantly consents to clean up the town; (6) Revenge and vigilantes: lead figure is violated and retaliates; (7) Chronicles of criminal careers: biographies and fictional characters; (8) Action films: lacking developed plots, series of episode transitions with fights and explosions, violent spectacles, epic heroes.

22.   Best and Hutchinson, "The Gang Initiation Rite as a Motif in Contemporary Crime Discourse," 388–389; and Sumser, *Morality and Social Order in Television Crime Drama,* 46.

23.   Best, *Images of Issues,* 332.

24.   Reinarman, "The Social Construction of an Alcohol Problem."

# CRIME AND CRIMINALITY

## CHAPTER OBJECTIVES

After reading Chapter 3, you should be able to describe the common portraits of criminality found in the media and understand the special attention that the media has given to the predatory criminality portrait. You should also see the link between the media portraits of criminality and various criminological theories, understand the issues and concepts associated with criminogenic media (media that generates crime), and have a basic introduction to the state of knowledge regarding violent media as a cause of social aggression, copycat crime, and terrorism and the media.

## CRIMINALS, CRIMES, AND CRIMINALITY

Portraits of crime and justice appear early in the media's history, and they have continued to be a staple. Historically, criminals, crime, and criminality have been a mainstay at least since classical Greek theater. Western literature continued the interest, with romantic and heroic criminals appearing as common figures in the ballads, plays, and folktales of medieval England. Similarly, crime and criminals have been ubiquitous elements in American media since the beginning of the republic. However, with large-scale industrialization, urbanization, and ethnic immigration in the nineteenth century, crime for the first time became one of the nation's principal social concerns.[1] Spurred by growing public worry about crime, by the second half of the nineteenth century the dominant image of the criminal in popular culture had shifted from the romantic, heroic portrait to conservative, negative images. The media of this period (newspapers, dime novels, and magazines) created the stereotypical portraits and themes of crime and justice that would later dominate movies and television—portraits and themes still common in today's media. What does this portrait of criminality look like?

## Criminals

Since the turn of the twentieth century, in addition to being the central theme of police, detective, robbery, and gangster stories, criminals and their crimes have often been secondary plot elements in love stories, Westerns, comedies, and dramas. In the pretelevision era, media criminals in films, radio, and print enjoyed full lives and were often decisive, intelligent, and attractive individuals. Whether basically good or bad, criminals were shown as active decision makers who went after what they wanted, be it money, sex, or power. They controlled their lives, lived

A 12-minute "Western" filmed in New Jersey, the 1903 film *The Great Train Robbery* was one of the first "narrative" movies (which aim to tell a story). The film introduced many features still common in today's crime media—gun-wielding criminals, brazen crimes, brutal murders, dramatic chase scenes, and violent fatal apprehension of the criminals. The robber's gun barrel view shown here had a profound effect on audiences as many people thought that they were actually about to be shot.

© Culver Pictures

The entertainment media's focus on white, middle-aged villains engaged in high-stakes crime has a long history, as shown here by actor James Cagney (*right*) in the 1931 film *Public Enemy.*

well, and decided their own fates, characteristics that made them more appealing and interesting than law-abiding citizens. These early dichotomous media portraits of criminals allowed audiences to shuttle back and forth between good and evil—to identify with the criminals until the end, at which point the criminal was usually shot and killed.[2] In a most basic way, early media criminals allowed the audience to savor the danger and sin of crime yet still see it ultimately punished.

This portrait began to change, however, with the decline of film and radio as the primary mass media in the late 1940s. The introduction of commercial television, a medium even more pervasive, direct, and influential, begin the shift to more one-dimensional heroes and villains. Criminality in the cinema and in radio, however, had provided a fifty-year pool of criminal portraits for television to tap. Not surprisingly, television programming at first constructed images of crime and justice similar to the ones found in film and radio but in much greater quantity, filling as much as 40 percent of prime time programming during the 1970s.

The portrait of criminals found in today's media has almost no correspondence with official statistics of persons arrested for crimes. The typical criminal portrayed in the entertainment media is mature, white, and of high social status, whereas statistically the typical arrestee is young, black, and poor—what they have in common is that both are male. The image of the criminal that the news media propagate is similar to that found in the entertainment media. Criminals tend to be of two types in the news media: violent predators or professional businessmen and bureaucrats. Furthermore, as in entertainment programming, they tend to be slightly older than reflected in official arrest statistics. In general, the news media underplay criminals' youth and their poverty while overplaying their violence.[3] Although other types of criminals are periodically shown, the violent and predatory street criminal is what the public takes away from the media's constructed image of criminality.[4] If there is a single media crime icon, it is predatory criminality—a construction that frames and dominates the media crime-and-justice world. In addition, while criminals are often portrayed in depth in the media, their victims frequently are not. Counterparts to the criminals—victims of crime—occupy a surprisingly low profile in the media. See Box 3.1 for a detailed look at how crime victims are commonly portrayed in the media.

## *Predatory Criminality*

In their entertainment, news, and infotainment components, the media construct **predatory criminality**—criminals who are animalistic, irrational, and innately predatory and who commit violent, sensational, and senseless crimes—as the dominant and most pressing crime problem in the nation. History reveals that the image of the predator criminal has dominated in the media for more than a century. Comparable to the hunting down of witches by the medieval church, modern mass media have given massive and disproportionate attention to pursuing innately predatory "outsiders" as the primary crime-and-justice goal.[5] Found in the media's content are repeated claims that crime is largely perpetrated by predatory individuals who are basically different from the rest of us and that criminality predominantly stems from individual deficiencies. Over the past one hundred years, media portraits of criminals have become more animalistic, irrational, and predatory and their crimes more violent, senseless, and sensational. The media have successfully raised the violent predator criminal from a rare offender in the real world to a common, ever-present image in constructed reality. The public is led by the media to see violence and predation between strangers as an expected fact of life. Nowhere is this image stronger than in the recent media social construction of the ultimate predator, the serial killer.

The social construction of the serial killer as a significant new type of criminal began in the 1980s and took off in the 1990s.[6] The commodification, public embrace, and effects on criminal justice policy from the media

## 3.1  Crime Victims in the Media

Although sometimes important for determining a crime's newsworthiness, crime victims are often ignored in crime news. When described, victims in the news tend to be portrayed as female, very young or old, or of high status such as celebrities (Chermak 1995; Mawby and Brown 1984; Meyers 1996; Pritchard and Hughes 1997; Reiner, Livingstone, and Allen 2003; Sorenson, Manz, and Berk 1998). News coverage also routinely depicts criminal violence against females differently from that against males (Meyers 1994, 1996) and underplays the victimization of minorities (Johnstone, Hawkins, and Michener 1994; Wilbanks 1984). Overall, the victimization rates of persons in the media, in fact, correlate more with fear of crime than with the public's actual victimization risk. In general, a typical victim is not a newsworthy nor entertaining one.

In the entertainment media, victims normally play one of two extreme roles. Victims are portrayed either as helpless fodder or as wronged heroic avengers. Entertainment crime victims are predominantly white and male—but the entertainment media also manages to overrepresent young women in excess of their real victimization rates. One trend in female victimization on television is that over time there are fewer female villains, more female assistant heroes, and many more female victims (Sumser 1996, 141). John Sumser (1996, 78) argues that television murder victims in particular are marginalized, and homicide frequently happens to characters who have absolutely no "character" and mean little to the other lead characters or to the audience. The audience is encouraged to react to television murders not with a "My God how horrible" response but with a "How curious, I wonder how it was done" reaction.

Common entertainment victim narratives also abound. One is the "Feeling Bad Victim." This is the victim, usually one of the first to die, who makes you mad at the villain and in turn makes you feel good when the villain meets a violent and gruesome death at the end. Another is the "Stupid Victim." This is someone being stupid, often a police officer, who is never smarter than the criminal or crime-fighting hero and ends up stumbling into his or her death. A good example of this is the off-duty police officer killed while trying to single-handedly capture all the criminals. Another is the "Shocker Victim." This is the one that really angers viewers; the victim is usually a child or the family pet. A final victim narrative is the "Lazy Victim." This is the one who is killed while doing something wrong or improperly—the security or correctional officer watching television instead of his area, for example.

This 1947 comic book story is an early example of the media portrait of predatory killers.

portrait of serial killers clearly demonstrate the media's crucial role in the social construction of criminality. With the construction of serial killers, the prior generic portrait of predators as dangerous but still human was supplanted by the portrait of animalistic killing machines more akin to gothic monsters than human offenders.[7] The media portrait also implied that these serial killers were everywhere and were the perpetrators of most violent crimes. Historian Philip Jenkins, however, reports that although there is some evidence of a small real increase in the number of active serial killers, in total serial killers account for no more than 300 to 400 victims each year, or 2 to 3 percent of all U.S. homicides.[8] However, media coverage of serial murderers and the success of fictional books and films about serial killers have swamped the picture of criminality the public receives. The result is that serial killers are commonly perceived as the dominant homicide problem in the United States and as symbols of a society overwhelmed by rampant, violent, incorrigible, predatory criminality.[9]

The myopic focus and immense public interest in violent predatory criminality intrinsic to this portrait of innate predation is ironically tied to a socially palatable explanation of crime. While constructing crime as a frightening (and hence entertaining) phenomenon, predator criminality also presents crime as largely caused by individual deficiencies. This individual focus frees the broader mainstream society from any causal responsibility. Such a perspective on criminal behavior leaves societal influences out of the causal equation and puts forth part of the crime problem (the individual) as if it were the whole problem. If one looks only at individual responsibility, one looks away from any social responsibility. Any social factions given credence tend to be marginalized such as devil worshiping or cult memberships. Predatory criminals are portrayed as springing into existence unconnected to any larger social, political, or economic forces. As constructed, the predatory killer is divorced from humanity and society.[10] Created by bizarre circumstances and individual flaws, irreparably separated from society and driven by alien needs, the predator criminal is both enjoyably evil and guiltlessly destroyed.

## Crimes

With predator criminals as the common grist for the media mill, it is not difficult to guess what crimes consumers are likely to find in the media. Not surprisingly, crimes that are most likely to be emphasized are those that are least likely to occur in real life. Property crime is underrepresented, and violent crime is overrepresented. In a classic representative content study of prime time television programs in the 1980s by media scholars Robert and Linda Lichter, murder, robbery, kidnapping, and aggravated assault made up 87 percent of all prime time television crimes, with murder accounting for nearly one-fourth of all television crimes.[11] In contrast, murders account for only one-sixth of 1 percent of the FBI Crime Index. At the other extreme, thefts account for nearly two-thirds of the FBI Crime Index, but only 6 percent of television crime. Although there are recent reports of declines in television program violence with fewer portrayals of both graphic and hero violence, due to the multimedia web and the constant recycling of content, total media content still greatly overemphasizes individual acts of violence.[12]

The content of crime news reveals a similarly distorted, inverted image. Crime news has been found to focus largely on violent personal street crimes such as murder, rape, and assault, with more common offenses such as burglary and theft often ignored. According to one study, murder and robbery account for approximately 45 percent of newspaper crime news and 80 percent of television crime news.[13] The irony is that violent crime's relative infrequency in the real world heightens its newsworthiness and leads to its frequent appearance in crime news. With consistent regularity, the news media take the rare crime event and turn it into the common crime image. Furthermore, trends that do occur over time in the amount of crime reported in the news have little relationship to trends in societal crime. Neither the content nor the total amount of crime news reflects changes in the crime rate. Crime news also focuses heavily on the details of specific individual crimes, whereas only a minuscule percentage of stories deal with the motivations of the criminal or the circumstances of victims. Even in the news, the focus is on entertainment with dramatic recitations of details about individual offenders and crime scenes.

Overall, crime is cast in the media within constructions where large differences exist between what the public is likely to experience in reality and what they are likely to gather from the media. Has the portrait changed over time? The portrait of criminals and crimes in the media does display a number of evolutionary trends. Criminals have become more evil, heroes have become more violent, victims have become more innocent, violence has become more graphic, and crimes have become more irrational.[14] This perhaps would not be a concern if the portraits of crime and justice in the media were balanced in other aspects and presented various competing explanations of crime. That, however, is not the case. As constructed, the most common and popular media crime narratives forward particular explanations of crime. They thereby encourage support for certain criminological theories and the disparagement of others. What are the criminological theories that do well in the media world of crime and justice?

## Criminological Theories and the Media

Before answering the question just posed, a brief overview of criminological theories is needed. Criminological theories can be grouped along a number of dimensions, one being where a theory locates the primary cause of crime. Applying that criterion, crime theories fall into five groups. The first group includes the **rational choice theories**, which state that

© Paramount/The Kobal Collection

Anthony Perkins in the 1960 film *Psycho* shower scene murder portrays the psychotic murderous criminal so popular with the public.

there is no cause of crime and no difference between the law-abiding and the criminal. Crime is seen simply as a rational, free-will decision that individuals will make when the gains from committing a crime outweigh the likely punishment from committing a crime. Criminals are essentially normal people making bad decisions. To control crime, these theories argue that society must deter crime by ensuring that punishments out-weigh the rewards of crime and that punishments are known beforehand and are certain to be implemented and quickly administered.

The second group is comprised of the **biological theories**, which place the cause of crime in the innate genetic or constitutional nature of criminals. The more primitive theories looked for specific physical traits (or Lombrosian-based atavisms) as signs of criminality; more recent ones look to genetic traits or biological trauma. Criminal justice policies asso-ciated with biological theories of crime focus on medical interventions and control of procreation. The appellation "natural born killers" is often applied by the media as a code phrase for these theories.

Group three are the **psychological theories**, which view crime as caused by defective personality development. Based on the work of various psychoanalytic and personality development theorists, Sigmund Freud being the best known, these theories explain criminality as the result of mental deficiencies or criminal personalities. In these theories, people commit crime because their "self" is ill formed. Associated policies

The 1972 film The *Godfather* and other films about organized crime portray crime as a violent type of business enterprise and criminals as deviant entrepreneurs.

are based around counseling and therapy. In the media, these theories come in "twisted psyche" and "sexual deviant" portraits best shown in Alfred Hitchcock films like *Psycho*.

Group four, **sociological theories**, look at social groups as the loci of the basic causes of crime. Criminals are criminals because of the people they associate with, or share a neighborhood or culture with. Whereas the psychological theories argue criminal personalities, the sociological ones argue criminal environments. These theories, and media renditions of them, argue that essentially normal people are forced or steered into crime by their social circumstances. Found most often in films that can profitably express society as part of the cause of crime, media portraits supporting sociological theories are found less often in other media. Strain, blocked opportunity, and culture conflict are the sociological theories that receive the most media play. Although there are hints of the need to change the social structure in these theories, their basic orientation is usually conservative. The means of fixing individual criminals, generated by bad environments, most often is to better fit and adjust criminals to law-abiding society, changing their socialization and only secondarily changing their social environment.

Finally, there are **political theories**, which emphasize the political and economic structure of a society as the root cause of crime. The distribution of political power; unequal access to influence and material goods; and racism, oppression, sexism, and elitism are all central to these theories. Unlike the other theory groups that tend to focus on the need for individual offenders to change, these explanations are more likely to argue for social changes, restructuring society relationships and revamping the criminal justice system.

Which of these five theoretical perspectives do well in the media and which are disparaged? A historical assessment of crime films suggests that different theories have been popular at different times. Commenting on crime movies, Nicole Rafter notes:

> The media tend to reflect the criminological theories popular at the time. During the 1930s, crime films tended to portray a social pathology [sociological theories] perspective which painted the urban ethnic inner city as the basic cause of criminality. The 1940 and 1950s films were Freudian based [psychological theories] with deviant personalities the root cause. The 1960s and 70s brought labeling and critical criminology [political theories] to the fore. The 1980s saw films indicting drugs and family violence [a mix of theoretical perspectives].[15]

## Criminality and Criminological Theories in Today's Media

Today the criminal portraits common in the media advance certain criminological theories over others. The most common media narrative portrait of criminality is the psychopathic criminal, sometimes given super-male traits to create seemingly indestructible murderous super-criminals popular in slasher and serial killer films.

**Psychotic super-male criminals** generally possess an evil, cunning intelligence and superior strength, endurance, and stealth. Crime is generally an act of twisted, lustful revenge or a random act of irrational violence. A historical trend has been to present psychotic criminals as more and more violent and bloodthirsty and to show their crimes more and more graphically. Hence, murderous violence that once typically took place completely off screen (for example, the murders of children in the classic film M in 1931) came to be represented in scenes that were violent but not graphic (such as the shower murder in Alfred Hitchcock's film *Psycho*). Since the 1980s, violence has been shown in graphic hyperviolent close-ups. As the most popular construction of criminality, the psychopathic criminal clearly supports the individually focused biological and psychological theories to the exclusion of other criminological perspectives. Crime is innate, an act of nature gone bad and not society's fault.

Less common but still popular narratives are those of **business and professional criminals**. The portraits of the criminal as businessman or professional are characterized in the media as shrewd, ruthless, often violent, ladies' men. If psychopathic criminals are mad dogs, these criminals are cunning wolves. The core message is that crime is simply another form of

© Morgan Creek/Warner Brothers/The Kobal Collection

Media portrayals of the heroic criminal Robin Hood such as Kevin Costner in the 1991 film *Robin Hood: Prince of Thieves* remain the standard for stories of the wronged hero forced into criminality to pursue justice against a corrupt establishment.

work or business, essentially similar to other careers but often more exciting and rewarding if, perhaps, more violent. The business and pro-fessional criminal portraits also forward individually based psychological theories of criminal personality and psychopathic explanations. However, the classical school of crime also does well, and elements of political and economic causes can be found. Thus these media portraits of criminality tend to be more complex and multi-theoretical, spreading the responsibility for crime over both the criminal and society. It is likely that this very complexity makes these narratives less popular than the more simplistic psychopathic criminal portrait.

A third group of popular criminality narratives are **victims and heroic criminals**. These portraits are the least common. They present an alternative perspective that supports sociological and political explanations. Although the criminal as hero and the criminal as victim appeared early and have been presented regularly throughout the history of the media, such narratives have always been less frequent in number than those of the criminal as a psychopath or businessman. Depending on how the portrait is structured, this "Robin Hood" criminality narrative supports strain, blocked opportunity, labeling, and critical criminology theories.

If you look closely, you will find that the media have attributed a wide range of factors as plausible causes of criminality and provided some support for every criminological theory. However, the dominant and loudest messages in terms of their frequency and popular appeal point to individually based theories of crime and away from social ones. In addition, while criminological theories come into and go out of popularity with criminologists, the criminological ideas imbedded in the media do not. Criminologists drop discredited theories, but the media recycle them.[16] Therefore, even primitive theories of crime such as demonic possession continue to be presented as credible explanations of crime in the media. "The devil made me do it" still carries weight in the media as a valid cause of crime.

Looking at the entire picture, the criminological theories that focus on individual characteristics as the cause of crime clearly fare the best. Of these, the psychological ones, often combined with political or biological elements, are the most popular. The single most common portrait of a criminal features an upper-middle-class person gone berserk with greed.[17] Indeed, greed, revenge, and mental illness are the basic motivations for criminality in the vast majority of crimes shown in the media. In addition, the psychotic criminals portrayed in the media frequently hold positions of political or economic power. The repeated message in the media is that crime is perpetrated by individuals who are different in substantially basic ways from the law-abiding, that criminality stems from individual problems, and that, when not in-born, criminal conduct is more often than not freely chosen behavior.

The dominant media construction of criminals, crimes, and criminality is thus simultaneously both unsettling and conservative. It is unsettling in its emphasis on violent predatory criminality, which is portrayed as random and largely unavoidable. It is conservative in that the explanations of criminality emphasize individual traits as causes and minimize social and structural ones. Social changes are called for far less frequently in the media world of crime and justice than is elimination of evil individuals. Not surprisingly, such a construction with its emphasis on predatory criminality has raised accompanying issues concerning its social effects. Specifically, what is the relationship of the media to crime and violence in society? Do we copy what the media constructs and we consume?

## CRIMINOGENIC MEDIA

**Criminogenic media** refers to media content that is hypothesized as a direct cause of crime. A basic, continually debated issue is the causal position of the media. Does exposure to media precede or parallel aggressive or criminal behavior? In other words, do the media cause changes in subjects or do predisposed individuals selectively seek out and attend to media content that supports their already preordained behaviors? The public long ago came to its conclusion. As early as 1908, worries appeared that the media (then newspapers and books) were creating an atmosphere of tolerance for criminality and causing juvenile delinquency, and ever since then public opinion polls have consistently reported the public's belief in the causal role of the media in crime and violence in society.[18] For example, when queried, a substantial portion of the public feels that television, movies, and even local television news contribute a lot to social violence.[19] More than two out of three Americans feel that television violence is a critical or very important cause of crime in the United States, and one-fourth feel that movies, television, and the Internet combined are a primary cause of gun violence in the country.[20] The media violence frame, as described by Theodore Sasson, continues to find substantial public support.[21]

Three contemporary criminogenic media issues are discussed here. The first area addressed is whether violent media generates aggressive behavior. There has been a great deal of research and public interest regarding this question, but the final answer is still being debated. However, most researchers today conclude that the media is a significant contributor to social aggression and as good a predictor of violence as other social factors. Most crime is nonviolent, though, and one can be aggressive without breaking the law (by being rude or pushy, for example), so even if the media are an important cause of social aggression, media still may not be an important cause of crime. Therefore, the next, more directly relevant discussion for crime and justice looks at the media as a cause of crime, focusing on the generation of copycat crime. The basic question is this: Does the presentation of crimes in the media result in people copying those crimes? The final discussion looks at the relationship between the mass media and terrorism. Media-oriented terrorist events have emerged as one of the most worrisome problems of the twenty-first century, and the relationship of the media to terrorism and the use of the media by terrorists is a critical contemporary issue.

## Violent Media and Aggression

Driven by the folk logic of "monkey see, monkey do," establishing whether "child see, child do" holds true in terms of the media and aggression has proved more difficult than first expected. Research on the link between media depictions of violence and social aggression initially revolved around two competing hypotheses: one conjecturing a cathartic effect and the other a stimulating effect. In brief, the cathartic effect hypothesizes that exposure to media violence acts as a therapeutic release for anger and self-hatred. In contrast, the stimulation effect hypothesizes that a diet of media violence stimulates violent behavior and fosters supportive moral and social values about violence.[22]

Researchers positing a stimulating effect have explored a number of causal mechanisms through which the media could cause aggression. The most commonly advanced mechanism involves imitation, in which viewers learn values and norms supportive of aggression and violence, learn techniques to be aggressive and violent, or learn acceptable social situations and targets for aggression. Advocates of a stimulating effect feel that children, in particular, learn aggression the same way they learn other cognitive and social skills—by watching parents, siblings, peers, teachers, and others. Accordingly, the more violence children see, the more accepting they become of aggressive behavior, and the more likely they are to act aggressively.

A few researchers have argued that the media are not a cause of aggression or violence.[23] They assert that to conclude that the media cause negative social behaviors such as violence is unjustified and premature. In their view, exposure to violent content and violent behavior is linked—but not causally. Rather, both stem from the predispositions of some media consumers who seek out violent content and act violently because of their predisposition to aggression. If this position is correct, eliminating portrayals of violence in the media will not reduce the level of violence in society because the number of individuals predisposed to violence will remain the same. Advocates of this model argue that the evidence of a link between violent content and social aggression has not been shown. Although experimental studies confirm that visual media violence can lead to short-term imitation, researchers do not know exactly how and to what extent the media cause long-term changes in aggressive behavior. Despite the general agreement that there is a persistent positive association between violence in the media and viewer aggression, the substantive importance of this relationship remains undetermined.

Why can't the media's effect on aggression be definitely measured? It is difficult to separate the effects of media on society or individuals from all the other forces that contribute to violent behavior. Media influences are so intertwined with other social forces that finding strong, direct causal effects should not be expected. However, after one hundred years of concern and seventy years of research, a modest but genuine causal association between media violence and aggression has been established beyond a reasonable doubt.[24] Violent media does cause social aggression; violent media is not the sole cause, or even the most important one, but it is a cause.

Another undeniable finding is that the cathartic-effect hypothesis has been discredited: people do not become less violent due to media violence. Contrary to what the catharsis theory predicts, when viewing is combined with frustration or arousal, viewers are more rather than less likely to behave aggressively. Current research is exploring the magnitude, mechanism, and significance of a stimulating effect. It is not yet clear whether media portrayals of violence increase the proportion of persons who behave aggressively, encourage already-aggressive persons to use aggression more often, encourage aggression-prone persons to use greater levels of aggression, or some combination of these outcomes.[25] We also do not fully understand who is most likely to respond to media violence, under what conditions a violence-enhancing effect will take place, and in what ways media content influences behavior. There is certainly a connection between violent media and social aggression, but its strength and configuration is simply not known at this time.

We are a more aggressive society because of our media, and violent media help create a more violent social reality. However, although some research does show a link,[26] social aggression is not necessarily criminal, nor is most crime violent. In addition to the stated unknowns concerning violent media and social violence, the greatest problem in applying the "violent media causes social aggression" research to the "media causes crime" question is that the validity of extrapolating from this research to a relationship between media and crime is highly questionable. Consequently, even if the media does significantly foster aggressive behavior, it is a separate question whether media influence extends beyond aggressiveness to cause increased criminal behavior.

## Media and Criminal Behavior

There are inherent difficulties in researching and examining possible relationships between the media and criminal behavior. First, experiments are even more difficult to conduct in this area than in the area of social aggression, so that most of the available evidence consists of anecdotal reports rather than empirical studies. Second, the ways in which media may be affecting crime are numerous. The media could be increasing the number of criminals by turning previously law-abiding persons into criminals. Media portrayals may be helping already active criminals successfully commit more crimes by teaching them better crime techniques. Media may be increasing the seriousness or harmfulness of the crimes that are committed by making criminals more selective or violent. They may be fostering theft and other property crimes by cultivating desires for unaffordable things. They may be making crime seem more exciting, satisfying, and socially acceptable. Any of these processes would result in more crime, or more criminals, or more costly crime. Third, research is also difficult because an aggregate, society-wide media criminogenic effect is likely to be small and intermixed with many other crime-generating factors. In addition, the pool of at-risk individuals who are likely to be criminally influenced by the media is probably small. All of these factors make identifying criminogenic effects and at-risk individuals difficult research questions to pursue.

Because of these difficulties, few empirical studies address the criminogenic effects of the media. In the best-designed empirical study of media effects on officially recorded crime, Karen Hennigan and her colleagues examined aggregate crime rates in the United States prior to and following the introduction of television in the 1950s. Hennigan's study examined the idea that television, at least initially, influences property rather than violent crime. They explain their empirical findings thusly:

> Lower classes and modest life-styles were rarely portrayed in a positive light on TV, yet the heaviest viewers have been and are poorer, less educated people. It is possible that in the 1950s television caused younger and poorer persons (the major perpetrators of theft) to compare their life-styles and possessions with (a) those of the wealthy television characters and (b) those portrayed in advertisements. Many of these viewers may have felt resentment and frustration over lacking the goods they could not afford, and some may have turned to crime as a way of obtaining the coveted goods and reducing any relative deprivation.[27]

Whether this process applies today is unknown because we can no longer separate mass media's influences from other social processes. Hennigan and her colleagues speculate that television still contributes to an increase in property crime rates to some unknown degree, although other research has failed to tie the media to aggregate crime levels. There does not appear to be a significant relationship between swings in media content and general criminality in society, but what about the influence of media portrayals on individual criminality?

## Copycat Crime

Historically, public interest in the relation of mass media to copycat crime emerged with the entertainment media of the nineteenth century.[28] One of the earliest examples of media specifically created to generate crime were the how-to manuals for terrorism published by anarchist Johann Most in 1885. In his book, *Revolutionary War Science*, Most provided instructions on how to make nitroglycerin, dynamite, inflammable liquids, and poisons and advocated their use in antigovernment bombings and attacks. The infamous 1886 Chicago Haymarket Square bombing is thought to have been a direct result.[29]

Growing concern that media messages could influence people to commit crime also sparked investigations and censorship drives against the media in the early 1920s. Partly in response to these concerns, in 1929 the Payne Foundation underwrote the first large-scale studies of the impact of mass media—at that time, the consequences of movies. Portions of this research examined the effects of movies on deviant, asocial, and violent behavior by juveniles. Combined with public concerns about the influence of the cinema, these research efforts prodded the film industry to create an internal review panel, the Hays Commission, to oversee the content of films and quell the increasing calls for government intervention.[30] The film industry adopted a self-imposed code that forbade crimes shown in film "to teach methods of crime, inspire potential criminals with a desire for imitation, or make criminals seem heroic and justified." A media-generated criminogenic effect was clearly not in doubt.

Despite these early concerns, research, and industry and government responses, specific knowledge about criminogenic media effects is still sparse. Ironically, despite the long ago conclusion that media can be criminogenic, there is no lack of information available today on how to commit crimes. Far more than in previous eras, a large body of material detailing how to commit specific crimes is readily available in films, on television, from the Internet, and in printed form. Texts come complete with diagrams and directions on how to commit robberies, murder, and numerous acts of terrorism, and countless visual examples are accessible. Why is the research so limited when the questionable content is so available and the concerns span five generations?

The reason research is limited is because what seems a simple matter— determining when a media-induced copycat crime has occurred—is complicated by the intrinsic nature of copycat crime. For a crime to be a **copycat crime**, it must have been inspired by an earlier, media-publicized or portrayed crime—that is, there must be a pair of crimes linked through the media. The perpetrator of a copycat crime must have been exposed to the media content of the original crime and must have incorporated major elements of that crime into his or her crime. The choice of victim, the motivation, or the technique in a copycat crime must have been lifted from the earlier, media-detailed crime.

These limits make identifying copycat crimes for study problematic because two independent but similar crimes may be erroneously labeled a copycat pair, and true copycat crimes may easily go unrecognized and unidentified. Too few copycat crimes or criminals have been identified to allow for generalization or for scientifically adequate research; the result is that although the term *copycat crime* has appeared for many years, little empirical research touches upon this phenomenon.[31] Instead, researchers have relied on anecdotal evidence to gauge the extent and nature of copycat crime. The slowly growing file of compiled anecdotal reports does indicate that criminal events that are rare in real life are sometimes committed soon after similar events are depicted in the media.[32] Collectively, these anecdotal examples provide a significant and growing body of evidence establishing the reality of copycat crime. Box 3.2 lists a number of examples of copycat crimes and criminals.

If there is a consensus regarding the nature of copycat crime, it is that a media criminogenic influence will concentrate in preexisting criminal populations. In the anecdotal case histories, most of the individuals who mimic media crimes have prior criminal records or histories of violence, suggesting that the effect of the media is more likely qualitative (affecting criminal behavior) rather than quantitative (affecting the number of criminals). The limited research also indicates a pragmatic use of the media by offenders, with borrowing media crime techniques as the most common practice. For example, criminologists Susan Pease and Craig Love conclude that except for isolated cases of mentally ill individuals, copycat offenders usually have the criminal intent to commit a particular crime before they copy a media-based technique.[33] Similarly, in a seminal study of copycat crime in the 1960s, media researchers Melvin Heller and Samuel Polsky state:

> A significant number of our subjects, already embarked on a criminal
> career, consciously recall and relate having imitated techniques of crimes.
> For such men, detailed portrayals of criminal techniques must be viewed as
> a learning process.[34]

Available research suggests that copycat crimes occur regularly at an unknown but significant rate. The studies further report that copycat crimes are largely limited to existing offender populations but that they influence a substantial proportion—20 to 40 percent—of offenders. Copycat criminals are also more likely to be career criminals involved in property offenses rather than first or violent offenders (although a violent copycat episode will usually receive a greater amount of media coverage when identified due to the greater newsworthiness of violent crime). The specific relationship between media coverage and the generation of crime remains unknown, as do the social context factors that are most important.

(*Continued on page 78*)

## 3.2  Copycat Crimes

- In Texas a group of kids imprisoned for a string of robberies claimed that they "got hyped" on rappers Easy E and N.W.A.
- Four youths who shot and wounded two Las Vegas police officers are alleged to have been motivated by Ice-T's rap song "Cop Killer."
- In 2003 a woman in Missouri robbed a bank saying she had a bomb wired around her neck in a copycat of a bank robbery the prior month in Pennsylvania that left a pizza delivery man dead.
- In June 1998 in Jasper, Texas, three white men drag James Byrd Jr., a black man, to his death behind their pickup truck. Within a week three white men in Illinois and three in Louisiana were charged with similar crimes, dragging a black man behind their vehicles.
- The film *A Clockwork Orange,* in which hoodlums rape a woman while one sings "Singing in the Rain," is followed by British youths raping a young woman while singing the same song. Director Stanley Kubrick bans the film from being shown in Great Britain.
- Two criminals forced five people to drink Drano during a holdup before shooting all five, killing three, claiming the film *Magnum Force,* in which a pimp forces a prostitute to drink Drano, inspired them.
- Four gunmen, ages seventeen to twenty-three, embarked on a killing spree, murdering four and wounding one after watching the TV movie *Helter Skelter,* a film about the Manson murders.
- Richard Miller allegedly shot and killed his former boss, reportedly after seeing the movie *First Blood* approximately twenty times. A psychologist at his trial testified, "He believes Rambo gives us approval to kill people."
- Nathaniel White, who slashed the first of his six murder victims, said that he did exactly what he saw in the movie *Robocop 2.*
- Nathan Martinez allegedly shot and killed his stepmother and half-sister after viewing the film *Natural Born Killers* at least six times. Martinez, who had shaved his head and wore granny glasses similar to the film's lead character Mickey Knox, reportedly told a friend, "It's nothing like the movies."
- In Elgin, Illinois, an ex-convict obsessed with guns and the film *Natural Born Killers* killed two people and wounded sixteen others in a bar.
- The film *Menace II Society* has been cited by a trial judge for providing a script for two youths accused of robbing and killing a

motorist, and four teenage boys told authorities that the same movie motivated them to steal a car, wound one man, and kill another.

- A sixteen-year-old California boy killed his mother and admitted to investigators that he got the idea from the movie *Scream*. Two young women in New Hampshire were murdered by acquaintances, one of whom was inspired by watching the same movie.
- A Kentucky high school student killed three and wounded five based on a scene from the movie *Basketball Diaries*.
- MTV cartoon characters Beavis and Butthead have been blamed for inciting children to start sometimes fatal fires.
- In 2001 a thirteen-year-old Connecticut youth attempted to imitate an episode of the MTV show *Jackass*, in which the host set himself on fire, and wound up with second and third degree burns.
- Three teenagers died when they imitated a stunt from the Disney film *The Program*.
- The film *New Jack City* has been associated with theater lobby fights, the killing of a teenager during a shootout outside a theater, and the exchange of gunshots outside other theaters.
- Three drunken men in Germany were jailed for throwing manhole covers from a highway bridge after reading about a similar prank in the papers.
- In France a seventeen-year-old boy was killed trying to make a bomb based on what he had seen in the TV show *MacGyver*.
- In Kentucky a thirteen-year-old boy evaded arrest and injured several police officers by booby-trapping his home based on scenes from the film *Home Alone*.
- In Seattle a fifteen-year-old girl laced a peanut butter sandwich with poison intended for an eleven-year-old playmate. She got the idea from the movie *Heathers*. The dispute was over a videotape of the same movie.
- Police credit the movie *Set It Off*, about a gang of female bank robbers, with inspiring a group of five female bank robbers in Olympia, Washington, in 1998.
- Two men armed with flammable liquid burned a clerk's booth inside a Brooklyn subway station, patterned on a crime in the movie *Money Train*.
- A Canadian boy attempted to extort $50,000 from a local mayor after watching an episode of *Starsky and Hutch*.

*Copycat Crimes (continued)*

- A nine-year-old girl was raped by several girls on a California beach a few days after a television movie was shown. In the movie a young female is raped in a similar fashion by three other teenagers in a juvenile reformatory.
- In Boston a woman was doused with gasoline and set afire following a movie on television in which teenage boys roamed Boston burning tramps for fun and amusement.
- The same evening that a television movie about a battered wife who pours gasoline on her sleeping husband was shown, a man poured gasoline on his sleeping wife and set her afire, saying he was trying to frighten her.
- Following a television movie called *Doomsday Flight,* airlines reported a number of extortion calls making bomb threats.
- The Tylenol copycat poisonings, in which the initial murders occurred after the victims had purchased Extra-Strength Tylenol that had been laced with cyanide, were followed within a short time by copycat poisonings and reports of product tampering across the nation.
- John Hinckley Jr.'s assassination attempt on President Reagan was generated when Hinckley emulated the main character in the movie *Taxi Driver.*
- Timothy McVeigh, convicted of bombing the Oklahoma City Federal Building, reportedly told interviewers that he was inspired by the movie *Red Dawn.*

---

*Sources:* Tim Purtell, "The Emulate Show: Movies that Inspired Copycat Crime," *Entertainment Weekly* (Issue 259, January 27, 1995); Heather J. Maher, "Imitation as Deadly Flattery," ABC News (June 21, 1998); Jeff Ferrel, "Criminalizing Popular Culture," in *Popular Culture, Crime and Justice,* eds. Frankie Bailey and Donna Hale (Belmont, CA: Wadsworth, 1998); J. Ostrow, "MTV's 'B and B' Ignites Call for Parental Guidance," *Denver Post* (October 12, 1993, E1); K. Tucker, "Reno and Butthead. Do Movies and Television Have an Image Problem?", *Entertainment Weekly* (No. 195, November 5: 1993, 44–47); *USA Today,* February 12, 1991; Reuters News Service, 1991; Associated Press, 1991; Perez-Pena, 1995; G. Nettler, *Killing One Another* (Cincinnati, OH: Anderson, 1982); Susan Pease and Craig Love, "The Copy-Cat Crime Phenomenon," in *Justice and the Media,* ed. Ray Surette (Springfield, IL: Thomas, 1984, 199–211); Alex Schmid and Jenny de Graaf, *Violence as Communication.* (Thousand Oaks, CA: Sage, 1982, 131–132); "Copycat Crime," *Issue Brief Series* (Studio City, CA: Mediascope Press, 2000).

There is no evidence of a direct media criminalizing effect on previously law-abiding individuals. The media influence how people commit a crime to a greater extent than they influence whether people commit a crime. In sum, media content is erroneously often described as a crime trigger where in reality the media is most often a crime rudder, molding crime's form rather than being its engine.

By what mechanism do the media generate copycat effects? Here again, knowledge is limited and speculation prevails. In that the concept implies the imitation of an initial crime, the obvious starting point in discussing copycat crime is imitation. Gabriel Tarde was first to offer a theoretical discussion of copycat crime in the late nineteenth and early twentieth century.[35] Focusing on violent crime and observing that sensational violent crime appears to prompt similar incidents, he coined the term *suggesto-imitative assaults* to describe the phenomenon. In a pithy summation, he concluded, "Epidemics of crime follow the line of the telegraph." Tarde's line of research was ignored in criminology until the 1970s, when a surge of copycat crimes involving airline hijackings and media interest in them led to renewed attention to the role of imitation in the generation of crime. Picking up directly from Tarde's earlier perspective, initial copycat crime researchers attributed copycat crime to a process of simple and direct imitation based on social learning tenets.

More recently, though, imitation has been criticized as too simplistic a process to fully explain copycat crime. It fails to explain why most children imitate aggression within socially acceptable limits and only a few imitate aggression with a real gun. Critics have also noted that imitation theory focuses on the copycat criminal and tends to downplay other social factors. Today imitation is considered a necessary but insufficient factor in the generation of copycat crime. The primary flaw in imitation theory is that it generally implies that the copycat behavior must physically resemble the portrayed behavior and therefore falls short in explaining any generalized effects or innovative applications.

Partly in response, Leonard Berkowitz posited another mechanism, more general than imitation, by which media portrayals activate similar behaviors.[36] Through this mechanism, termed a **priming** effect, the portrayals of certain behaviors by the media activate a cluster of associated ideas and concepts within the potential copycat offender that increase the likelihood that he or she will behave similarly but not necessarily identically.[37] Priming holds that when people read or hear or witness an event via the mass media, ideas within their minds having a similar meaning are activated for a short time, and these thoughts can result in related actions. Thus after viewing violent media, individuals will be primed to have more hostile thoughts, to see aggression as justified, and to behave more aggressively.[38] Priming can be understood within the perspective of this work as providing a set of ideas and beliefs that construct a particular social reality—the perception that the nature of the world is such that a particular type of crime is appropriate, justified, and likely to be successful.

A study by Allen Mazur offers an example of priming in the area of crime.[39] Mazur reported that bomb threats directed at nuclear energy facilities increased significantly following increases in news coverage of nuclear power issues. Mazur's study is important in that it indicates that the media may initiate crimes even when they don't provide precise models

## 3.3  John Hinckley's Copycat Crime

The shooting of President Reagan by John Hinckley Jr., a crime ideal for exploitation as infotainment, is also a good example of a copycat crime. Hinckley's assassination attempt on President Reagan and Hinckley's bizarre life fit the psychotic-killer narrative popular in crime-related entertainment. Because of this overlap, the Hinckley story provided the media with both great entertainment and news material, having elements of drama, celebrities, money, and filmed violence. The entertainment media provided the role model and reality structure Hinckley followed in formulating his assassination attempt, which the news media used to frame the resulting coverage. In a study of the media coverage of the assassination attempt, Robert Snow observed:

> Hinckley's story was perfect for news media, and television news in particular, as it went beyond the usual character of a major news story. The Hinckley case not only had drama, a famous person, and filmed violence; it had an unexpected and fascinating twist. [Hinckley] was motivated by an apparent irrational desire to impress a movie star. As reported by network television news, Hinckley was characterized much like the psychotic killer in a fictional television drama.

The Hinckley saga displays the full range of possible effects by the media on crime and justice, from creating a tolerant atmosphere for violence, to providing criminal role models and techniques, to influencing the public reaction to the justice system's processing of the case, to fostering a copycat crime for notoriety.

---

*Source:* Robert Snow, "Crime and Justice in Prime-Time News: The John Hinckley, Jr. Case," in *Justice and the Media*, ed. Ray Surette (Springfield, IL: Thomas, 1984), 226.

to copy; the bomb threats to nuclear facilities followed news stories that were not bomb-related. In Berkowitz's conceptualization, the news media coverage primed some people to make bomb threats even though the coverage did not provide a specific bomb-threat model to copy. John Hinckley's assassination attempt on President Reagan is a well-known anecdotal example of a crime where media priming also occurred (see Box 3.3).

At this time, copycat crime appears to be concentrated in predisposed, at-risk individuals primed by media characterizations of crime. This proposition leads to the model of copycat crime shown in Figure 3.1. Copycat crime is seen as the result of the interaction of four factors: the initial crime and criminal, subsequent media coverage, the social context,

FIGURE 3.1
A Reiterative Model of Copycat Crime

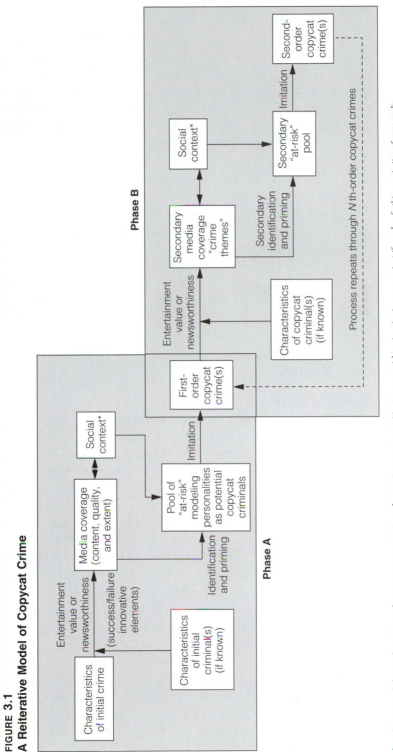

*Social context includes social norms regarding crime, news reporting and entertainment; opportunities to copy; social tensions (racism, economic strife, and so forth); organization of mass media (state, private, profit, nonprofit, accessibility, regulation, audience size, and credibility).

and the characteristics of the copycat criminal. The model denotes a process in which select, usually successful, highly newsworthy crimes shown in popular entertainment or news media emerge as candidates for copying. The media coverage and portrayals first affect individuals by inviting them to identify with the initial crime and criminal and thereby prime a pool of potential copycat criminals. A susceptible **modeling personality**—that is, a person who sees other people and the media as profitable crime information sources—is thought to exist and to be at special risk for copycat behavior.[40] The size of this pool is affected both by the level of media attention and by other social context factors such as social norms regarding deviance and violence; the preexistence of social conflicts; the number of opportunities available to the potential offender to copy a crime technique (there are more opportunities to copy a car theft technique, for example, than a bank robbery technique); the nature, credibility, and pervasiveness of the mass media; and the size of the preexisting criminal population. Unfortunately, contemporary U.S. society scores high on all of these criteria; therefore, the generation of copycat crimes should be high in the United States compared to other countries. After the at-risk copycat pool emerges, the first wave of copycat crimes results through a process of generalized primed imitation, limited by and adapted to the copycat criminal's opportunities (Phase A).

Should these first-order copycat crimes receive further media attention, and particularly should they be incorporated into a news media crime theme, the likelihood of additional copycat crime increases (Phase B). This extended reiterative process is regarded as much more likely to occur with violent crime because of the high news value of violence. Thus the model reflects a paradox. The process is more common for property crime and property offenders through first-order copycat crimes (Phase A). But violent copycat crime and offenders are most likely to generate second and higher-order imitations (Phase B) as they are more likely to become the focus of intensive news media attention. Once more the media take the rare real-world event, the violent copycat crime, and make it the more significant, better known event in the public's constructed reality. The accepted social construction of a copycat crime is more likely to be of a violent crime such as a bombing even though in actuality copycat property crimes are probably far more common.

It is clear that copycat crimes occur fairly regularly, but the number of such crimes generated by the media is not known. Even before the September 11, 2001, World Trade Center and Pentagon attacks, the copycat crimes that generated the most concern were those related to terrorism. Today, terrorism's relationship to the media is the leading cause of anxiety in the media, crime, and justice area.

## Media-Oriented Terrorism

Terrorism's relationship with the media epitomizes the dangers of copycat effects. Carlos Marighella, a Communist insurgent terrorist in the 1960s, described the terrorists' aim in their interactions with media:

> These actions, carried out with specific and determined objectives, inevitably become propaganda material for the mass communication system. . . . The war of nerves or psychological war is an aggressive technique, based on the direct or indirect use of mass means of communication and news in order to demoralize the government. In psychological warfare, the government is always at a disadvantage since it imposes censorship on the mass media and winds up in a defensive position by not allowing anything against it to filter through. At this point it becomes desperate, is involved in great contradictions and loss of prestige, and loses time and energy in an exhausting effort at control which is subject to being broken at any moment.[41]

The strength of the symbiotic media–terrorism relationship is such that in many ways the modern terrorist is the creation of the media. If mass media did not exist, terrorists would have to invent them.[42] Media and terrorists share several needs. Most fundamentally, both are trying to reach the greatest number of people possible. Driven by their mutual goal to maximize audience size, a new type of terrorist act has emerged—the **media-oriented terrorist event** (or MOTE), where violence is scripted to earn publicity.[43] **Media-oriented terrorism** is "propaganda by deed," a purposely symbolic crime, and today a steady stream of terrorist acts can be identified as media-oriented terrorist events characterized by the selection of high-visibility targets, graphic terrorist acts, preevent contact with media outlets, and postevent videos, interviews, and other media accommodations.

Like politicians, media-oriented terrorists have learned to manipulate coverage to bypass the editing and contextual formatting of journalists and go directly to the public with their message.[44] In the process, terrorism has become a form of infotainment and public theater. On the other side, the media can be thought of as innately "terrorism oriented" in terms of the commercial value of terrorist events. Due to the huge audience it attracts, media-oriented terrorism is highly valuable to media organizations.

> For the media, terrorism is dramatic, often violent, visual, and timely. Unlike wars which are usually protracted and highly complex events . . . acts of terrorist violence normally have a beginning and an end, can be encompassed in a few minutes of air time, possess a large degree of drama, involve participants who are perceived by the viewing public as unambiguous, and are not so complex as to be unintelligible to those who tune in only briefly.[45]

All of this transforms terrorism into high ratings and readership levels for the media. And as the media pursued terrorists, terrorists became

© Reuters/Landov

The September 11, 2001 attacks on the World Trade Center towers and the Pentagon are examples of media-oriented terrorist events.

media wise. They now understand the dynamics of newsworthiness and the benefits of news coverage: increased legitimacy and political status; heightened perception of their strength and threat; and an increased ability to attract resources, support, and recruits.

   Contemporary media-oriented terrorists are guided by five principles.[46] First, their acts are not tactical in nature but are aimed at distant external audiences. Second, victims are chosen for symbolic meaning to maximize fear and public impact. Third, the media are eager to cover terrorist violence and will devote significant resources to reporting media-oriented terrorist events. Fourth, the media can be activated, directed, and manipulated for propaganda effects. Fifth, target governments are at a disadvantage because their choice is usually between censorship and allowing terrorists to use the media. The application of these principles has resulted in the spread of media-oriented terrorism around the world. In the research literature on terrorism, no doubts are expressed that the media motivate copycat terrorist acts or that a substantial number of terrorist events are aimed primarily at garnering publicity.[47] The media are seen as providing the potential terrorist with all the ingredients needed to engage in terrorism by reducing inhibitions against the use of violence, offering models and technical know-how, and providing a host of benefits to their cause from subsequent publicity.

Even after the galvanizing impact of September 11, 2001, gaining media attention is not guaranteed, particularly for terrorist groups not linked to al-Qaeda. Worldwide, many more acts of terrorism are committed than are reported in the media, and U.S. media give more coverage to terrorism aimed at U.S. citizens or property.[48] The resulting competition for media attention causes terrorists to escalate their violence because more violent and more dramatic acts are necessary to gain news coverage as the shock value of ordinary terrorism diminishes. Occupation of a building, for example, no longer garners world or even national coverage in many instances. As long as news reporting is a commercial product whose content is influenced by sensationalism, excessive coverage will afford the more violent terrorist acts disproportionate significance. Media-oriented terrorist events can be expected to be increasingly violent.

In the end, the impact of media coverage on terrorism is twofold. First, coverage of a terrorist act encourages copycats. As with general copycat crime, there is much anecdotal evidence that terrorist events such as kidnappings, bank robberies in which hostages are taken, plane hijackings, parachute hijackings, planting altitude bombs on airplanes, and suicide bombings occur in clusters. These copycat effects are especially strong following a well-publicized successful terrorist act using a novel approach. Second, media-oriented terrorism contributes an additional impact. Terrorism performed for media has become a staple of the twenty-first century. Although their numbers wax and wane, the pattern of these violent performances suggests that media-oriented terrorism has been a persistent element of the total terrorism picture since the 1972 Olympics when Palestine Liberation Organization terrorists killed members of the Israeli Olympic team. Copycat events combined with media-oriented terrorist crimes will continue to significantly influence the quantity and nature of terrorism.

Today terrorism is less tactical and more a twisted public relations "infotainment" effort on the part of terrorists. Like other types of crime, we would still have terrorism if the media disappeared, but the media–terrorism relationship exacerbates the amount and types of these crimes.

## CRIMINOGENIC INFOTAINMENT

The public's high interest in crime-related media, the large proportion of media that is crime related, and the skewed content of the media have raised alarms about media that have become criminogenic and infotainment focused. The greatest concerns are associated with the media's predatory portrait of criminality and a media criminogenic effect. The cumulative result of the violent predator image, which favors individually based criminological theories as the best explanations of crime, constructs a social reality in which broad-based social and structural causes of crime are disparaged. It also creates a social reality wherein criminogenic media effects are plausible and likely.

Where does the research about violent, criminogenic, and terrorism-related media lead? The existing research suggests the following propositions. Most people exposed to pernicious media will show no negative effects. Some small proportion of people—the proportion is not clear—will show slight effects, concentrated more in attitudes than in behaviors. Strong behavioral effects are relatively rare and are most likely to appear in at-risk individuals predisposed to crime, but the reality of long-term effects on a large number of people remains a distinct possibility. In addition, the media's ability to generate greater numbers of predisposed at-risk individuals also appears to be real. Therefore, in the future, the media's criminogenic effects will be enhanced as their current crime-and-violence content contribute to an increased number of people at risk for negative media influences due to racial strife, income disparities, and poor social conditions. Violence-prone children and adults are especially at risk for emulating media violence. When sex and violence are linked, hyper-masculine males are most influenced. When the news media sensationalize crime and make celebrities of criminals, the danger of imitation for notoriety increases. And when successful crime is detailed either in print or visual media, criminals will emulate it. When a successful terrorist event is shown or a terrorist group is able to gain the attention of the media, media-oriented terrorism will increase.

Whether criminogenic effects, such as copycat crime, emerge in any particular individual depends on the highly idiosyncratic interactions of the content of a particular media product (its characterizations of crime and criminals), the individual's predispositions (personal criminal history, family, and environmental factors), and the media's social context (pre-existing cultural norms, crime opportunities, and pervasiveness of the mass media). A media-generated criminogenic effect ultimately depends on the combined influences of social context, media content, and audience characteristics. The more heavily the consumer relies on the media for information about the world and the greater his or her predisposition to criminal behavior, the greater the likelihood of an effect.

Media effects are real, but it is also apparent that the media alone cannot make someone a criminal. You can get an idea of what it would be like if the media went away by looking at the country before the mass media existed. What you will find is a violent land with many violent people.[49] That fact is the core reason it does not make sense to blame the media for the bulk of our violence and crime today. Based on our heritage, we would certainly be a violent and crime-burdened society today without the media's influences, but are we more violent and criminal because of them? This is also true. Violent media alone does not make a violent person, but violent media can make a violent person more often violent. Criminogenic media won't make a law-abiding person a criminal, but a preexisting criminal may become a greater threat. The media play their role after the biological, economic, and social variables factor in. To blame only the media is like blaming the bread for how the ham, cheese, baloney, turkey, and mustard sandwich tastes. But while you can argue that the media is not the main ingredient in our crime sandwich, media do facilitate the widespread packaging and delivery of a criminogenic meal.

In the end, the media's influence on the behavior of most of us is to cause us *not* to do certain things. The media do not turn law-abiding people into criminals or nonviolent people into assaulters, but they keep people from flying or taking a vacation in Europe or going downtown or opening the door for local trick or treaters. It makes us wary of each other and in doing so makes us more isolated and subsequently more dependent on the media for our knowledge about crime.

Media should not be painted as the dominant cause of crime in society, but their portraits of criminality cannot be ignored. By painting crime in a particular hue, the media color the actual world as violent, predatory, and dangerous. They supply criminal role models and techniques, create a conducive social atmosphere for the predisposed few to emulate the crimes they see, hear, and read about, and provide the theoretical ideas that explain it all to the public while largely absolving that public of any social responsibility. With this image of criminality in mind, Chapter 4 looks at the relationship of the media and the first line of response to crime, law enforcement.

## DISCUSSION QUESTIONS

1.  How much of the crime and violence in society would disappear if there were no crime-and-justice media?
2.  Do you feel that some types of media (films or books, for example) are more criminogenic than others? Is some content more dangerous than other content? Describe the content you think is most dangerous, and explain why you think it is.
3.  What public policies would you support to reduce media criminogenic influences? What policies would you be adamantly against?
4.  Why does the predator criminal enjoy such lasting popularity?

## IN-CLASS ACTIVITY

Watch the film *The Silence of the Lambs* as a basis to discuss predatory criminals in the media.

## ASSIGNMENT

Watch an entertainment film based on a real serial killer and write a brief essay comparing the media rendition with historical facts about the case. Here are some examples to get you started: Ted Bundy and the film *The Stranger Beside Me*; Charlie Starkweather and the films *Badlands* and *Murder in the Heartland*; Aileen Wuornos and the film *Monster*; Henry Lee Lucus and the film *Henry: Portrait of a Serial Killer*.

## SUGGESTED READINGS

Karen Boyle. 2005. *Media and Violence: Gendering the Debates*. Thousand Oaks, CA: Sage.

Thomas Leitch and Barry Grant. 2002. *Crime Films*. Cambridge, UK: Cambridge University Press.

Nicole Rafter. 2000. *Shots in the Mirror: Crime Films and Society*. Oxford, UK: Oxford University Press.

Dennis Rome. 2004. *Black Demons: The Media's Depiction of the African American Male Criminal Stereotype*. Westport, CT: Praeger.

Philip Simpson. 2000. *Psycho Paths: Tracking the Serial Killer through Contemporary American Film and Fiction*. Carbondale, IL: Southern Illinois University Press.

John Sumser. 1996. *Morality and Social Order in Television Crime Drama*. Jefferson, NC: McFarland.

Joseph Tuman. 2003. *Communicating Terror: The Rhetorical Dimensions of Terrorism*. Thousand Oaks, CA: Sage.

## NOTES

1. Stark, "Perry Mason Meets Sonny Crockett," 236.

2. Rafter, *Shots in the Mirror*; see also Leitch and Grant, *Crime Films*.

3. Lynch, Stretesky, and Hammond found, for example, that regarding chemical crimes, a very small percentage of events are reported as news; those that are reported are likely to be cast as caused by an individual and the harm of the event downplayed ("Media Coverage of Chemical Crimes," 121–122).

4. Graber, *Crime News and the Public*.

5. Curran, "Communications, Power and Social Order," 227.

6. For example, Eric Hickey (*Serial Murderers and Their Victims*, 3) tracks the number of serial murder themed films: 2 (1920s), 3 (1930s), 3 (1940s), 4 (1950s), 12 (1960s), 20 (1970s), 23 (1980s), and 117 (1990s). Yvonne Jewkes (*Media and Crime*, 94–105) describes an analogous process in Britain concerning pedophiles.

7. Simpson, *Psycho Paths*.

8. Jenkins, *Moral Panic*.

9. For discussions of the culture that has developed around serial killers, see Ian Conrich, "Mass Media/Mass Murder"; and Schechter, *The Serial Killer Files*, 369–402.

10. The popularity of violent predatory crime is also likely associated with a downward comparison effect. *Downward comparison* is a psychological process in which people feel better about their own situation when they see someone in a worse one. Therefore, a media image of violent urban crime would have a soothing effect on middle-class suburban Americans by holding up to them a crime-and-justice construction of reality that is more violent and dangerous than what they are experiencing. And, as this violent crime is shown as due to individual deficiencies like greed and innate evil, the apparently better-off-by-comparison rest of America can enjoy a guilt-free boost regarding their crime situation while being encouraged to purchase security products.

11. Lichter and Lichter, *Prime Time Crime*. Robert Reiner points out that, ironically, in relation to property crime risk, television has become safer than the real world ("Media Made Criminality," 391).

12. Wilson et al., "Violence in Television Programming Overall."

13. Shelly and Ashkins, "Crime, Crime News, and Crime Views"; see also Dowler, "Comparing American and Canadian Local Television Crime Shows," 583; Duwe, "Body-Count Journalism"; Reiner, Livingstone, and Allen, "No More Happy Endings?", 114–115.

14. Shipley and Cavender, "Murder and Mayhem at the Movies."

15. Rafter, *Shots in the Mirror*, 48.

16. Ibid.

17. Lichter and Lichter, *Prime Time Crime.*

18. Thomas, "The Psychology of Yellow Journalism," 491.

19. *Sourcebook of Criminal Justice Statistics—2000.* "Table 2.44: Attitudes toward Contributors to Violence in Society."

20. *Sourcebook of Criminal Justice Statistics—2000.* "Table 2.42 Attitudes toward the Causes of Crime in the United States," and "Table 2.45: Respondents Perceptions about the Primary Cause of Gun Violence."

21. Sasson, *Crime Talk*, 161.

22. Sparks and Sparks list five theoretical groups: catharsis, priming, arousal, desensitization, and cultivation as potential violent media effect mechanisms ("Effects of Media Violence," 278–280). For a recent review of the media violence debate, see Boyle, *Media and Violence: Gendering the Debates.*

23. A recent summary of this research is offered by Huesmann and his colleagues: "Childhood exposure to media violence predicts young adult aggressive behavior for both males and females. Identification with aggressive television characters and perceived realism of TV violence also predict later aggression. These relations persist even when the effects of socioeconomic status, intellectual ability, and a variety of parenting factors are controlled" ("Longitudinal Relations between Children's Exposure to TV Violence and Their Aggressive and Violent Behavior," 201). See also Freedman, *Media Violence and Its Effect on Aggression.*

24. See, for example Heath, Bresolin, and Rinaldi, "Effects of Media Violence on Children"; and Wilson et al., "Violence in Television Programming Overall," 3–267.

25. Wilson and Herrnstein, *Crime and Human Behavior*, 343.

26. Huesmann, Moise-Titus, Podolski, and Eron, "Longitudinal Relations between Children's Exposure to TV Violence and Their Aggressive and Violent Behavior," 210.

27. Hennigan et al., "Impact of the Introduction of Television on Crime in the United States," 474.

28. Bleyer, *Main Currents in the History of American Journalism.*

29. Papke, *Framing the Criminal*, 171–172.

30. Hays, *President's Report to the Motion Picture Producers and Distributors' Association.*

31. Toplin, *Unchallenged Violence: An American Ordeal.*

32. Cook, Kendzierski, and Thomas, "The Implicit Assumptions of Television Research"; Canter, Sheehan, Alpers, and Mullen, "Media and Mass Homicides."

33.  Pease and Love, "The Copy-Cat Crime Phenomenon."

34.  Heller and Polsky, *Studies in Violence and Television,* 151–152.

35.  Tarde, *Penal Philosophy,* 137.

36.  Berkowitz, "Some Effects of Thoughts on Anti- and Prosocial Influences of Media Events"; see also Berkowitz and Rogers, "A Priming Effect Analysis of Media Influences."

37.  Roskos-Ewoldsen, Roskos-Ewoldsen, and Carpentier, "Media Priming: A Synthesis."

38.  Jo and Berkowitz, "A Priming Effect Analysis of Media Influences," 46.

39.  Mazur, "Bomb Threats and the Mass Media."

40.  Surette, "Self-Reported Copy Cat Crime among a Population of Serious Violent Juvenile Offenders." In addition, few differences have been found between juvenile offenders and nonoffenders in media consumption and use. See Hagell and Newburn, *Young Offenders and the Media.*

41.  As cited in Alexander, "Terrorism and the Media," 161.

42.  For a specific example of the complicated relationship between the media and terrorism, see Hayes, "Political Violence, Irish Republicanism and the British Media."

43.  Surette and Noble, "Working Paper: Media Oriented Terrorism"; Tuman, *Communicating Terror*; and Weimann and Winn, *The Theater of Terror: Mass Media and International Terrorism,* 47.

44.  See Paletz and Schmid, *Terrorism and the Media,* for an overview.

45.  Livingstone, *The War against Terrorism,* 62.

46.  Weimann and Winn, *The Theater of Terror,* 57.

47.  Poland, *Understanding Terrorism,* 47; and Weimann and Winn, *The Theater of Terror.*

48.  Schmid and de Graaf, *Violence as Communication*; and Weimann and Winn, *The Theater of Terror.*

49.  Courtwright, *Violent Land: Single Men and Social Disorder from the Frontier to the Inner City.* A wry comment on the level of violence in pre–mass media society in the United States is provided by the Salt Lake *Deseret News* in the 1860s: "The place is rapidly becoming civilized. Several men having been killed there already" (as cited in Ambrose, *Nothing Like It in the World,* 337).

# CRIME FIGHTERS

## CHAPTER OBJECTIVES

After completing Chapter 4, you will be able to describe the major divisions in the media portrait of law enforcement and discuss the differences and similarities between professional crime fighters who work for the criminal justice system and the civilian crime fighters who do not. Regarding the law enforcement narratives found in the media— lampooned police, G-men and procedurals, and street cops—you will be able to differentiate between each genre and understand the core differences between police work as shown in the media and real police work. You will be able to compare the portraits of private eyes and private citizens as crime fighters in the media with those of police officers. Finally, you will understand the link between media portraits of crime fighting and public support of anticrime policies.

## LAW ENFORCEMENT: A HOUSE DIVIDED

After criminality, the media pays the most attention to fighting crime. In the United States, law enforcement has high visibility coupled with low public knowledge.[1] That is, the public is exposed to large amounts of crime-fighting content in news, entertainment, and infotainment, most of it terribly distorted if not plain wrong. The first problem with the media construction of law enforcement is that it is schizophrenic, persistently presenting two competing law enforcement frames of "good cop" or "bad cop." In the good cop frame, the criminal justice system, particularly the police, are part of a justice machine with dedicated professionals using the latest technology to repeatedly prove that crime does not pay. In the competing and more common "bad cop" frame, the criminal justice system and its police are so inefficient and bound by regulations, politics, corruption, and incompetence that only the outsider rogue cop or citizen crime fighter can get anything positive accomplished.

In addition to the good cop/bad cop schizophrenia, another secondary split exists in the media's portrait of law enforcement. In the media, crime is fought by either professional or citizen soldiers. These soldiers either expertly or incompetently (depending on whether they are within a good cop or bad cop frame) wage a war against predatory violent crime. The terms *war* and *soldier* are not used here simply as colorful adjectives; across the media spectrum crime fighting is depicted as a never-ending battle against evil doers.[2] The enemy is everywhere, the battlegrounds can be anywhere, and anyone may be caught in the crossfire at any time. The media portraits of law enforcement reflect these two basic divisions and the overarching construction of effective anticrime policies as warlike rather than socially restorative and reconstructive.

The professional soldiers in the media war on crime usually occupy law enforcement positions, but lawyers, judges, wardens, and corrections officers also sometimes morph into crime fighters. These are the professional, career soldiers in the media's portrait of the war on crime, and they are often matched up with a competent criminal justice system filled with effective crime scene technicians and experts in criminalistics to help solve crimes. When the professionals of the criminal justice system are the main crime fighters in the media, civilians usually have a minor role, frequently serving solely as hapless victims.

On the other hand, when civilian crime fighters are portrayed as the primary crime fighters, the police and the criminal justice system are downplayed and often disparaged. Civilian crime fighters are unavoidably enhanced when paired with an incompetent criminal justice system. The traditional criminal justice components and personnel, especially the police, are often shown as part of the crime problem, either through corruption or ineptitude, when civilian crime fighters are on the scene. The "citizen soldiers" in the war on crime are shown to be successful where the bureaucratic, hampered, and often not so bright, career law enforcers are not.

This media house divided subsequently projects two conflicting messages about law enforcement. The first is that the expertise to deal with crime can only be found in the criminal justice system. Enhancement of the criminal justice system and unleashing the police is one core message in the media's construction of crime fighting. The second and opposite core message is that the incompetence of the criminal justice system and its people requires that individuals protect their own homes and communities and solve crime problems themselves. In the first social construction, we are told to wait for heroes to save us, in the second we are told we had better save ourselves. What the two messages share is that the solutions will require violence.

Whether a criminal justice or a civilian hero is emphasized is not, for the most part, related to the type of crime being portrayed. Most types of crime stories are comfortable with either official or civilian heroes. Popular mystery and detective tales in which the search for clues is the key story element have employed both private investigators and police as their heroic sleuths. Similarly, crime thrillers that feature endangered victims and heroes; modernized Westerns in which heroic outsiders reluctantly clean up a town; crime, revenge, and vigilante stories in which a victim-hero is injured and retaliates; and action crime stories that feature superhero crime fighters all utilize both criminal justice employees and private citizens as heroes.[3] Within these stories both civilian and professional crime fighters can be either law-abiding role models (good cops) or less straight-and-narrow adventurers, gunfighters, loners, and sometimes criminals themselves (bad cops). The first group represents the incorruptible all-American hero narrative; the more ambiguous individualistic and self-reliant second group represents our cultural admiration of the rebel. The rebels seem to enjoy themselves more and appear to be effective more quickly (not having to wait for search warrants or worry about repercussions from using entrapment or coercion), so it is not surprising that they far outnumber the law-abiding crime fighters in the media. As the largely inaccurate legends of Jesse James, Bonnie and Clyde, Wild Bill Hickok, Eliot Ness, and Al Capone exemplify, media reconstructions have habitually made folk heroes out of criminals and heroic crime fighters out of less than stellar individuals. By-the-book crime fighters are usually outdistanced by kick-your-butt, recently suspended, or wanted ones. Be it professionals or civilians, good cops or bad cops, it is undeniable that the media supplies a great number of law enforcement depictions. Solving crimes and apprehending criminals is an immensely popular media pastime.

## MEDIA CONSTRUCTS OF PROFESSIONAL SOLDIERS IN THE WAR ON CRIME

Culturally, we have long been fascinated with the police and their work. We relish and devour media that is **front-end loaded**, which concentrates on the origins of crime and crime's investigation and solution. Our first crime-and-justice love is media constructions of crime and criminality (discussed in Chapter 3). Once crimes have been committed, the people who enforce the laws and pursue the criminals are second in media and public interest. We particularly relish the investigation, pursuit, and capture of criminals by formal agents of the law. Police dramas on television, for example, are nearly twice as frequent in number and duration as civilian crime fighter private eye shows.[4] Three stereotypes of professional law enforcement are found in the media: lampooned police, G-men, and cops.[5] Like most media constructions, once created all three survived and compete for influence today, and each contributes in its own way to the social construction of law enforcement.

## Lampooned Police

Lampooned police appeared soon after the birth of the film industry and initially were introduced by the Keystone Kops and Charlie Chaplin films in the 1920s. **Lampooned police** is a popular media frame that satirized law enforcement as foolish, slapstick police officers in television characters like Barney Fife and films in the *Police Academy* genre. These depictions continue to be popular with the public, if not always with real police. Some of these early portrayals of the police so upset the International Association of the Chiefs of Police, for example, that its members passed a resolution at their 1913 meeting pledging to change the depictions.[6] The Barney Fifes, Inspector Clouseaus, and Vaudeville styled *Police Academy* and *Naked Gun* films all provide escapist entertainment. Like gallows humor, they allow serious issues of police power and crime control to be discussed indirectly and in less threatening portraits. A police force that can be poked fun at is not one that must be feared. Similarly, crime that can be resolved by cartoon violence is less threatening. However, when the satire is felt to reflect a reality of incompetence or when it undermines the public support of police, these images raise an outcry among the public and law enforcement professionals.

## G-Men and Police Procedurals

G-men, also historically known as "crime-busters," arose during the Depression and have periodically been invigorated by media attempts to appear more realistic. **G-men** represent a media law enforcement frame that focuses on effective, professional crime-busters. Tough federal agents emerged in the 1930s media as Hollywood responded to the Payne Fund research on the film industry and its social impact.[7] The resulting Hays Commission heavily criticized the movies for glorifying criminals and encouraging copycat crime (see Box 4.1).[8]

In response, the movie and radio industry shifted to G-man portrayals, in which federal law enforcement agents rather than criminals were the heroes.

The lampooning of police officers and formal law enforcement is found in some of the earliest silent movies. Shown are the Keystone Kops, a popular early media lampoon of the police first seen in 1912.

Stars such as James Cagney, who had previously played criminals, now found themselves cast as heroic crime fighters. These crime fighters were shown as professional, straight-laced, and Cagney aside, usually boring. This change in the construction of law enforcers marks the media shift from the local neighborhood "officer friendly" portrait of police officers, who were well meaning but largely incompetent against serious crime, to that of professional federal crime-busters. Previously, if police officers were shown at all,

## 4.1   *The Hays Code in Hollywood*

The Hays Code, adopted by major American movie studios in response to the criticisms voiced by the Hays Commission, imposed severe limitations on celluloid crime and justice:

> *General Principles:* 1. No picture shall be produced that will lower the moral standards of those who see it. Hence the sympathy of the audience should never be thrown to the side of crime, wrongdoing, evil or sin. 2. Correct standards of life, subject only to the requirements of drama and entertainment, shall be presented. 3. Law, natural or human, shall not be ridiculed, nor shall sympathy be created for its violation. . . .
>
> *Crimes Against the Law.* These shall never be presented in such a way as to throw sympathy with the crime as against law and justice or to inspire others with a desire for imitation. 1. Murder: a. The technique of murder must be presented in a way that will not inspire imitation. b. Brutal killings are not to be presented in detail. c. Revenge in modern times shall not be justified. 2. Methods of Crime should not be explicitly presented:
> a. Theft, robbery, safe-cracking, and dynamiting of trains, mines, buildings, etc., should not be detailed in method. b. Arson must subject to the same safeguards. c. The use of firearms should be restricted to the essentials. d. Methods of smuggling should not be presented. 3. Illegal drug traffic must never be presented.

*Source:* Will H. Hays, *President's Report to the Motion Picture Producers and Distributors' Association* (Washington, DC: U.S. Government Printing Office, 1932).

more often than not they were just there, walking a beat, personable but largely irrelevant. In contrast, the new crime fighters were aggressive, smart, and proactive. Because they were clearly not local police officers, the shift to G-men crime-busters also marks the beginning of a long-term denigration of local law enforcement. The "G," after all, stood for "government" and that government was the one in Washington, D.C. With the exception of local sheriffs in Westerns, local street police would not commonly be presented as capable of dealing with serious crime again until the 1970s. The tradition of professional, crime-busting portraits successfully made the transfer in the 1950s to television and continued as the dominant crime-fighting narrative frame. The *Naked City* on radio, *Dragnet* on radio and then television, and *Dick Tracy* in the comics are well-known early examples.

© Warner Brothers/The Kobal Collection

Based on the investigation of cases by two Los Angeles Police Department detectives, *Dragnet* was one of the first and most successful police procedural-style crime programs. Originating on radio in the late 1940s and running on television from 1952 to 1959 and again from 1967 to 1970, *Dragnet* emphasized police jargon and the technical aspects of law enforcement. Episodes began with the promise that "the story you are about to see is true; the names have been changed to protect the innocent."

Beginning a bit after and then paralleling the G-men portraits, the **police procedural** originated in the United States in the 1940s. Police procedurals attempt to portray the back-stage realities of police investigations in dramatic media portraits. They were, in essence, the first infotainment docudramas produced on criminal justice work. The crime fighters in these portraits normally rely heavily on teamwork and criminalistics to solve crimes. Especially well suited to television's stereotyping, simple story lines, and preference for short-term violent events, the police procedural presents policing in infotainment-based constructions in which a continuous response to an unending series of violent criminal acts is needed. Crime and the fight against it is constructed as the reserve of professional experts (see Box 4.2). Civilians and other law enforcement personal should not get involved, and do so at their peril. Analogous to the manner in which real and fictional crimes and criminals coalesced in the 1980s to socially construct serial killers, the G-men and the police procedurals portraits and the ongoing real-world police reform movement of the first half of the twentieth century collectively constructed criminality as a threat to middle-class lifestyles while encouraging a faith in expert police knowledge as the crime solution. The combined effect of the media portraits and the police professionalism movement was the social construction of aggressive proactive policing as the best policy course to address an apparently burgeoning crime problem.[9]

## *Cops*

The cops frame originated in the 1970s with the return of media portraits of professional, competent, local law enforcement heroes, which had disappeared from the media with the demise of the Western local sheriffs in the 1950s. In a small number of television shows, like *Dragnet* and *The Untouchables*, the professional police hero was kept alive until the 1970s when the cop narrative emerged. With the release of the film *Dirty Harry* in 1971, the premiere of the television show *Police Story* in 1973, and the publication of the novel *The New Centurions* in 1970, local street police as heroes was once again in vogue.

The new **cops** construction portrayed the local police as aggressive, crime-fighting, take-no-prisoners, frontline soldiers in the war on crime. Far from irrelevant, they were now the combat grunts who fought the crime war battles. Community policing, public service, traffic, and order maintenance duties were nowhere to be found in this new construction of the local police. Police became paramilitary units, citizens became civilians and collateral damage, and crime fighting became urban warfare. Local "cops" emerge in this construction as professional, seasoned soldiers engaged in proactive law and order battles—combat-hardened lifers in an unpopular war. Within the cop construction, criminality was simultaneously portrayed as the result of evil and weak individuals making bad choices. The criminals were clearly enemies, not citizens who had broken a law, and they had to be defeated as opposed to being deterred or rehabilitated.

## 4.2   The CSI Effect: Forensic Science and the Modern Police Procedural

Police dramas are having an unexpected impact in the real world: The public thinks every crime can be solved, and solved now—just like on television.

The scene, on TV, is of a dead kid in a high school bathroom. This, in itself, is not funny. What cracks up the senior forensic criminalist at the State Police Crime Laboratory is watching the forensic crew work a case on CBS's drama *CSI: Crime Scene Investigations*.

Crime scene investigators don't tackle murder suspects or pack heat. They don't storm into the lab demanding DNA reports. They don't prance around in leather pants and a halter top. It can take days to fingerprint a scene, months to process a single DNA sample. Most of that used to be inside crime scene stuff—shoptalk for cops and forensic scientists. Then *CSI* and a handful of bloodstained copycats took over prime time.

Real-life investigators are watching this gross new world and bracing for each boob-tube breakthrough. They call it the *"CSI* effect," a phenomenon in which actual investigations are driven by the expectations of the millions of people who watch fake whodunits on TV. It has contributed to jurors' desires to see more forensic testimony from the stand. Academic programs are springing up to accommodate people who now want to be forensic scientists. And it has spurred a phenomenon that defense lawyers call "junk science," in which high-paid, underqualified consultants are hired to lend a little razzle-dazzle to a case because in prime time we've learned that virtually anything left behind can solve a crime: sofa cushions, a dead insect, lint.

Jurors watch TV shows in which investigators walk onto scenes soaked with forensic evidence. Then they want to know why there's no DNA on the suspect's shirt collar or blood on his hands. Why aren't the hairs at the scene a match for those found inside the accused's cap? Even in the face of eyewitness testimony, juries are starting to say, "If all the possible forensic tests weren't done in a case, maybe somebody else committed the crime."

---

*Source:* Excerpted from Carlene Hempel, "TV's Whodunit Effect," *The Boston Globe Magazine*, February 9, 2003.

© Warner Brothers/Photofest

The character Dirty Harry marks the return of effective and aggressive local police to the media portrait of law enforcement in the 1970s.

Within this constructed world of domestic combat, the special socialization by an effective veteran crime fighter was needed to change the naïve civilian police recruit into the professional frontline crime-fighting soldier.[10] Police, like the combat veteran, have to be initiated into the police culture and instilled with the special knowledge and skills needed to survive in combat and deal with rampant criminality. Gaining this special knowledge frequently involved a violent unlearning of prior social conceptions picked up in the civilian world and the police academy. To survive, cops adopted the antibureaucracy attitude of the World War II -era private eye. Middle-class status, liberal attitudes, those college criminology and criminal justice courses, official police department procedures—all must be forgotten. As Dirty Harry says to his new Mexican American partner, "Don't go letting that sociology degree get you killed."[11] In Table 4.1, David Perlmutter's basic differences between media cops and real-world street officers are summarized. This media image of policing generates unrealistic public expectations about the real police and dissatisfaction when police don't act like their media portraits.[12]

Highly popular, seven different cop narratives are found today (see Table 4.2).[13] One of the most popular is the "rogues," officers who go off on their own in their pursuit of criminals and justice. Throwing off the

| TABLE 4.1 | Differences between Media Cops and Real Cops | |
| --- | --- | --- |
| | Media Cops | Real Cops |
| Action | Never a dull moment. They are doing something, about to do something, or planning to do something. | Tedium and adrenaline are both experienced. Filling out forms is the norm. Action is unexpected, not predictable. |
| Crime | Fighting serious crime is foremost. Felonies are most common. Each crime is unique and exceptional. Cops are attuned to these nuances and pay attention. | Felony arrests are rare; officers often spend time preventing crime and defusing social situations. The repetitive scripts of excuses and explanations for breaking the law rapidly dull their impact and the believability of suspects. |
| Violence | Cops are violent. They menace, fight, and shoot and kill with relative impunity. Physical force, even brutality, is part of their tool kit for solving crimes. | Officers also live in a mean world, but usually one of potential rather than actual violence. |
| Heroes and villains | Clearly defined good and evil with any ambiguities resolved by program's end. | The good and the bad is mostly gray. Good people do bad things; bad people sometimes perform good acts. Most people have elements of both. |
| Status | Patrolmen are often the dumb background foil; plainsclothes detectives are the brilliant problem solvers. | Officers are gatekeepers of the criminal justice system who make the first and crucial early decisions. |
| Insight | With an almost psychic awareness of what people are thinking and where the clues are, they overwhelmingly uncover the truth. Omniscient qualities allow them to defy procedures and still triumph. | Officers are given almost no advance data for encounters and are under great pressure to obey procedures and policy. |
| Closure | There are almost no unsolved cases on TV, (even on the shows with titles like *Unsolved Mysteries*). | Events have a middle, but no beginning and no end. Cops arrive when incidents are in progress and rarely see the resolution of cases they confront. |
| Justice | Cops rarely deal with law, which is more often seen as the obstacle to justice, a legal technicality pulled out by a shyster lawyer. The hero cop directly dispenses justice, makes things right, and avenges wrongs. | Real cops must obey the law. Because of the complexity of the law and the emphasis on due process rights, its glacial pace leaves cops enforcing rules they do not think work. |
| Back stage | Sanitized back stage. No matter how crude, the hero cop rarely alienates an audience. | Sex, lies, and stupidity are common themes. Cops often make fun of, complain about, or criticize many of the people they encounter, both victims and suspects. |

| TABLE 4.1 | Differences between Media Cops and Real Cops (Continued) | |
|---|---|---|
| | **Media Cops** | **Real Cops** |
| Chronology | Time compression. Events are edited to render swifter progress of the narrative and more rapid resolution. | The forever war with long periods of stasis. Cops understand how long it can take the system to resolve an issue. |
| Audience and public awareness | Godlike powers of observation by audience who see clues, overhear conversations, perceive revealing facial close-ups, and receive voice-overs with insider information kept from the cops. The audience ends up knowing more than the cops. | Uniformed police are first on the scene. They see what no one in the public sees except the perpetrators and victims, misery and blood at close quarters. |

Source: David Perlmutter, *Policing the Media* (Belmont, CA: Sage, 2000), 41–52.

restraints of agency approval, due process, and legal procedures, they display single-mindedness in a less than legal but usually moral crusade. Also common are the "corrupt cop" narratives, which have the officers taking the extra step and actually joining the dark-side forces of crime and evil. At the other extreme are "honest cop" narratives, which trace the hardships of cops trying to do the right thing in a corrupt police culture. "Buddy cop" stories work off the conflicts and complications from opposite personalities forced to work together; mismatched racial partners are a standard. "Comedy" and "action comedy" cop narratives toss reality to the winds. Comedy portrayals incorporate harmless slapstick violence in which bullets and punches fly but no one gets seriously hurt. Action comedies liberally add in explosions and spectacular stunts in which only the bad guys are seriously injured. Two recent additions to this family are "female cop" stories and "aging cop" stories. Female cop narratives have the positive, if yet unfulfilled, potential to lift women from their stereotypical crime-and-justice portraits as pseudomasculine or hyperfeminine creatures to equal crime-fighting heroes. "Aging cop" stories are a market response to the aging of the baby boom generation and the need to provide heroes they can identify with. In these stories, a weathered but still virile (mentally, physically, and sexually) police officer manages to be successful on all fronts. Except for the woman cop story lines, successful hypermasculinity is the common thread throughout the cop narratives. These portraits collectively reduce the crime issue to a contest between individuals. Not only is a social solution not needed, in the cop narratives crime is no longer even an agency problem. To solve crime, you don't need a criminal justice system, or even a police department. You don't even need a few good men, just one good cop will do.

| TABLE 4.2 | Film Examples of Cop Narratives |
|-----------|--------------------------------|
| **Narrative Type** | **Films** |
| Rogue cops | *Dirty Harry* (1971) |
| | *The French Connection* (1971) |
| Corrupt cops | *Training Day* (2001) |
| | *Unlawful Entry* (1992) |
| Honest cops | *Serpico* (1973) |
| | *The Untouchables* (1987) |
| Buddy cops | *48 Hours* (1982) |
| | *New Jack City* (1991) |
| Comedy cops | *Police Academy* (1984) |
| | *The Naked Gun* (1988) |
| Action comedy cops | *The Erasure* (1996) |
| | *Rush Hour* (1998) |
| Female cops | *Blue Steel* (1990) |
| | *Point of No Return* (1993) |
| Aging cops | *The Line of Fire* (2003) |
| | *Twilight* (1998) |

On the journalism print side, the constructed combat police officer was accompanied and enhanced with the marketing of **true crime** books, many written by newspaper crime reporters. These reporter memoirs are traditionally initiation narratives about a reporter's introduction into the cop world.[14] Similar to the necessity for police recruits to discard misleading knowledge acquired in the police academy and college to become effective combat cops, in these true crime narratives journalists have to be socialized into the ways of the street police. In the process they have to leave behind their journalistic sensibilities and social values and learn that the modern predatory criminal is a different creature.

In these true crime books the crime is usually homicide, and the reader looks over the cops' shoulders as they pursue criminals and clean up after violent messy events. (Of course, the other popular view in the true crime tradition looks over the shoulders of criminals while they violently create messy events. Not surprisingly, an interest in crime fighters is only exceeded by fascination with predator criminals. Tales of serial killer narratives naturally dominate the true crime genre.) The cop-oriented true crime memoirs contribute to the comforting illusion of police expertise, that crime, while pervasive, is effectively being handled by dogged, heroic police work.[15]

Turning to the news portrait of professional crime fighters, despite great interest in law enforcement, the news, particularly the visual news media, rarely focus on individual crime fighters.[16] Instead, the news media prefer to focus on crimes and criminals. In the news, law enforcement is normally referred to as generic agencies rather than individual crime fighters. When individuals are interviewed, they are most frequently administrators or media-relations specialists. Therefore, most individual crime-fighter portraits come not from traditional news but from either the pure entertainment content discussed previously or infotainment products. Infotainment programming fills in whatever gap exists between the entertainment and news portraits in the public's construction of the modern professional crime fighter. Reality police shows, a subset of infotainment programming, are of special interest because these shows are promoted as delivering a slice of unaltered crime fighting and, unlike the news, focus heavily on individual crime fighters.

## Police as Infotainment: "Who you gonna call?"

First appearing in 1989, **police reality programs** have become a regular part of the crime-and-justice media, with the theme song of one show, *COPS*, becoming a pop hit in 1993.[17] In these productions viewers are invited to share a street cop's point of view as a partner officer. Not surprisingly, the demographic that most future police officers will be recruited from—young, white males—are their largest audience component. The attraction of these shows is clearly voyeuristic, with content running the gamut from dealing with ordinary street crime to the unusual violent predation. The cooperating police departments also have editorial control over the end product and routinely eliminate any scenes of police violence, malfeasance, or ineptitude. Thus, in her study of these shows, Pamela Donovan found that the final construction invariably shows the police as sensitive, knowledgeable, and competent, never careless, corrupt, foul-mouthed, or overwhelmed.[18] In a companion study, Aaron Doyle points out the highly selective picture of criminal justice found in these programs, which overrepresents both violent crime and the proportion of crime solved by police.[19] One police infotainment show, *COPS*, was found to grossly overrepresent violent crime; murder, rape, aggravated assault, and robbery made up 43 percent of all the crimes shown.[20] Reflecting the operation of the **backwards law**—that the media will present the opposite of crime-and-justice reality—Table 4.3 compares the distribution of violent and property crimes on the show with their distribution in the Uniform Crime Report statistics for one selected year.

| TABLE 4.3 | Index Crimes on *COPS* and in the UCR (1994) | | | |
|---|---|---|---|---|
| | **COPS** | | **UCR** | |
| **Type of Crime** | **Number** | **%** | **Number** | **%** |
| Violent | 58 | 84 | 1,864,168 | 13 |
| Property | 11 | 16 | 12,127,507 | 87 |
| Total | 69 | 100 | 13,991,675 | 100 |

Source: Kooistra, Mahoney, and Westervelt, "The World of Crime According to *COPS*," Table 4.2, 148.

Crime selection aside, how realistically do these reality shows portray police work? In the view of Paul Kooistra and his colleagues, "Crime [fighting] on these shows is a caricature that is shaped more by the organizational demands of television than by carefully documented representations of reality."[21] Unlike the traditional news, where you can see the commentators and reporters and where editing decisions are more apparent, reality programming works from a different process in its format, style, and texture. In these shows, there are no production clues, narrators, actors, scripts, or hosts to suggest editing or formatting. The infotainment audience does not easily realize and are not given hints that they are receiving a heavily reconstructed piece of reality. As shown in Figure 4.1, because the content is presented as if unaltered, the constructed reality found in reality programming is more misleading than the constructed reality portrayed in the news where the editing and production decisions are clearly visible.

For reality shows, production techniques are borrowed from entertainment shows. These programs are formatted to unobtrusively fill in missing facts and scenes to hide the editing and molding of their content. Time gaps are smoothed over, and holes in knowledge or action are filled. It is through their production techniques that these shows can grossly misrepresent police work and still manage to come across as reality programming. As criminologist Gray Cavender points out, realism is achieved in these efforts by mimicking the early entertainment "police procedural" films of the 1940s and 1950s and applying an entertainment style of "gritty realism."[22] Employing low-cost production values establishes an atmosphere of "being there" for the viewer. Ironically, producing reality programs cheaply results in increasing their believability.

The demographics on these shows constructs crime so that nonwhites account for more than half of all suspects shown, about two-thirds of the

FIGURE **4.1**
## Crime News Compared with Police Reality Programming

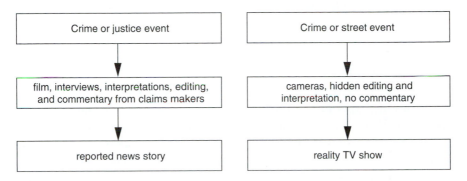

**Crime News**

With crime news it is clear that you are getting a condensed event, usually described and explained to you by someone clearly in a position of authority.

**Infotainment Police Reality Programming**

With reality programming the molding of content is hidden and difficult to discern. A live documentary feel is given to the portrait of police work, and you are encouraged to believe you are seeing unedited raw video footage.

| Crime or justice event |
| --- |

↓

| film, interviews, interpretations, editing, and commentary from claims makers |
| --- |

↓

| reported news story |
| --- |

| Crime or street event |
| --- |

↓

| cameras, hidden editing and interpretation, no commentary |
| --- |

↓

| reality TV show |
| --- |

police are white, and more than half of the victims shown are white. These shows construct a reality in which the most typical police crime-fighting events are white police battling nonwhite criminals while protecting white victims. In addition, almost 75 percent of the crimes portrayed in these infotainment shows are cleared by arrest, compared with the 18 percent clearance rate for property crime and 44 percent clearance rate for violent crime reported in the UCR statistics. Because of these factors, reality police programs most closely resemble pure entertainment media portrayals of crime fighting. The media crime-and-justice backwards law is equally applicable to police reality shows.

The backwards law results in these infotainment shows promoting two claims about crime fighting.[23] The carefully chosen and edited footage encourages the claims that:

- The police are in a contest with criminals who are unlike law-abiding citizens. Reality police shows further encourage the construction of criminals as predatory deviant others, people who are utterly unlike the rest of us.
- The police invariably get it right. The people they stop really are criminals. Viewers never get to see the police battering down doors to the wrong apartment or arresting the wrong person. Legal rules invariably hamper the police needlessly and get in the way of effective law enforcement. There appears to be no reason to place

legal checks on how the police do their job, and constitutional safeguards make no sense.

In the end, crime control is applauded, due process is disparaged. Individual causes of crime, assumed guilt of suspects, and an "us" versus "them" portrait dominates these constructions. The police emerge as our best defense, but they need help—in this constructed world, the audience, the police, and television must work together to fight crime. Analogous to videogames, viewers are prodded to become interactive—to be on the lookout, call in tips, and help catch fugitives—to, in effect, enlist in the crime war effort.

What is the effect of these shows? Aaron Doyle reports that most see the shows as realistic and think of them as informational rather than entertainment, as more similar to local news than to fictional TV storytelling.[24] Society is seen to be in decline and in a constant state of crisis because of spiraling crime, particularly violent street crimes committed by lower class offenders, and aggressive law enforcement is shown as the last hope. Another concern with the portrait of police work found in police reality programming comes from its effect on real police. Doyle reports that, like courtroom cameras influencing trial attorneys, there is anecdotal evidence of police tailoring their behavior for the cameras, behaving not as they actually do but as they believe the audience expects them to. Shows like *COPS* appear as a fantasy come true for police officers raised on the media's fictional police heroics found in entertainment crime dramas.[25] Here is the law enforcement career as they were led to believe it would be, full of crime-busting excitement. Finally, the solution proffered in police infotainment programming is drawn from the faulty system frame: Crime is out of control because the criminal justice system is misaligned. Society needs tougher crime control: due process and civil rights are part of the problem, and more unfettered police are needed.

## Police and the Media

In the 1990s there was a transition to community policing in the real police world and a media fixation on criminal profiling in the media-constructed one. In the resulting mix, the media did not simply lionize police professionalism or technical expertise. Criticisms of the police abound in the media, but as the media drifted into infotainment content, media dependence on police cooperation increased. The police are sought, quoted, and catered to on one hand, marginalized and criticized on the other. Factual and fictional cop narratives remain popular and, as shown by the development of women and aging cop portraits, are flexible enough to evolve and to respond to changing demographics and market needs. In addition to female lead crime fighters, the emergence and acceptance of minority actors as lead heroic cops is another healthy trend. The media-constructed world of professional crime-fighting soldiers is secure. Ironically, this world is largely constructed in the entertainment and infotainment segments of the media. The traditional news media do not normally focus on crime fighters except when they suffer a personal fall from grace or are killed. That is, individual crime fighters become newsworthy when they become criminals or victims. This lack of traditional news media attention is also true for their counterparts, the citizen soldiers in the war on crime.

## MEDIA CONSTRUCTS OF CITIZEN SOLDIERS IN THE WAR ON CRIME

The second major brigade of media crime solvers comes not from the official world of criminal justice and government agencies but from the ranks of citizens. When portrayed, these "citizen soldiers" in the war on crime often save the day for bungling police officers. Other times they battle the corrupt forces of government and official law enforcement.

### Private Investigators

One division of these civilian crime fighters occupies the boundary between civilians and police officers. They are the independent contractors of law enforcement, the **private investigators** or PIs. Private investigators were popularized in film noir movies in the 1940s. Historically male, sexual, debonair, hard-boiled, and smart, the PI lives on the borderline between criminality and the law-abiding, solving crimes with inside knowledge combined with the freedom to act outside the restraints of agency policies and due process rules. A classic film example of the noir PI is Humphrey Bogart as Sam Spade in the 1941 movie *The Maltese Falcon*. In addition to these semiprofessional private eyes, another group of personally motivated private citizens take on solving crimes as a hobby or due to some personal connection with a crime victim.

### Private Citizens

Predating the private eyes, private citizens have been successful media crime fighters for at least 600 years, as can be seen in the tales of Robin

| TABLE 4.4 | Citizen Crime-Fighting Narratives and Film Examples |
|-----------|------------------------------------------------------|
| **Narrative** | **Films** |
| Heroic | *Billy Jack* (1971) |
|  | *The Princess Bride* (1987) |
| Avengers | *Lipstick* (1976) |
|  | *Collateral Damage* (2002) |
| Vigilantes | *Death Wish* (1974) |
|  | *Boondock Saints* (1999) |
| Robin Hoods | *Robin Hood: Prince of Thieves* (1991) |
|  | *The Mark of Zorro* (1920, 1940) |
| Superheroes | *Unbreakable* (2000) |
|  | *Spider Man* (2002) |

Hood and other citizen heroes. Although usually adult white males, **citizen crime fighters** in the media include a diverse group: elderly female novelists (Angela Lansbury in *Murder She Wrote*), teenagers (the *Bobbsey Twins* and *Hardy Boys*), and even children (Tom Sawyer) and cartoon dogs (Scooby-Doo, for example).

The citizen crime fighter can be found in a number of entertainment narratives that share the characteristic of being outside of and sometimes in conflict with the traditional criminal justice system (see Table 4.4). Originating in the Western, "heroic" outsiders are a crime-fighting narrative that remains highly popular. Unfettered by official red tape and due process considerations, the heroic outsider can cut to the heart of the crime problem and quickly and usually violently deal with it. Riding or driving off into the sunset, as it were, after his work is done. Avengers and vigilantes are related to the victim crime-fighter narrative. In these portrayals, the citizen crime fighter has a personal interest or has been personally wronged by a criminal. At the extreme are tales where the citizen hero has actually been unjustly criminalized by the official criminal justice system. These criminal Robin Hood heroes are among the oldest Western citizen crime-fighter narratives available. A more recent citizen crime-fighter narrative is the superhero, which originated in Depression era comic books and today is found in action films. Still cartoonlike and clearly functioning as an escape from reality for their audiences, these crime fighters are the most "outside" of the outsiders. Mutants, aliens, ninjas, or just "regular" people who apparently are impossible to kill or defeat, these superheroes overcome massive odds to prevail and, as Superman states, defend "truth, justice, and the American way."

The success that private citizens and private investigators have enjoyed when solving crime in the media has been impressive. For example, media researchers Robert and Linda Lichter found that private citizens and private investigators solved many of the crimes shown in prime time television programming in the 1980s.[26] Crime fighters of every other type failed to capture the criminal more often than they succeeded. Cops, being rule bound, cannot possibly be as effective as private investigators. By contrast, private eyes and private citizens proved almost incapable of failure. This tradition of citizen success coupled to official police failure has deep roots. Penned in the 1840s by Edgar Allan Poe, the very first detective stories had the French police fumble and fail while citizen-hero, outsider American detective Dupin solved crimes.[27]

Combined with the media's proclivity to show professional crime fighters as loners and mavericks, as not fitting comfortably into their agencies, the cumulative media message clearly is that it is outsiders who save the day and that ordinary law enforcers are unequal to the task of fighting crime. Collectively, the citizen soldier crime fighters further reveal the media tendency to present crime not as a social problem but as an individual contest. In these portraits private citizens supplant the task of the entire criminal justice system. Crime fighting becomes a private issue of good versus evil between autonomous individuals. The larger society, and particularly its formal institutions, is little involved if not a direct obstacle to successful crime fighting. The message is that if you have a crime problem the regular police are unlikely to be helpful, and you had best deal with it on your own.

## PROFESSIONAL VERSUS CITIZEN CRIME FIGHTERS

The basic distinction between media crime fighters is whether the crime fighter is a member of the established criminal justice system or a citizen. If one combines the citizen crime fighter with the rogue, special-unit, maverick law enforcers, criminal justice system outsiders and marginalized employees are far more common and more successful in the media-constructed world of crime fighting than traditional mainstream criminal justice system personnel. Successful crime fighters are usually portrayed as antisocial, unattached loners even when they are members of an established law enforcement agency—the icon of Clint Eastwood's *Dirty Harry* is a prime example. The media super-cop is accordingly usually not a regular cop at all but someone from outside the system or a maverick officer within it. Whether an outsider or not, the successful crime fighter is usually a heroic white man of action. Media crime fighters are portrayed as very effective in solving crimes and apprehending criminals but not at all effective in preventing crime. They are better agents of punishment than deterrence. The basic crime-fighting narrative is that early crimes are successful and that a criminal enterprise has been ongoing for years. Only later, after the hero has arrived on the scene, are crimes unsuccessful. Similar to the manner in which crime is covered in the news, media crime fighters are reactive and incident driven rather than proactive and community problem oriented.

The main message these crime-fighter constructions convey about crime is that crime is not a social problem to be solved at the community level. Instead it is an invading social evil that must be destroyed. The social construction of law enforcement repeatedly points out that a crime "war" is being waged, and society needs crime "fighters," not "peace officers" or God-help-us, legal due process protections, social services, or community-based rehabilitation programs—all of which come across as blatantly naïve and wrong-headed. Because of crime's insidious nature, the traditional criminal justice system's due process constraints and rehabilitation mandates make it unable to cope with crime. The system needs the assistance of either a rebellious law enforcement insider who is willing to ignore or bend the law or an unencumbered civilian outsider. Justice, which in the media means law enforcement, is achieved by individual stars, not by the criminal justice system. Effective conformist law enforcement officers are rare, and when they are portrayed, they normally have to resort to innovative special tactics, weapons, technology, and support units to successfully deal with crime. The media world of crime fighting is not a world for standard operating procedures and community-oriented police officers, or for the unarmed, the hesitant, or the faint-hearted. The media message concerning crime fighting is one of "legitimized corruption"; solving crimes requires breaking the rules.[28]

A word should be said about the role of crime victims in these professional and citizen crime-fighter constructions. As described in previous chapters, in addition to victim portraits in the media being demographically mismatched on age and gender with official victim statistics, greater proportions of both news and entertainment media victims tend to be portrayed as randomly selected, having no prior associations with their assailants, as innocent, and as noncontributory to their victimization.[29] Aside from these misleading constructions of victimization, which have the tendency to paint crime as a random unavoidable event, victims are of secondary importance in the media. Only if they transform into crime fighters in the entertainment media or have a preexisting newsworthiness (are already famous or are especially vulnerable such as a child or pregnant woman) are they focused on and developed by the news media.[30] Unlike the real world of crime, where existing relationships between victims and criminals are the most significant factor in the generation of violence, in the media-constructed world it is more important to develop the relationship between the crime fighter and the criminal. This holds true even in police reality programming where the interactions between the police and offenders/suspects dominate the shows. Overall, most victims in the media exist only to be victimized; once that function is fulfilled, if still alive, they are shunted aside to allow the central contest between the heroic crime fighter and the evil criminal to be played out.

Also significant in media portrayals of law enforcement is the use of violence. Violence has been an element in the depiction of crime and justice throughout media history, but in the twentieth century the entertainment media came to portray both crime fighters and criminals as more violent and aggressive and to show this violence more graphically. Since the 1960s, a distinct style known as **ultraviolence**— which entails slow motion injuries, detonating blood capsules, and multiple camera views—has become common entertainment media content. Indeed, so brutal have media crime fighters become over the course of the last century that they now have more similarities to older gangster portraits than to older crime-fighting heroes. In today's media, the distinction between the crime fighter and the criminal has all but disappeared in regard to who initiates violence and how much force is used.

Finally, the increasing emphasis on graphic violence has resulted in a kind of **media weapons cult**. Over the years, weapons have become increasingly more technical and sophisticated but less realistic. More important, guns are shown as useful problem solvers and necessary crime-fighting tools in modern America. In the media, the people who get their way, both heroes and villains, are the ones who have the guns. Furthermore, weapons—especially handguns—tend to be portrayed as either ridiculously benign, so that misses are common and wounds minor and painless when the crime fighter is the target, or ridiculously deadly, so that shots from handguns accurately hit moving, distant people, killing them quickly and without extensive suffering when the crime fighter is shooting. People in crime-and-justice media who use guns seldom suffer social or legal repercussions. A gun battle is played out in the street, and everyone is back at work the next day. Adding to the unreality, when a gunshot victim is described, rarely is the victim's pain or that of the victim's family or friends shown.[31] In general, the media play up the violence and play down the pain and suffering associated with criminal violence and gunplay.

In conclusion, the construction of law enforcement as a criminal justice endeavor dominates over the courts and corrections and is portrayed as a glamorous, action-filled process of pursuit and detection that legitimizes and glorifies the use of violence. Dealing with crime is a battle of good versus evil. Historically this battle was invariably won by the good guys, but today an increasing minority of evil criminals escape; corrupt, brutal police officers have become more common; and crime control goals are advanced over due process considerations.[32] Civil liberties are ignored and degraded as mushy-headed hindrances that result in a less safe, more violent society. Professional crime fighters compete with citizen crime fighters for attention and effectiveness, but in both groups individual loners tend to be the most successful. Translated to the real world, the need for special undercover police units, vigilantes, and individual armed protection is implied. In the end, the media's social construction of crime fighting shows crime not as a social problem at all but as an individual concern to be solved by force and technology by either a core of beleaguered frontline cops, special tactic federal officers, or individual well-armed civilians.

## DISCUSSION QUESTIONS

1. Discuss the connection between the portrayal of guns, violence, and victims and the crime-fighting policies that are implied in these portrayals.
2. Discuss some of the possible reasons that civilians are portrayed so often as successful crime fighters and the traditional police are portrayed as unsuccessful in the entertainment media.
3. What are the policy repercussions of the media portraying crime fighting as an individual battle between good and evil? Support for what types of policies is encouraged and discouraged by this portrait?

## IN-CLASS ACTIVITIES

1. Come up with additional differences between media police and real police beyond the ones mentioned by David Perlmutter, or differences

between real and media crime scene technicians as described in Box 4.2. Apply the same exercise to other criminal justice positions.

2. Watch the film *Dirty Harry* and discuss the law enforcement stereotypes and narratives portrayed. If all someone knew about the crime problem was based on this film, what criminal justice policies would be advanced?

3. Watch an episode of the show *COPS* and discuss the use of editing, formatting, and the portrayal of police work, offenders, and victims.

4. Invite a local criminal justice Public Information Officer to speak to the class about his or her daily routine, relationship with local news media, and how a crisis is handled.

## ASSIGNMENTS

1. Watch a different crime-fighting show for five consecutive nights and summarize the portrait of crime fighters shown.

2. If possible, participate in a ride-along with local police and compare the experience with your prior media impressions of policing.

## SUGGESTED READINGS

Aaron Doyle. 2003. *Arresting Images: Crime and Policing in Front of the Television Camera*. Toronto: University of Toronto Press.

Mark Fishman and Gray Cavender, editors. 1998. *Entertaining Crime: Television Reality Programs*. New York: Aldine de Gruyter.

Regina Lawrence. 2000. *The Politics of Force: Media and the Construction of Police Brutality*. Berkeley, CA: University of California Press.

Frank Leishman and Paul Mason. 2003. *Policing and the Media*. Devon, UK: Willan.

David Perlmutter. 2000. *Policing the Media*. Thousand Oaks, CA: Sage.

Christopher Wilson. 2000. *Cop Knowledge*. Chicago, IL: University of Chicago Press.

## NOTES

1. Wilson, *Cop Knowledge*.
2. Gorelick, "Join Our War."
3. Rafter, *Shots in the Mirror*.
4. Inciardi and Dee, "From the Keystone Cops to Miami Vice."

5.  Reiner, "Keystone to Kojak."

6.  Stark, "Perry Mason Meets Sonny Crockett," 239.

7.  See Blumer, *The Movies and Conduct*; Blumer, and Hauser, *Movies, Delinquency, and Crime;* Charter, *Motion Pictures and Youth: A Summary*; Dale, *Children's Attendance at Motion Pictures;* Holaday and Stoddard, *Getting Ideas from the Movies;* Peterson and Thurstone, *Motion Pictures and the Social Attitudes of Children*; and Shuttleworth and May, *The Social Conduct and Attitudes of Movie Fans.* For a summary of the Payne Fund studies, see Lowery, and DeFleur, "Milestones," chapter 2.

8.  Hays, *President's Report to the Motion Picture Producers and Distributors' Association.*

9.  Wilson, *Cop Knowledge*, 91.

10. Wilson, *Cop Knowledge*, 118.

11. *Dirty Harry*, 1971.

12. Perlmutter, *Policing the Media.*

13. The discussion on cop narratives draws on ideas from Wilson, *Cop Knowledge.* In a similar vein, Robert Reiner (*The Politics of the Police*, 150–152) offers twelve ideal-type models of law enforcement stories found in the media.

14. Wilson, *Cop Knowledge*, 134.

15. Wilson, *Cop Knowledge*, 134; and Eschholz, Mallard, and Flynn, "Images of Prime Time Justice."

16. Brown and Benedict, "Perceptions of the Police"; Mawby, "Completing the 'Half-Formed Picture'? Media Images of Policing." See also Lawrence, *The Politics of Force,* 15.

17. *Bad Boys* (1993) by Inner Circle, Atlantic Records.

18. Donovan, "Armed with the Power of Television."

19. Doyle, *Arresting Images.*

20. Kooistra, Mahoney, and Westervelt, "The World of Crime According to 'COPS,'" Table 2: Index Crimes on "COPS" and in the UCR (1994), 148.

21. Ibid., 153.

22. Cavender, "In the Shadow of Shadow."

23. Sherwin, *When Law Goes Pop*, 184–185.

24. Doyle, "Cops: Television Policing as Policing Reality."

25. Hallett and Powell, "Backstage with *COPS*."

26. Lichter and Lichter, *Prime Time Crime.* Reiner, Livingstone, and Allen ("No More Happy Endings?", 115–116) found a decline in civilian heroes in films over the latter half of the twentieth century.

27. The Chevalier C. Auguste Dupin, an American amateur detective living in France, appeared in three stories: *The Murders in the Rue Morgue, The Mystery of Marie Roget,* and *The Purloined Letter.* He is described in the *Oxford Companion to Crime and Mystery Writing* (Herbert, 126): "Dupin is an isolated figure. Well aware of his intellectual superiority, Dupin is particularly contemptuous of the unimaginative methods of the police."

28. Leishman and Mason, *Policing and the Media*, 70, 74.

29. Chermak, *Victims in the News*; Meyers, News Coverage of *Violence against Women*.

30. Chermak, *Victims in the News*, 107. Reiner, Livingstone, and Allen ("No More Happy Endings?", 118) found, however, that since WW II crime films have become more likely to show victims in a central role.

31. Price, Merrill, and Clause, "The Depiction of Guns on Prime Time Television."

32. Reiner, "Media Made Criminality," 392.

# THE COURTS

## CHAPTER OBJECTIVES

After reading Chapter 5, you will be able to describe and discuss the media portrait of the judicial system, judges, and attorneys. You will have in-depth knowledge of the concept of media trials—heavily covered and marketed cases—and their effect on nonpublicized cases. You will also have an appreciation of the unique love-hate relationship between television and the courts and will be able to discuss the differences and similarities between judicial mechanisms to deal with publicity and media access to judicial proceedings and media strategies to limit government access to media-held information.

## MEDIA, INFOTAINMENT, AND THE COURTS

Commenting on the relationship between the courts and contemporary media, legal scholar Richard Sherwin remarks, "Law in our time has entered the age of images, legal reality can no longer be properly understood, or assessed, apart from what appears on the screen."[1] For many in today's world, mass media images are their primary source of knowledge about law, lawyers, and the legal system. In addition to being an important source of knowledge about the judicial system, judicial images found in the media are significant in another way. Courtrooms are a society's formal social construction arena where the significance and meaning of a wide range of social behaviors are determined—for example, the courts have recently defined, or at least attempted to define, what is or is not insane behavior, proper or improper child care, and intrusive or acceptable government law enforcement policies. Judicial proceedings function, therefore, not only as mechanisms for resolving individual disputes but also as mechanisms for legitimizing the broader society's laws, policies, government agencies, and social structure. Accordingly, anything that influences the public image of the courts invariably

© NBC/Photofest

Much of the public's knowledge of the judicial system comes from media portraits found in commercial films and television shows like *Law and Order*.

influences the courts' ability to be a legitimizing mechanism and to fulfill their function as definers of acceptable social boundaries.

If the media's renditions of court proceedings influence how the public sees the courts, in turn, the public's perception of the courts result in expectations of how judicial proceedings should look and play out. Media-induced public expectations cycle back to affect the real courts. How the judicial system conducts procedures, how attorneys and judges try cases, and how participants behave in courtrooms are all influenced. The mass media portrait of the judicial system constructs a reality that the public comes to expect and the courts subsequently strive to fulfill.

The judicial portrait found in the media is examined in three realms: the entertainment media's construction of the courtroom; the development of infotainment style media trials; and the concerns associated with pretrial publicity, government access to media-held information, and media access to government-held information. The end result of the collective media portrait of the courts is the modern construction of the judicial system as a source of high drama and infotainment.

## COURTS AND ATTORNEYS

Directly and indirectly, the media paint a distorted image of the courts. When portrayed indirectly as in the law enforcement focused media, the courts are often alluded to as soft on crime, easy on criminals, due process–laden institutions that repeatedly release the obviously guilty and danger-ous.[2] In law enforcement portraits of crime fighting, most of the criminals being fought are recidivists, which implies that criminals go through the court system and return to the streets undeterred and unrehabilitated. When shown directly, court officers are often more engaged in fighting crime than in practicing law.[3] When shown practicing law, they are usually immersed in high-stakes dramatic trials. In accordance with the media's myopic concentration on the rare event in reality such as murder, media-rendered court procedures emphasize the rare-in-reality adversarial criminal trial as the most common judicial proceeding.[4] Seldom are pre-liminary procedures or informal plea bargaining shown, and posttrial steps are even less common. In contrast to real court systems, in the media most defendants go to trial. The courts and the law are constructed in the media as complicated, arcane contests practiced by expert professionals and beyond the understanding of everyday citizens. The confrontations, ora-tory, and deliberations in the media courtroom are in stark opposition to the criminal justice system's daily reality of plea bargains, compromises, and assembly-line justice. None of the media judicial images you are likely to see come close to representing the reality of the courts.

As with most components of the criminal justice system, the dominant popular image of courtrooms was initially constructed within Hollywood films. The construction of judicial justice in the cinema differs in some basic ways from the media construction of crime and law enforcement. For one, courtroom films more often locate the obstacles to justice in society and the legal system rather than within individual offenders. And because they also frequently show the impediments to justice being overcome, trial films do not require an incorrigible criminal who must be destroyed. Courtroom films, however, do reflect the operation of the backwards law regarding crime and justice in the media; that is, they present the opposite of crime-and-justice reality. Films feature the ever-popular narratives of murder, abuse of power, and sex, not the more mundane matters generally before the courts.

Historically, many courtroom films presented real cases in liberally adapted infotainment productions formatted to look like dramatic documentaries. *Judgment at Nuremberg, Inherit the Wind, I Want to Live,* and many other trial movies are based on true stories adapted from past famous and infamous trials. (Box 5.1 provides a list of popular courtroom film narratives.)

Although movies loosely based on actual events are still popular, recent courtroom portraits have evolved from the highly unrealistic media courtrooms where attorneys investigate and solve crimes by eliciting confessions during cross-examination to showing more nontrial, backstage aspects of practicing law. This trend can be traced to Hollywood's need since the 1960s to appeal to audiences that have been raised on television. Television programmers, in turn, followed suit and have applied a soap opera format to TV courtroom dramas. Scriptwriters and television programmers attempted to add more realism to their shows by revealing more of the backstage behavior and private lives of their crime-fighting lawyers.[5] The next step for television was to develop courtroom docudramas in which real cases are reenacted, infotainmentized, and tried in realistic-looking courtroom scenes. Spurred by the immense popularity and profits of the O. J. Simpson trial in the 1990s, the infotainment format has been incorporated into a number of contemporary media court-based productions. Currently, the social construction of the courts is rendered through a triumvirate of trial and law films, infotainment style pseudojudicial programs, and heavily publicized media co-opted live cases. All of these media judicial portraits emphasize rare events (trials), uncommon charges (homicide), and unlikely interactions (dramatic adversarial confrontations) to collectively present a heavily skewed unrealistic picture of the courts and the rendering of the law. How are the attorneys, the practitioners of law, portrayed in these renditions?

## Crime-Fighting Attorneys

Although criminal law is only one area of law and in the real world most attorneys practice other specialties, most lawyers in the media are criminal lawyers and specialize in criminal law.[6] Based on the most prominent media images of courtrooms, most law school graduates apparently really wanted to attend the police academy. In the media, the protectors of due process are also frequently advocates of crime control. Thus, although shown less frequently than police officers in the entertainment media, attorneys and judges, when they star, like their law enforcement counterparts often expend

(*Continued on page 124*)

## 5.1   Popular Courtroom Film Narratives

REAL-LIFE CASES

*Judgment at Nuremberg* (1961) was based on the war crime trials
   in Germany that followed World War II.
*I Want to Live* (1958) was based on the trial and execution of
   Barbara Graham, one of four women to die in California's gas
   chamber.
*Inherit the Wind* (1960) was based on a 1925 trial that pitted
   William Jennings Bryan against Clarence Darrow in a case
   that tested a Tennessee law forbidding the teaching of evo-
   lution in public schools. It is often referred to as the "Scopes
   Monkey Trial."

MILITARY JUSTICE

*The Caine Mutiny* (1954) depicted the mutiny trial of naval
   officers who seized control of a ship from a deranged captain.
*A Few Good Men* (1992) showed the court martial of two
   marines charged with murder.
*Billy Budd* (1962) described the court martial of an impressed
   seaman for the murder of a sadistic officer.

COMEDY

*Adam's Rib* (1949) portrayed husband and wife attorneys who
   are adversaries in an attempted murder case.
*Bananas* (1971) put Woody Allen on trial for treason.
*My Cousin Vinny* (1992) told the story of a New York lawyer
   defending his cousin, accused of murder, in a small Alabama
   town.

HEROIC LAWYERS

*And Justice for All* (1979) portrays a criminal defense attorney
   who chooses justice over law when defending a rapist judge.
*Philadelphia* (1992) follows a gay attorney stricken with AIDS
   who sues his law firm for wrongful termination.

*To Kill a Mockingbird* (1962) shows lawyer Atticus Finch defending an innocent black man accused of rape in a classic trial movie.

IMPROPER CLIENT–LAWYER RELATIONS

*Jagged Edge* (1985) follows the story of a politically ambitious prosecutor who battles a defense attorney who has fallen in love with her socialite client.

*Guilty as Sin* (1993) depicts a beautiful trial attorney who is fascinated and repulsed by her client who is charged with murder.

UNUSUAL JUDGES AND JURORS

*The Devil and Daniel Webster* (1941) follows the devil's hand-picked judge and jurors as they decide whether a "sell your soul" contract is valid.

*Twelve Angry Men* (1957) depicts a jury that reinvestigates a murder case during deliberations.

*The Star Chamber* (1983) portrays angry judges meeting secretly to reconsider cases dismissed on technicalities; their findings of guilt result in hiring hit-men to kill the offenders.

*M* (1931) shows German criminals who catch and try a serial killer who preys on children.

CIVIL CASES

*Kramer vs. Kramer* (1979) shows an absentee mother who returns and begins a child custody case against her ex-husband.

*Losing Isaiah* (1995) follows Caucasian adoptive parents and an African American birth mother as they fight for custody of a child.

*Whose Life Is It Anyway?* (1981) portrays a paralyzed accident victim who sues to be allowed to die.

*Source:* Paul Bergman and Michael Asimow, *Reel Justice: The Courtroom Goes to the Movies.* Kansas City, MO: Andrews and McMeel, 1996.

as much effort solving crimes and pursuing criminals as they do interpreting and practicing law.[7]

The crime-fighting lawyer has not always been the dominant image. In earlier generally uncritical portraits of the judicial system such as the film classic *To Kill a Mockingbird,* lawyers were constructed as homespun, simple yet crafty all-American jurists. In the contemporary period, legal skill and justice have become less important and have been replaced by attorneys hunting down predator psychopaths or involved in sundry action scenes. Trial scenes are now more likely to be episodes imbedded within a thriller, and heroic lawyers are as likely to appear in fight and chase scenes as in court proceedings.[8]

When they aren't the crime fighters, attorneys can expect to be portrayed negatively. For example, Robert and Linda Lichter found that in prime time television programming attorneys are more likely than police officers to be shown as greedy and nearly as likely to be shown as corrupt. In sum, in another backwards portrait, attorneys in the media are not shown spending much of their time practicing law, and when they do practice law, it is overwhelmingly criminal law. A group that has particularly suffered its media constructions are female attorneys.

## Female Attorneys

Similar to the portrayals of policewomen, female attorneys—while enjoying a longer tradition in the media—are frequently defeminized as career women or projected as creatures dominated by sexual conflicts or repression. The media construction of the female lawyer frequently assumes the incompatibility of the social roles of attorney and woman. Even so, female attorneys appear to fare better than media policewomen in that some aspects of their likely real-world experiences are portrayed.[9] The scarcity of female lawyers, the gender-based attitudes prevalent toward women lawyers, and the social friction generated by the clashing of traditional female social roles and their functioning as effective attorneys can all be found in their media constructions. However, like policewomen, their sexuality and unresolved sexual tensions are likely to dominate their media portrayals. Female attorneys are more often shown as young, white, single, childless, and in lower echelon positions in their law firms and criminal justice agencies. They also share with male attorney portrayals an unrealistic level of involvement in dangerous and sensational criminal law cases.

In sum, the courts and attorneys are usually unrealistically constructed in the media. Rare real-world events and activities are common in media judicial portraits; common judicial procedures and attorney duties are rare in the media. Although not as wildly inaccurate as the image of police, the courts and attorneys are still more often shown in crime-fighting narratives than in more realistic story lines. Even when the portrayals are based on real cases, the infotainment criteria that drive the selection of cases culls out the usual and nonviolent case in favor of the abnormal and predatory. Some of these selected cases become multimedia, pop culture bonanzas, generating enormous markets, profits, and spinoffs for news, entertainment, and infotainment media. Termed "media trials," these judicial miniseries have become the most important single contributor to the social construction of the courts in America.

## MEDIA TRIALS

Media trials involve the social construction of select criminal justice cases as massive infotainment products that are taken up by the media, commodified, and mass marketed. The first notorious mass-mediated trial in the United States was the 1859 trial of anarchist John Brown, which attracted daily coverage and widespread dissemination via telegraph and newspaper. A later example is the 1875 trial of nationally known preacher Henry Ward Beecher, a narrative of a spectacular adultery trial. The Lizzie Borden 1893 trial for the ax murders of her parents foreshadowed the lurid murder trials of celebrities like O. J. Simpson.

Contemporary media trials are distinguished from typical judicial news by the massive and intensive coverage that begins either with the discovery of the crime or the arrest of the accused.[10] The media cover all aspects of the case, often highlighting extralegal facts. Judges, lawyers, police, witnesses, jurors, and particularly defendants are interviewed, photographed, and frequently raised to celebrity status. Personalities, personal relationships, physical appearances, and idiosyncrasies are commented on regardless of legal relevance. Coverage is live whenever possible, pictures are preferred over text, and text is characterized by conjecture and sensationalism.[11] In their coverage of these trials, the media offer direct and simple explanations of crime: lust, greed, immorality, jealousy, revenge, and insanity.

One factor behind the recent increase in the number of media trials is that news organizations competing for ratings increasingly structure the news along entertainment lines, presenting it within frames, formats, and explanations originally found solely in entertainment programming. Eventually fast-paced, dramatic, superficial presentations and simplistic explanations became the norm. As this trend developed, some criminal trials came to be covered more intensely, and news organizations expanded their coverage from hard factual presentations to soft human interest news,

© Bettmann/Corbis

In 1927 Charles Lindbergh made the first solo, nonstop New York to Paris flight in the airplane *Spirit of St. Louis.* He returned an international hero and the most famous man in the world, becoming, in effect, the first mass media celebrity. The kidnapping and murder of his infant son in 1932, and the subsequent trial and execution of Bruno Hauptmann for the crime, foreshadowed today's massive coverage of media trials. Shown are the reporters gathered to cover the 1935 trial of Bruno Hauptmann.

emphasizing extralegal human interest elements. Thomas Mathieson observes that today, "It is primarily the sensational and dramatic 'legal news' which is transmitted through the media—particularly sensational or titillating cases."[12] The process culminates in the total combining of news and entertainment in the media trial. Media trials have been a consistent presence in the media, crime, and justice world and were constructed every three to five years over the entire course of the twentieth century. Increasing in frequency as the century ended, they show no evidence of decline in the twenty-first century.

## Media Trial Effects

When media trials began to be televised in the 1960s, heightened concern arose over their effects. In the Estes case in 1965 (which resulted in banning television cameras in courtrooms), Chief Justice Earl Warren stated: "Should the television industry become an integral part of our system of criminal justice, it would not be unnatural for the public to attribute the shortcomings of the industry to the trial process itself."[13] The passage of time has not reduced this concern. The basic issue is whether attorneys, judges, and other participants react to the presence of television cameras by altering their courtroom behavior. The fear is that participants will change the way they testify, argue, and construct their cases to fit the needs of the electronic visual media and that attorneys will audition for massive external television audiences rather than litigate before much smaller courtroom audiences. Media-driven changes have already been documented in religion, sports, and politics; small live audiences are often less important (and sometimes skipped entirely) in preference for large, external media-supplied ones.[14]

The relationship between the media and the justice system is further strained by media trials because different considerations and values govern the means by which each obtains knowledge and evaluates its worth. The criminal justice system is guided by legislative and constitutional mandates, and the courts have the task of separating legally relevant from irrelevant information. Media, however, respond primarily to newsworthiness and entertainment considerations. Each side's considerations dictate what facts are presented as well as when and how they are disclosed. Traditionally, in the courtroom information is imparted in a form and by a process quite different from that preferred by the media. Courtroom knowledge is extracted point by point in long story lines following legal procedures and rules of evidence. Moreover, the information is specially prepared for a limited audience of a judge or jury.

In contrast, media renditions are outwardly directed and developed in accordance with entertainment values rather than legal relevance. They are brief, time- and space-limited constructions that must make their points quickly, and they are built around whatever film or dramatic elements are available. In sum, the courts have traditionally presented internally controlled, frontstage events to a small, specific audience of judges and jurors, whereas media-produced products tend to present dramatic backstage information to an external, general mass audience. This inherent conflict between media and justice systems crystallizes in the media trial where the courthouse becomes the production stage for the media. With the ascendance of media trials, the traditional courtroom audience became secondary to the external media audience both inside and outside of the courtroom.

For these reasons, despite their relatively small numbers, media trials are crucial in the social construction of crime-and-justice reality. They serve as massive public stages to disseminate crime-and-justice knowledge as they explicitly compare competing constructions of reality before vast audiences of ordinary citizens.[15] In a media trial, both the jury and the vicariously attending public can decide between one reality constructed by the state in which the accused is guilty and another constructed by the defense in which the defendant is not guilty. As the dominant delivery medium of these trials, television directs the facts that are selected, constructed, and presented to the public. Not surprisingly, media trials involve cases that contain the same elements popular in entertainment programming—human interest laced with mystery, sex, bizarre circumstances, and famous or powerful people (see Box 5.2). In their coverage the media simplify the task of reporting, interpreting, and explaining a trial. As in the entertainment media, recurrent themes dominate media trial constructions, and crime is nearly universally attributed to individual failings rather than to social conditions. The three most common types of media trials utilize narratives taken directly from entertainment media: abuse of power, the sinful rich, and evil strangers.[16] These themes provide the news media with powerful preestablished conceptual frameworks to present and mold the various aspects of a trial's coverage.[17]

Media trials that fit the **abuse of power** theme include those cases in which the defendant occupies a position of trust, prestige, or authority. The general rule is the higher the rank, the more media interest in the case. Cases involving police corruption and justice system personnel in general are especially attractive to the media. **Sinful rich media trials** include cases in which socially prominent defendants are involved in bizarre or sexually related crimes. These trials have a voyeuristic appeal, and the media coverage aims to persuade the public that they are being given a rare glimpse into the backstage sordid world of the upper class and powerful. Love triangles, deviant sex, and inheritance-motivated killings among the rich and famous are primary examples.[18] The category of **evil strangers** is composed of two subgroups: non-Americans and psychotic killers. Non-American evil stranger media trials may involve—depending on the time and political climate—immigrants, blacks, Jews, socialists, union and labor leaders, anarchists, the poor, members of counterculture groups, members of minority religions, or political activists and advocates of unpopular causes. Foreign terrorists provide recent examples. Psychotic killer media trials usually focus on bizarre murder cases in which the defendant is portrayed as a maddened, predatory killer—exemplified historically by Lizzie Borden (in spite of her acquittal) and more recently by Jeffery Dahmer, John Wayne Gacy, and other serial killers.

All three media trial types have long histories in popular entertainment narratives, and these preestablished entertainment narratives help determine the content of the coverage in the real cases. Entertainment story lines provide the news media with the structural frameworks by which to

## 5.2  O. J. Simpson

The Simpson trial was of the sinful rich genre. The trial's story line could be found in numerous novels and Hollywood films: handsome, rich, successful ex-athlete is accused of murdering his ex-wife and her friend in a jealous rage amid a sea of rumored drug abuse, sexual deviance, and fascinating subcharacters—racists cops, beautiful women, and offbeat friends and acquaintances. Indeed, a large part of the enduring interest and ultimate social impact of this trial stems from the way it became a long-running mass media entertainment vehicle—a drama-in-real-life, covered more along the lines of a sports spectacle than a criminal trial.

In terms of legal and social significance, it is clearly not the trial of the century as it was

(*continued*)

The media co-optation of a criminal trial. Television trucks and temporary studios create a media "tent city" across from the Criminal Courts Building in downtown Los Angeles in 1995 at the start of the O. J. Simpson double-murder trial.

© AP Photos/ Mark J. Terrill

An example of the commodification and marketing of a media trial. Books, films, photos, souvenirs, songs, toys, and games are all spinoffs of a high-profile, intensely covered trial.

© Fred Prouser/Sipa Press

129

*O. J. Simpson (continued)*

christened by the media—it is better described as the signal television
event of the century, demanding hundreds, if not thousands, of hours of
coverage. Regarding the trial's social impact, most commentators focused
on race relations, with few reporting any positive effects. Other concerns
specific to the judicial system generated from the coverage included the
prospect of more criminal defendants refusing to plea bargain, a new
skepticism about police testimony, more judicial gag orders on trial participants and less camera access, restrictions on attorneys' use of political
rhetoric in front of juries, and the general degrading in the public's eye of
judges, juries, attorneys, and the judicial system. Coverage of the trial
represented American culture at one of its lowest ebbs, and the reputation
and dignity of the judicial system continues to require rehabilitation after
the televising, marketing, and exploitation of the "trial of the twentieth
century."

---

*Sources:* G. Bains, "The Criminal Trial as a Sports Spectacle." *Mclean's* 108 (February 20, 1995): 55; G. Barak, ed.,
*Media, Process, and the Social Construction of Crime.* New York: Garland, 1995; S. Gaines, "O. J. Simpson, Mark
Fuhrman, and the Moral 'Low Ground' of Ethnic/Race Relations in the United States." *Black Scholar* 25 (1995):
46–48; J. Garvey, "Race and the Simpson Verdict." *Commonwealth* 122 (1995): 6; D. Gelernter, "The Real Story of
Orenthal James." *National Review* (October 9, 1995): 45–47; B. Handy, "Our Mutual Houseguest." *Time* 146
(October 16, 1995): 108; S. Pillsbury, "Time, TV, and Criminal Justice: Second Thoughts on the Simpson Trial."
*Criminal Law Bulletin* 59(3) 1997: 3–28; R. Rosenblatt, "A Nation of Painted Hearts." *Time* (October 16, 1995):
40–46; F. Schmalleger, *Trial of the Century.* Englewood Cliffs, NJ: Prentice Hall, 1996; J. Walsh, "Special Report:
The Simpson Verdict." *Time* 146 (October 16, 1995): 62–64; and M. Whitaker, "Whites v. Blacks." *Newsweek* 126
(October 16, 1995): 28–34.

measure, choose, and mold aspects of real trials that will be reported and
highlighted. Media trials reinforce the similarity between news and entertainment, inspiring news personnel to structure their coverage along
familiar entertainment story lines and entertainment personnel to author
the distorted images that are frequently referenced in the news. From both,
the public receives the responsibility-diverting message that the rich are
immoral in their use of sex, drugs, and violence; that people in power are
evil, greedy, and should not be trusted; and that strangers and those with
different lifestyles or values are inherently dangerous. Table 5.1 lists some
well-known examples of media trials and their outcomes.

## Merging Judicial News with Entertainment

Media trials represent the final step in a long process of merging judicial
news and entertainment—a process that today results in multimedia products and extensive commercial exploitation. The Internet has extended this

*(Continued on page 134)*

| TABLE 5.1 | Media Trial Examples |
|-----------|---------------------|

| Defendants | Trial | Verdict |
|------------|-------|---------|
| **Abuse of Power** | | |
| Nuremberg trials (1946) | The trial of the major German war criminals by an International Military Tribunal of the victorious allies following World War II. | The 1947 verdicts sentence eleven of the twenty-one defendants to death. Hermann Goering committed suicide prior to execution. The remaining ten war criminals were hanged in Nuremberg in late 1947. |
| My Lai courts martial (1970) | Lieutenant William Calley was accused of killing unarmed civilians in March of 1968. | Convicted and sentenced to life, Calley's sentence was later reduced and he was paroled in 1974 after serving three and a half years. |
| McMartin Preschool (1987, 1990) | Two owners of a preschool were accused and tried for sexual abuse of children left in their care. | Two trials were conducted. Neither owner was found guilty on any of more than 50 counts. The two prosecutions cost the state of California $15 million. |
| Rodney King beating (1992) | Four Los Angeles police officers were accused of using excessive force in arresting Rodney King following a car chase. | In the state trial, the jury acquitted three of the officers of all charges and was unable to reach a verdict on one charge against the fourth officer. |
| | The acquittals in the state trial set off riots in Los Angeles, leaving fifty-three people dead, more than 7,000 arrested, and more than $1 billion in property damage. | In a subsequent 1993 federal trial on charges of violation of civil rights, a federal jury convicts two of the officers and finds the other two not guilty. No disturbances follow the verdict. |
| Clinton impeachment (1999) | President Clinton is accused of obstruction of justice and perjury while attempting to conceal an affair with a White House intern. | The president is found innocent of the charges as U.S. Senate votes on both articles of impeachment fall short of the two-thirds majority required to convict. |
| **Sinful Rich** | | |
| Leopold and Loeb (1924) | Nineteen-year-old Richard Loeb, the privileged son of a Sears Roebuck vice president, and nineteen-year-old Nathan Leopold, the son of a millionaire box manufacturer, were accused of kidnapping and murdering a fourteen-year-old boy from one of Chicago's most prominent families. | Both were convicted and sentenced to life in prison. In 1936 Loeb was slashed and killed with a razor while in Joliet penitentiary. In 1958, after thirty-four years of confinement, Leopold was released from prison. He died peacefully in August 1971. |

*(Continued)*

| TABLE 5.1 | Media Trial Examples (*Continued*) | |
|---|---|---|
| **Defendants** | **Trial** | **Verdict** |
| Roscoe "Fatty" Arbuckle (1921) | This popular silent-screen comedian was tried for the murder of a young starlet, Virginia Rappe. | He was acquitted after two trials, but his movie career was ruined. Arbuckle died of a heart attack in June 1933 at 46 years of age. |
| Sam Sheppard | An Ohio doctor who was tried for the 1954 murder of his wife Marilyn. | Found guilty by a jury of murder in the second degree and sentenced to life in prison, Sheppard won a retrial in 1966 after a successful U.S. Supreme Court appeal arguing prejudicial impact from news coverage surrounding the first trial. He was acquitted by the jury in the second trial and died in 1970 at the age of 46 of liver failure. |
| Patty Hearst (1976) | The granddaughter of newspaper publisher William Hearst, she was kidnapped by a left-wing radical group (Symbionese Liberation Army) and held for ransom. After months in SLA captivity she appeared in a bank robbery surveillance video carrying a weapon. | She was convicted of bank robbery and served nearly two years in prison. She was pardoned by President Clinton. |
| William Kennedy Smith (1991) | He was accused of date rape. | Smith was acquitted by a jury in Palm Beach, Florida. |
| O. J. Simpson (1995) | He was tried for the 1994 murder of his ex-wife and her acquaintance. | Simpson was found not guilty in the criminal trial but later was found guilty in a civil case. |
| Kobe Bryant (2004) | Professional basketball player, he was charged with sexual assault of a nineteen-year-old woman in a Colorado hotel where she worked. | Criminal charges were dropped and a civil lawsuit against Bryant was settled out of court. |

**Evil Strangers**

*Non-Americans*

| | | |
|---|---|---|
| Nicola Sacco and Bartolomeo Vanzetti (1921) | Two Italian immigrants associated with anarchists, they were accused in a 1920 robbery and murder at a Massachusetts shoe company. | Sacco and Vanzetti were both found guilty of murder in the first degree and were electrocuted in August 1927. |
| Julius and Ethel Rosenberg (1951) | They were charged with conspiracy to commit espionage for selling information about the atomic bomb to the Russians. | Both were found guilty and were executed in June 1953. |

| TABLE 5.1 | Media Trial Examples (Continued) | |
|---|---|---|
| **Defendants** | **Trial** | **Verdict** |
| Bruno Hauptmann (1935) | Accused of the 1932 kidnapping and murder of the infant son of aviator Charles Lindbergh. | He was found guilty and electrocuted in 1936. |
| Chicago 7 (1969) | Seven members of an anti-Vietnam War and counterculture group were accused of inciting riots during the 1968 Democratic National Convention in Chicago. | The jury found five of the seven defendants guilty of violating the Anti-Riot Act of 1968. Their convictions were reversed on appeal in 1972. |
| Timothy McVeigh (1997) | A right-wing terrorist and former U.S. military member, he was accused of bombing the Oklahoma City Federal Building, which killed 167 people. | He was convicted and executed in June 2001. |
| Ramzi Yousef (1997) | An al-Qaeda–linked terrorist accused of the 1993 bombing of the World Trade Center, which killed six people. | He was found guilty and sentenced to life plus 240 years. |
| **Psychotic Killers** | | |
| Lizzie Borden (1893) | She was accused of the 1892 ax murder of her father and stepmother. | She was acquitted by a jury and died in 1927 at the age of 67. |
| Charles Manson (1970) | As head of the "Manson Family," he and his followers were accused of killing at least nine people in Southern California between July 27 and August 26, 1969. | Initially sentenced to death, his sentence was later commuted to life. |
| Ted Bundy (1979) | He confessed to more than twenty murders committed across the country from 1973 to 1978. | He was executed in Florida in 1989 for the 1978 murder of twelve-year-old Kimberly Leach. |
| Jeffrey Dahmer (1992) | A cannibalistic serial killer who preyed on young men in Milwaukee from 1987 to 1991, he was accused of killing seventeen men. | Sentenced to fifteen consecutive life terms, he was killed in prison by another inmate in 1994. |
| Aileen Wuornos (1992) | She was accused of killing seven men who had solicited her as a prostitute. | She was found guilty and executed in Florida in 2002. |
| Scott Peterson (2004) | He was tried for the murder of his pregnant wife, Laci Peterson, and his unborn son. | He was convicted and sentenced to death. |

process and provides detailed information about these cases to a much greater degree than was previously available. The Internet also provides a vehicle for the public to become active trial participants in dedicated trial chat rooms, complete with votes on guilt or innocence. If early coverage of media trials resembled a miniseries, today it's becoming more like a game show. Along with this extensive interest, the money to be made from a popular long-running media trial is enormous. That the source of media trials is the judicial system eases the merger and heightens the profits, for media trials allow the news media to attract and entertain large audiences while maintaining their preferred image as objective and neutral. A trial is also a natural stage for presenting drama and comes supplied with tax-supported sets, lead and secondary characters, extras, and dialogue. Media trials provide the media with ready-made entertainment-style themes that give shape and direction to their coverage. They further supply fodder for entertainment vehicles in the form of movie scripts, episodes for weekly crime and law dramas, and content for infotainment talk shows, books, and other commercial spinoffs. They become, in effect, an entire media industry line.

The social impact and importance of media trials is seldom connected to the extent of harm resulting from the crimes. Their significance comes from the massive attention they receive and the public debate they engender. The social impact of media trials comes not from what happened during the commission of the crime but from the immense focus on what happens during the trial proceedings. These trials are significant because they influence the public's attitudes and views regarding crime, justice, and society for years.[19] A specific concern for the criminal justice system associated with medial trials is their generation of echo effects.

## Echo Effects

Following a media trial, an **echo effect** influences the processing and disposition of similar but unpublicized cases.[20] This effect was first described by John Loften in 1996:

> But while the impact of the press is most direct on specific cases covered, there is good reason to believe that [its] sway extends considerably beyond the cases actually appearing. . . . From the cases that are covered, officials become conditioned to expect demands for stern treatment from the press, and in the unpublicized cases they probably act accordingly.[21]

And later John Kaplan and Jerome Skolnick concurred in this evaluation:

> This unwillingness [to plea bargain] appears to occur relatively infrequently. It is most likely to occur when there is strong pressure upon the prosecution

to obtain maximum sentences for a particular class of crime: for example, after a notorious case of child rape, the prosecutor may refuse to bargain, for a time, with those charged with sex offenses involving children; after a series of highly publicized drug arrests, for a time, to engage in reduction of charges from sales to possession.[22]

The implication of echo effects is that media attention influences the disposition of a large number of cases, the majority of which receive no coverage. Echo effects are, of course, heightened when live television is part of the media trial package.

## Live Television in Courtrooms

Often a component in the construction of media trials, live television coverage of judicial proceedings represents the most intrusive media interaction with the judicial system. The schizophrenic judicial posture toward televised proceedings is shown by its embracement in the O. J. Simpson criminal trial and its banishment from his civil trial. The judiciary has long been skeptical about visual coverage of trials. Recognition of its unique potential for disruption originated with Bruno Hauptmann's trial for the kidnapping and murder of Charles Lindbergh's baby son in the 1930s.[23] In response to problems that arose during this trial, the American Bar Association in 1937 issued a new rule (or canon) regarding the use of photographic equipment at trials:

> Proceedings in court should be conducted with fitting dignity and decorum. The taking of photographs in the courtroom, during sessions of the court or recesses between sessions, and the broadcasting of court proceedings are calculated to detract from the essential dignity of the proceedings, degrade the court and create misconceptions in the mind of the public and should not be permitted.[24]

This recommended ban on photography in the courtroom was widely adopted and was extended in 1952 to include television cameras as well. Despite the extension of the ABA rules (which are, in reality, unenforced recommended standards of expected conduct), the first trial to receive television coverage took place in 1953 in Oklahoma City, and the first to receive live coverage in 1955 was in Waco, Texas. These cases stand as exceptions to the more broadly upheld aversion to television in the courts that existed into the 1980s.

The Supreme Court first reviewed the question of television access to courtrooms in *Estes v. Texas* in 1965.[25] The Estes trial received intense regional television coverage with nightly news reports broadcast from the courthouse. The Court reversed Estes's conviction, ruling that television was unavoidably disruptive and should be banned from the courthouse: "Television in its present state and by its very nature, reaches into a variety of areas in which it may cause prejudice to an accused. . . . The televising of criminal trials is inherently a denial of due process."[26] In the Estes after-math, most states severely limited television's access to their courts, and many simply banned all TV coverage.

However, encouraged by the development of less obtrusive television equipment, various states continued to experiment with televising pro-ceedings. In 1979 the Florida Supreme Court allowed television reporting from trial courts without requiring the permission of defendants. Florida's procedures were reviewed by the Supreme Court in 1981 in *Chandler v. Florida*.[27] At that time, the Court rejected many of the assumptions about television it had forwarded sixteen years earlier. The most significant assumption it rejected was that televising a criminal trial without the defendant's consent is an inherent denial of due process. Emphasizing the modernization of the medium, the lack of evidence of a psychological impact from televised coverage on trial participants, and an increase in the public acceptance of television as a fact of everyday life, the Court upheld the *Chandler* conviction.

Unstated by the Supreme Court, additional reasons for this reversal also developed in the years between *Estes* and *Chandler*. Backed by surveys of the public, during this period there was growing concern among the judiciary that the public lacked confidence in the courts' ability to confront crime and criminals.[28] The courts were viewed as part of the cause of a steadily increasing crime rate. In this negative atmosphere, televising trials began to look like a possible counterweight to negative public perceptions. As frontstage events constructed for public con-sumption, trials show the justice system at its best. It was increasingly felt that the cameras would show impartial justice, fair procedure, conviction of the guilty, and imposition of fair sentences. By contrast, the seamy backstage of the criminal justice process—the plea bargaining, the pro-cedural inefficiency, the arbitrary decision making inherent in police and prosecutor discretion—would go unseen. Televising trials, in other words, was seen as unlikely to hurt and likely to be potentially helpful in shoring up the court's poor social image. By the 1980s, the courts saw televised trials as a means of presenting controlled, formal frontstage events to the public while protecting their backstage assembly-line processes from exposure.

The basic question of whether or not to allow television cameras in the courtroom was never whether the media had the freedom to report courtroom matters—broadcast journalists could attend and report trials on the same basis as other reporters, that is, without their cameras—but concerned the effect of expanding the trial audience to include persons not in the courtroom. In the 1960s—at the time of the *Estes* ruling—the court feared the effects of this expansion on both the trial participants and the expanded electronic audience. By the 1980s the courts felt that a broadly expanded audience of external spectators was a good thing that would have a positive impact on the social image of the judicial system. In addition, judges came to accept the news media and became more comfortable with the measures necessary to control media behavior during trials.

As predatory criminality became the dominant social construction of crime and began to influence criminal justice policy, the constitutional importance given to defendants' rights diminished in favor of general social interests and thus increased support for media access. As a result, opposition to courtroom television evaporated. The *Chandler* decision marks a remarkable shift in the attitude of the judicial system toward the presence of television in courtrooms. In 1976 all but two states prohibited cameras in courtrooms. Today, nearly every state allows cameras in their courts at either the appellate or trial level or both. The *Chandler* decision is seen as a broad victory for the electronic media and the assumption of media access to judicial proceedings.

The effects of cameras on actual courtroom proceedings are no longer seen as a prime concern, but the effects of those cameras on those outside the courtroom is still worrisome. Most worrisome is that public disturbances and full-scale riots have been triggered by court decisions in highly publicized cases.[29] Other unresolved issues include a chilling effect on victims reporting crimes, particularly victims of rape, witnesses seeking to avoid embarrassing coverage being reluctant to testify, heightening the public's fear of crime, distorting the public's beliefs about the workings of the judicial system, encouraging copycat crimes, and publicly pillorying defendants who are eventually found innocent. However, the infotainment value of media trials is too great, the television ratings too high, and none of the negative effects or speculated concerns severe enough to curtail televised coverage. In fact, the social and economic pressures to grant media access are so great that even in trials that are influenced by massive coverage, as in the O. J. Simpson criminal trial, the cameras and intense media scrutiny are usually allowed.

So it is that today intensive, and sometimes intrusive, news coverage is accepted as a fact of life in the judiciary. Future clashes between the two are to be expected as the media seek access to previously backstage judicial proceedings and as media technology makes recording and marketing them easier. These clashes will continue to revolve around the social construction of the judiciary. The media are aided in this process by the society-wide effects of the electronic visual mass media over the last fifty years, which has undermined the social legitimacy of closed social institutions. Country clubs, golf courses, prisons, bars, fraternal organizations, and a host of other institutions, as well as the courts, have been less successful in claiming a traditional right to insulate themselves from broad public and media access. Currently the evolution of the media and the judiciary's unsteady relationship has three areas of concern and unresolved conflict—the effect of pretrial publicity, the appropriate judicial mechanisms to be used by the courts when they are faced with intense media attention, and access by both sides to information held by the other.

# PRETRIAL PUBLICITY, JUDICIAL CONTROLS, AND ACCESS

## Pretrial Publicity

In 1807 Aaron Burr's attorney claimed that jurors could not properly decide his client's case because of prejudicial newspaper articles.[30] From this initial point of contention, the media and courts have continued to joust over pretrial publicity. Ironically, despite their adversarial history and contentious interactions, the media and the judicial system react to criminal events in much the same manner. Both concentrate on constructing a particular version of reality to be presented to a specific audience—jurors, viewers, or readers. The relationship between the media and the judicial system is sometimes cooperative, but more often each jealously guards its information while attempting to discover what the other knows. This is particularly true during the investigative and pretrial period of a case. Publicity before and during a trial may so affect a community and its courts that a fair trial becomes impossible and due process protections such as the presumption of innocence are destroyed. The media especially create problems when they publish information that is inadmissible in the courtroom and construct a community atmosphere in which finding and impaneling impartial jurors is not possible.

Unfortunately it is not always clear when particular media content is prejudicial. **Prejudicial publicity** can take two forms: factual information that bears on the guilt of a defendant and emotional information without evidentiary relevance that simply arouses passions. Factual information includes allusions to confessions, performances on polygraph or other inadmissible tests, and past criminal records and convictions. Emotional information includes stories that question the credibility of witnesses or present the personal feelings of witnesses about prosecutors, police, victims, or judges: stories about the defendant's character (he hates children and dogs), associates (she hangs around with known syndicate gunmen), or personality (he's a mean-spirited, bad-tempered degenerate), and stories that inflame the general public (someone has to be punished for this!).

Despite the concerns about prejudicial coverage, the U.S. Supreme Court has not operationally defined prejudicial coverage for the lower courts. Faced with ambiguity and forced to render largely subjective determinations, both trial and appellate courts have focused on jurors as the key to determining the fairness of a trial. In practice, the operational definition of an impartial juror is derived from the 1807 Aaron Burr case: "An impartial juror is one free from the dominant influence of knowledge acquired outside the courtroom, free from strong and deep impressions which close the mind."[31] Though not a precise rule, this definition does eliminate ignorance of a case or a total lack of exposure to media coverage as a requirement for impartiality. Jurors can be exposed to extensive media content regarding a case and still be considered impartial. If a jury is deemed impartial and uninfluenced by media coverage, then the proceedings are usually considered fair.

Paralleling this issue is the concern that trial publicity will result in unwarranted harm to a defendant. Appeals courts have thus far not recognized media coverage as a mitigating factor in sentencing decisions. Left unaddressed are cases in which a defendant is found innocent of criminal charges but has his or her career or reputation permanently ruined by publicity. The consequence of publicity has been described in this way in relation to government officials who have been investigated:

> Once again the tendency to portray public officials accused of criminal or unethical activities as guilty [is displayed]. . . . We find it appalling that long after many of these individuals have been found innocent of the accusations against them, the disproved accusations continue to be repeated as almost a permanent addendum to their name in news stories.[32]

The concern is that live television coverage incites such negative feelings against defendants that, even if they are later acquitted, the feelings are irreversible. The modern mass media have constructed a new verdict: legally innocent but socially guilty. In the process, media coverage confounds the concepts of **legal guilt** (is the defendant legally responsible for a crime?) and **factual guilt** (did the defendant actually commit the criminal behavior?). Factual guilt is not always equivalent to legal guilt, and the general public little understands and is poorly instructed by the media in the differences between the two. If defendants who have been found innocent are subsequently still punished by losing their career or reputation because of publicity, then the criminal justice system loses legitimacy with those who identify with these defendants.

## Judicial Mechanisms to Deal with Pretrial Publicity

Faced with a case that will generate significant pretrial publicity, the courts have two strategies they can pursue. One is proactive and seeks to limit the availability of potentially prejudicial material to the media. The second is reactive and seeks to limit the effects of the material on the proceeding after it has been disseminated to the public by the media. Under the first strategy, if a court deems information to be prejudicial, it acts to restrict either media access to the information or, if the material is already in the media's possession, restricts the publication of the information. **Proactive mechanisms** include closure and restrictive and protective orders (see Box 5.3). This approach directly clashes with the First Amendment protection of freedom of the press and has been vigorously resisted by the media. It has also not been a favored strategy of the appellate courts, as shown in test cases in which the Supreme Court has been more likely to uphold appeals by the media where a proactive strategy has been used.

Appeals by the media have been less successful when the courts employ a reactive strategy, allowing the news media access and publication but attempting to compensate for any negative effects from the resulting publicity. In this approach, trial court judges can invoke a number of reactive steps to limit the negative effects from information reported by the media. These **reactive mechanisms** are generally preferred over closure, restrictive orders, and protective orders because they do not directly limit the activities of the media and thus do not directly undermine the First Amendment freedom of the press.[33] They rest on the premise that even if most of the public may be influenced and biased by media information, an unbiased jury can still be assembled and an unbiased trial conducted. Applying a reactive strategy, judges can expand jury selection (the voir dire), grant trial continuances, grant changes of venue, sequester jurors, and give special instructions to the jury to counteract the effects of publicity (see Box 5.4).

Current case law and legislation provide little direction concerning the appropriate use of these reactive mechanisms, and little empirical research is available regarding their relative effectiveness. Therefore, although each mechanism has recognized strengths and weaknesses, its application is based on unproved but commonly accepted assumptions concerning its

## 5.3  *Proactive Judicial Mechanisms to Control Prejudicial Publicity*

| Mechanism | Description of Procedure |
| --- | --- |
| Closure | Closure involves isolating judicial proceedings from outside (public and press) attendance. Closure is felt to be a very effective means of preventing prejudicial coverage once a proceeding has begun because there can be no prejudice if there is no coverage. In opposing closure, the media argue that they are proxies for the general public and therefore have a right of access to the court proceedings under the open trial provision of the Sixth Amendment. |
| Restrictive orders | The next most effective step available to control prejudicial materials is the use of restrictive orders (also termed prior restraint or gag orders). Restrictive orders prevent the media from printing or broadcasting information. If information is not published, it cannot cause bias. Not surprisingly, the media have argued vigorously for the right to publish what they have already discovered, and this right has generally been upheld. |
| Protective orders | The third judicial mechanism used to limit the availability of prejudicial materials is the protective order. Trial participants are a common source of prejudicial information. By issuing a protective order, the trial judge prohibits attorneys and others from making statements outside the courtroom. These orders are most effective in the early stages of a case. The legal rationale behind protective orders allowing speech to be restricted is that trial participants possess privileged information regarding a criminal case and no longer have the same First Amendment right to freely speak as a member of the general public. As it now stands, it is currently easier for a trial judge to restrict the speech of a trial's participants, excluding the defendant, than to close a proceeding or to restrain the media from publicizing information and statements they have obtained. |

effectiveness and appropriate use. Given the pervasiveness and intrusiveness of the media, these after-the-fact attempts to compensate are often costly and disruptive, and, most important, of questionable effectiveness in massively covered media trials.[34] Proactive mechanisms are more effective, but they tend to close off the judicial system and therefore run counter to the society-wide, media-driven trend to open social institutions. They also preclude any positive social effects that might be generated from media attention to the judicial system. Although sometimes employed, proactive mechanisms are likely to continue to lag in popularity, reserved for the rare and unusual case and challenged whenever used.

## 5.4  Reactive Judicial Mechanisms to Control Prejudicial Publicity

| Mechanism | Description of Procedure |
|---|---|
| Voir dire | Voir dire, "to speak the truth," is a process in which prospective jurors are queried regarding prejudice. Attorneys can prevent jurors from serving either through challenges for cause, where they must state a valid reason for eliminating a juror, or through peremptory challenges (normally limited in number) that do not have to be supported by a reason. Voir dire will only identify those jurors who admit knowledge and prejudice about a case, and it is based on the premise that jurors will recognize themselves as biased and truthfully admit it. |
| Continuance | Continuance is simply a delay in the start of a trial until media coverage and its effects are thought to have subsided enough to allow an unbiased trial. The practice is based on the premise that media interest in the case will wane and that jurors will forget details of past media reports. Disadvantages include that it is inconsistence with the defendant's right to a speedy trial and the possibility that witnesses and evidence may not be available at a later time. |
| Change of venue | A trial may be moved from a location in which the case has received heavy media coverage to one in which it has received less coverage and is of less interest, and where residents are assumed to be less biased. Although costly and questionable in effectiveness, venue changes are deemed necessary in certain cases—for example, in rural areas where the jury pool is limited and a major crime is likely to be the dominant news story for a long time. |
| Sequestration | Isolating a jury to control the information that reaches it can be very effective if the jury has not been exposed to prejudicial information prior to being impaneled. However, it is costly and disruptive to jurors and is felt to generate animosity toward the accused. |
| Jury instructions | The simplest and least expensive judicial mechanism that can be invoked, jury instructions comprise the directions the trial judge gives to the jury. They fundamentally consist of telling jurors to ignore media coverage. Empirical studies that have examined this mechanism suggest, however, that for the most part standard jury warnings do not eliminate publicity-generated bias and that juries commonly discuss prejudicial information despite instructions not to. |

Regardless of which strategy judges employ, to enforce their decisions trial judges rely on contempt-of-court rulings to deter and punish those ignoring their orders regarding media publicity. In practice, the threat of a contempt finding works better with local criminal justice system personnel, as they have to consider future dealings with the court, and less well with jurors, witnesses, reporters (especially those from other jurisdictions), and other temporary participants. As a last resort, a mistrial can be declared and a retrial ordered if jurors are exposed to or admit to being influenced by prejudicial news once a trial has begun. A retrial can be thought of as the ultimate reactive judicial remedy for media publicity—but it also represents an expensive failure of the judicial system and does not prevent the recurrence of renewed massive coverage.

In addition to pretrial publicity and strategies to deal with the media, access to files, records, notes, photos, and databases have raised concerns. Issues here take two forms: those related to the media desiring access to government controlled and collected information and those related to government agencies gaining access to media collected and controlled information.

## Media Access to Government Information

In a significant number of instances, a government agency has possession of information that the media deems newsworthy. Oftentimes the government is reluctant to release such information, and in response the press has worked to increase its access to government-held data and files. The first national response to obtaining information held by the government was the federal **Freedom of Information Act**, adopted in 1966. This act opened up numerous government files to the media and the public. A later associated law was the **Government in Sunshine Act**, passed in 1976, which prohibits closed government meetings that concern public policy. Both of these efforts have been duplicated in numerous states but have had mixed results in easing the news media's access to government files and information.

Part of the cause of the mixed impact of the laws targeted at access stems from the federal **Privacy Act** in 1974. Concerns over privacy and misuse of information collected by government regarding individuals led to support for a counterbalance. The goal was to control the misuse of government information and to restrict access to certain information in criminal files and judicial records. Information required to be disclosed under the Freedom of Information Act cannot be withheld under the auspices of the Privacy Act, but the boundary between the two acts has always been blurred. Further muddying the water, the effects of the Patriot Act of 2001 and the Homeland Security Act of 2002 on media access to government-held information are not yet clear. As in other areas regarding the media, the lower courts, agency personnel, and the media operate without clear rules in determining when privacy supersedes public interests, and decisions are rendered on a case-by-case basis. To date the overall effect of this legislation has been more symbolic than significant, and today the media's access to government-held files and information varies significantly by jurisdiction.

## *Reporters' Privilege and Shield Laws*

On the opposite side of the knowledge control issue, the media sometimes possess information that the courts or law enforcement officials want but that reporters do not want to provide. Controversy generally revolves around journalists' claims to the right of a **privileged conversation**. Journalists argue that they should be protected from having to divulge information or identify their sources to the same extent that communications between husbands and wives, attorneys and clients, priests and penitents, and psychiatrists and patients are protected. In each of the latter relationships, the courts cannot compel disclosure. Journalists argue that to fulfill their constitutional function as watchdogs of government activities and to guarantee their access to information, their news sources must be similarly protected.

Opponents to the extension of privileged protection to media sources have argued that the media should have no more protections or privileges than the average citizen, whose duty to provide testimony in criminal matters has been regularly affirmed.

Paralleling media efforts for recognition of a constitutional right to privileged conversation protection, the media has also lobbied for **shield laws**, or legislative protection from forced divulgence. The first reporters' shield law was passed in Baltimore, Maryland, in 1896. Since then, the media have continued to lobby successfully for shield laws, and currently more than half the states have enacted some form of shield law. Most qualify the protection afforded reporters and provide a judicial test to be applied to assess whether the media's information is relevant and whether it can be obtained from other sources.[35] The effectiveness of shield laws is questionable, though, as the protection they afford the media is subject to state court interpretations and judicial rulings. Often the degree to which reporters are shielded depends not on what a state's laws say but on a judge's attitude toward the press.[36] A second serious deficiency with state shield laws is that they operate only within each state, and contemporary news organizations are national and international in scope. Because of these deficiencies, few journalists believe their state's shield laws provide substantial help in protecting confidential files or preventing forced testimony.

Currently, the media are seldom asked to provide information. But due to the absence of new Supreme Court decisions, a narrow interpretation of shield statutes at the state level has occurred. When judges and law enforcement personnel do request information, reporters can usually be forced to divulge it—especially if the information can be shown to be central to a case and is unavailable from other sources. The media's efforts have made obtaining their information more costly, time consuming, and difficult, and in that sense they have successfully increased control of their knowledge. But like the courts themselves, the media are now also more open to inspection and more often pressed for access and information from nongovernmental sources such as citizen and lobby groups. Ironically, the very process of access the media initiated has cycled back to affect their own social reality.

## THE COURTS AS TWENTY-FIRST-CENTURY ENTERTAINMENT

Today phrases such as "government in the sunshine" and "freedom of information" reflect a larger, media-driven social trend toward greater openness of public institutions. The two social institutions involved in this trend, the media and the criminal justice system, play critical roles. That the courts, as central players in these struggles, would be pressured by the media, especially the electronic media, to open their institutions to scrutiny was inevitable. Simultaneously, the media have also felt the pressure to open their institutions, processes, and files and have suffered through their own exposés of backstage activities. For better or worse, the courts and media are tightly coupled as we begin the twenty-first century, and both internal courthouse and external media audiences dance to an infotainment tune.

The place where the change in the dance is most readily observed is in the courtroom. In the process of defending or prosecuting, lawyers construct reality. In the courtroom, they reach into the popular culture for images and symbols. The popular characters and plot lines serve as the building blocks for courtroom social reality construction by evoking what "everybody knows" about the world. As displayed in the O. J. Simpson trial, prosecuting attorneys invoked the mystery narrative to deliver an evidence-based story to jurors; defense attorneys countered with the beleaguered hero narrative to construct their client as the innocent victim of state power.[37] As the dominant media in the United States have moved from print to visuals, so has the style of legal story construction. Today, one is much more likely to see visual representations in courtrooms: videos, computer-based animations, and reenactments that reflect the influence of the visual electronic mass media. The end result is that infotainment has worked its way into court proceedings.

Commenting on this process regarding the Amy Fisher case (which involved a baby-sitter's affair with a father and her attempt to eliminate her competition for him by shooting his wife), Richard Sherwin states:

> The role of the litigator, unlike that of journalist, is to come up with a narrative truth [or social construction] that can successfully compete against a

counter-narrative [a competing social construction] offered by the other side. Consider the case of Amy Fisher. In the sense of the prosecution Amy Fisher represented threats to the established moral order. As a consequence, [she] would have to pay the penalty for her transgression. On the side of the defense, Fisher would be framed within a counter-narrative. The image of Lolita gives way to "the poor unfortunate," the victim.... In Fisher's case, it is a story of psychological disturbance and parental complacency in the face of her increasingly desperate, and futile, cries for help ... [established social] myths and archetypes contribute to this process. When a crime occurs, the media, and in time the lawyers for the parties involved, struggle to come up with the most compelling means [to present their construction] conveying what occurred and what it means. In this way, Amy Fisher comes to be known as "the Long Island Lolita."[38]

The courts provide a perfect small-scale model of the social construction process. For the internal judicial audience, two constructions of reality are created by competing claims makers who use factual and interpretative claims (evidence and explanations) and submit them to an audience (judges and jurors) that chooses and validates one or the other (guilty or not guilty verdicts). The media have tapped into this internal judicial social construction process and transformed the judicial system into a massive public infotainment machine. Attorneys, judges, defendants, witnesses, and victims sometimes protest, but more often they embrace their celebrity status and the chance to play a leading role. The courts have found their place in the twenty-first-century world of media, crime, and justice, and it's as a combination studio and production company where the most popular and gripping crime-and-justice dramas are cast and marketed.

All these developments can be understood as a social reconstruction of the courts by the media. The judicial reconstruction process has been simultaneously carried on within entertainment, news, and infotainment media. The notable transformation of attorneys from lawyers to crime fighters in the entertainment media is one indicator of the wider social process of the shift of the courts from a judicial system to a source of public entertainment. Today, the courts struggle to construct public images that better align with their traditional social reality—that of the courts as fair, impartial institutions that determine truth and dispense justice by the rule of law. To what extent the media will degrade this historical construction remains to be determined, but the current public expectations and media content are clearly steered by infotainment values. For the near future, at least, the judicial system will be seen more as a source of entertainment than a source of justice. Another set of criminal justice institutions would also like to reconstruct its media portrait. Corrections have fared even worse than the courts; Chapter 6 explores the historically poor media–corrections relationship.

## Discussion Questions

1. How is the trial by jury process of determining guilt or innocence a small-scale example of social constructionism?
2. Is the law shown in a positive or a negative light in the media?
3. In that the courts actually determine what happens to offenders, why are media portraits of the courts fewer in number than those of law enforcement?

## In-Class Activities

1. Watch and discuss one of the films from the courtroom narratives (Box 5.1).
2. Invite a local prosecuting attorney to speak to the class about the effects of publicity on cases.

## Assignments

1. Attend a session of first appearances at the local courthouse and compare the processing of cases there with judicial processing shown in the media.
2. Watch a week's worth of crime shows and note violations of and adherence to due process protections. Also note and summarize pro and con comments on civil liberties, judges, attorneys, and the judicial system.

## Suggested Readings

Frankie Bailey and Steven Chermak, 2004. *Famous American Crimes and Trials*. Westport, CT: Praeger.

Paul Bergman and Michael Asimow. 1996. *Reel Justice: The Courtroom Goes to the Movies*. Kansas City, MO: Andrews and McMeel.

Hedieh Nasheri. 2002. *Crime and Justice in the Age of Court TV*. New York: LFB Scholarly Publishing LLC.

Richard Sherwin. 2000. *When Law Goes Pop*. Chicago, IL: University of Chicago Press.

Jon Bruschke and William Loges. 2004. *Free Press vs. Fair Trials: Examining Publicity's Roles in Trial Outcomes*. Mahwah, NJ: Lawrence Erlbaum.

# NOTES

1.    Sherwin, *When Law Goes Pop.*

2.    Matthew Robinson (*Justice Blind?*, 133) characterizes the content of the media as constructing due process protections as if they were a cause of crime in the United States.

3.    Rafter, "American Criminal Trial Films," 9.

4.    Stark, "Perry Mason Meets Sonny Crockett"; Surette, "Media Trials."

5.    Stark, "Perry Mason Meets Sonny Crockett," 275.

6.    Lichter and Lichter, *Prime Time Crime*; Rafter, "American Criminal Trial Films," 9.

7.    Greenfield and Osborn, "Film Lawyers"; Stark, "Perry Mason Meets Sonny Crockett."

8.    Rafter, *Shots in the Mirror.*

9.    Bailey, Pollock, and Schroeder, "The Best Defense."

10.   Andie Tucher ("Framing the Criminal," 908) cites an 1836 New York trial of a teenage clerk for the murder of a prostitute as the first media circus trial in America due to extensive coverage in the New York penny press.

11.   Barber, *News Cameras in the Courtroom*, 112–114; Nasheri, *Crime and Justice in the Age of Court TV.*

12.   Mathiesen, *Prison on Trial*, 66–67.

13.   *Estes v. Texas,* 381 U.S. 532, at 570 (1965).

14.   Altheide and Snow, *Media Worlds in the Postjournalism Era.*

15.   Hariman, "Performing the Laws: Popular Trials and Social Knowledge," 23.

16.   Surette, "Media Trials."

17.   David Papke (*Framing the Criminal*, 22) reports that similar themes existed in the 1830s. Popular pamphlets portrayed crime within two long-standing themes—the rogue (a semi-hero who commits property fraud) and the fiend (a diabolical, frenzied villain). This period saw the creation of a new theme—the fiendish rogue. An example from the early part of the twentieth century is the 1913 Leo Frank case involving the strangulation of a fourteen-year-old female factory worker in Georgia. As was common in such cases, coverage was heavily biased against the defendant. An Atlanta paper was typical: "Our little girl—ours by the Eternal God! has been pursued to a hideous death and bloody grave by this filthy, perverted Jew of New York." The commutation of Frank's sentence from death to life imprisonment led to Georgia's governor being driven out of office. A year after his conviction, Frank was taken from a prison farm by a band of men, driven 125 miles to the scene of the murder, and lynched.

18.   Like many things in life, it appears that being rich and famous and accused of a crime is double-edged. Access to a top-notch defense assures that your case will follow strict due process procedures and that every step in the criminal justice process will be exercised. It wasn't the race card that helped O. J. Simpson in his criminal trial, it was the money card. The rich can depend on a strong, aggressive defense. The poor are much more likely to plea bargain and be adjudicated guilty. However, if you are rich

and famous and are found guilty, you are likely to receive a stern sentence. Judges and the state do not want to appear to be favoring rich guilty defendants. Contrary to usual sentencing practices, this appears to be especially true for female defendants of late. Leona Helmsley, Patty Hearst, and Martha Stewart all received jail time as first offenders. In sum, money and fame help you avoid guilty verdicts, but if you are found guilty, you are more likely to be made an example of.

19.  Drucker, "The Televised Mediated Trial."

20.  Surette, "Media Echoes."

21.  Loften, *Justice and the Press*, 138; M. K. Wisehart ("Newspapers and Criminal Justice") makes the earliest historical references to echolike effects from media coverage in 1922.

22.  Kaplan and Skolnick, *Criminal Justice*, 467–468.

23.  Marcus, "The Media in the Courtroom," 276.

24.  62 A.B.A. Rep, 1134–1135 (1937) cited by Kirtley, "A Leap Not Supported by History."

25.  In a case important in Texas due to Estes's political associations, Texas financier Billie Sol Estes was accused of a salad-oil swindle. Cameramen crowded into a tiny courtroom and seriously disrupted the proceedings. After a trial of great notoriety, which was televised despite his objection, Estes appealed his conviction, arguing that the presence of television cameras denied him a fair trial. The Supreme Court agreed and reversed the decision, reversing its own decision sixteen years later in *Chandler v. Florida*.

26.  *Estes v. Texas*, at 538 and 544.

27.  Florida policeman Noel Chandler was tried and convicted with another police officer for a series of burglaries. The case received a large amount of regional media attention and was televised over Chandler's objection as part of a Florida pilot program for televising judicial proceedings. The Supreme Court held that if other constitutional due process guarantees are met, a state could provide for television coverage of a criminal trial over the objection of defendants.

28.  "Public Confidence in Selected Institutions, 1973–1996," table 2.9.

29.  Examples include the 1992 Los Angeles riots following the not guilty verdict for the police officers involved in the Rodney King beating; the 1980 Miami riots following the acquittal of police officers charged in the beating death of black motorist Arthur McDuffie; and the 1989 Miami riots following the shooting death of a black motorcyclist by police officer William Lozano (acquitted in 1993).

30.  *United States v. Burr*, cited in Marcus, "The Media in the Courtroom," 237.

31.  *U.S. v. Burr*, 25 F. Cas 49, 49. (1807).

32.  "Trial by Media," *U.S. Press.*

33.  For an overview and discussion of the research and issues associated with pretrial publicity and fair trials, see Bruschke and Loges, *Free Press vs. Fair Trials*. They note a discrepancy between laboratory research, which generally concludes that pretrial publicity biases trials, and field research, which reports that such effects are not common and occur only when the publicity is excessive and includes persuasive information and when trial evidence is inconclusive.

34.   Bruschke and Loges (*Free Press vs. Fair Trials*, 137) argue that combinations of reactive judicial remedies appear to be effective and that pretrial publicity will only bias a trial outcome in rare circumstances.

35.   Kirtley, "Shield Laws and Reporter's Privilege," 164.

36.   Ibid., 170.

37.   Sherwin, *When Law Goes Pop,* 219.

38.   Ibid., 34–35. Amy Fisher, the seventeen-year-old "Long Island Lolita" who shot the wife of her thirty-eight-year-old boyfriend, Joey Buttafuoco, in 1992 became a tabloid legend. She was released from prison in 1999.

# CORRECTIONS

**CHAPTER OBJECTIVES**

After reading Chapter 6, you will be able to describe the common portrait of corrections found in the entertainment media, which is dominated by prison films, and understand why television and infotainment programming have given corrections little attention. You will be able to discuss the news portrait of corrections as an example of the media backwards law, comprehend the concerns of correctional personnel with regard to negative news coverage, and know the media factors that influence the extent and nature of news coverage of correctional issues. Finally, you will understand how support for public correctional policy is connected to the combined entertainment and news media portraits of prisoners, correctional officers, and correctional institutions.

## HISTORICAL PERSPECTIVE

"What we've got here is a failure to communicate" (*Cool Hand Luke,* 1967). These words of the warden in the film *Cool Hand Luke* apply as much to the social construction of corrections as they did to Paul Newman's film character. The last step in the criminal justice system, the field of corrections is also the last thought. Society has always been more interested in catching criminals and holding media trials than in what happens to convicted offenders in our correctional institutions.

In colonial America, jails and prisons were places to hold offenders until they could be otherwise punished, usually by a corporal method such as branding, flogging, or hanging. Corrections were of little interest as institutions or as symbols of criminal justice policy. Following the enlightenment, when loss of freedom became the punishment rather than

**151**

just the precursor to punishment, societal interest in prisons, prison programs, and prison conditions increased, but never to the level of interest held by policing or courtroom proceedings. Corrections has always been the stepchild of the criminal justice system. The police got the glory and the courts got the public spectacles, but corrections—both monetarily in the real world and symbolically in the media-constructed one—got the shaft.

Like a plain child who puts his worst face forward for the camera, correctional institutions have historically suffered from their own lack of media sophistication. Correctional personnel have been notorious for poor media and public relations, frequently blocking access to inmates and staff, withholding information, and stonewalling in times of crisis. In the words of criminologist Robert Freeman: "Fortress corrections has been both a mentality and a philosophy in the field."[1]

Despite the correctional field's historic adversarial relationship with the media, the media have played a strong role in correction's public image. It is a tenet of social constructionism that the more remote the subject, the more the public perception of it will be shaped by media imagery. Unlike experiences with the police who are seen in public daily and the courts whose institutions are prominently displayed in our cities and can be easily visited, few people have direct knowledge about corrections. Most of the general public has neither experience knowledge (from having visited a jail or served a correctional sentence) nor conversational knowledge (from talking with people who work or have been in prison). The public is severely limited, therefore, in the amount of non–media rendered information it has about prisons, jails, prisoners, probation and parole, and other correctional programs. Access to direct non-mediated knowledge of corrections is concentrated in the poor. The affluent, who influence correctional policy more, construct their corrections reality largely from media renditions.[2]

Adding to the significance of this lack of direct experienced or conversational knowledge about corrections is the historical distrust between corrections personnel and the news media. The information flow from corrections to the media can be kindly described as a trickle.[3] The scarcity of information about corrections from correctional personnel compounds the public's lack of experienced and conversational knowledge. Combined, the public's lack of direct information about corrections and the correctional field's inability to successfully get realistic correctional information into play in the news and infotainment media makes the public dependent on the unrealistic correctional images and stereotypes found in the entertainment media. Driven by profit motives, the entertainment media have not been overly concerned with projecting an accurate image of corrections. Instead, the entertainment media use the institutions as backdrops to construct stories of social power and personal morality that often have little connection to correctional issues.

Lacking other sources of knowledge, the public constructs its perception of corrections from the source most easily and consistently available. The limited visual images of corrections found in television programming, news, and infotainment shows and the print-based descriptions of corrections contribute to the public perception, but prison films are by far the most influential sources for determining the social construction of corrections.[4] The importance of the prison film is due to the fact that books and magazines are less widely distributed and lack the visual impact of film. For its part, television has produced only a handful of programs based on corrections that have lasted beyond one season (the most successful being the HBO cable program *Oz*, which ran from 1997 to 2003). News stories and documentaries about corrections tend to be few in number and negative in content. Infotainment media that touch upon corrections are also rare and usually divorced from reality, dominated by violent "escape from prison" videogames. This leaves commercial films as the primary medium that creates and supports the dominant social construction of corrections.

## SOURCES OF CORRECTIONAL KNOWLEDGE

### *Prison Films*

Unlike most of the media, the film industry has not ignored corrections and, as stated previously, motion pictures are the primary source of knowledge about correctional issues.[5] The attraction of prison movies lies in their ability to combine escapist fantasies that purport to reveal the backstage brutal realities of incarceration with tales of adventure and heroism. Although one of the longest running genres (movies have been made about corrections since the early 1900s), prison films make up only about 1 percent of all films. Unfortunately, the image of corrections found in this small percentage is largely negative. Correctional movies commonly show either harsh, brutal places of legalized torture or uncontrolled human zoos that barely contain their animalistic criminals.[6] And unlike crime films, which also focus on crime fighters and even occasionally on victims as well as on the criminals, correctional films nearly universally focus on the inmates.

Within this fixation a particularly twisted construction of U.S. corrections dominates. Narrative staples of the genre include convict buddies, evil wardens, cruel guards, craven snitches, bloodthirsty convicts, and inmate heroes. Nearly all prison films dwell on stories of injustice and the effect of harsh treatment on individuals, and the focus is usually on an inmate's reaction, adjustment, and triumph over the correctional system.

Despite their stereotypes and inaccuracies, commercial movies about prison continue to be a prime source of the public's perceptions about corrections.

The movie world of corrections is a place where long-suffering virtue is rewarded and where, ironically, one usually has to look to the prisoners to find moral, honest men.

These correctional archetypes exist within fantasies about sex, violence, and salvation built around cinematic constructions marketed as "insider views" of the realties of prison life. Unique to correctional films are pervasive promotional claims of "based on a true story or actual event." Lacking other information sources, claims of being true and accurate are stressed more with prison films than with films about any other part of the criminal justice system. As criminologist Nicole Rafter observes, "No other genre so loudly proclaims its truthfulness."[7] But despite their claims of verisimilitude, prison films distort their subject more than other criminal justice movies. Except perhaps for the media portrait of superhero crime fighters, the construction of reality found in prison films is more distant from the real world than the entertainment realities constructed for criminality, law enforcement, and the courts. However, due to their validity claims and the lack of other information sources to counter them, prison movies remain the most influential correctional social construction source for the general public.

In an extensive content analysis study, Derral Cheatwood found four distinct narratives in prison films: the nature of confinement, the pursuit of justice, authority and control, and freedom and release.[8] These narratives dominate and guide the stories of correctional life found in the media. While the themes take differing tacks in portraying prison life, all four invariably focus on inmates and take an inmate's perspective. These narratives are found across the history of prison films, but Cheatwood identifies four eras in which a specific perspective dominates.

**Nature of confinement correctional films** (1929 to 1942) dominate the first era and are exemplified by classic films such as *The Big House, I Am a Fugitive from a Chain Gang*, and *20,000 Years in Sing Sing*. In this perspective, inmates appear as victims of injustice, either as good men framed or imprisoned by a chance accident or pushed into crime by powerful societal forces. A recurrent message in these films is the corrupt values of the correctional system and its administrators. This first era established and cemented the unique correctional backwards law common to prison films. In prison films the **corrections backwards law** works through a role reversal derived from the dynamic of the underdog, wrongly jailed inmates pitted against oppressive correctional employees. The inmate-hero was born in this era and has since dominated the portrait of corrections.

**Pursuit of justice correctional films** (1943 to 1962) dominated the second era, and *The Birdman of Alcatraz* and *Riot in Cell Block 11* are typical examples. A focus on violence in prison is shared with the nature of confinement films, but in this era offenders were personally responsible for their actions and were portrayed less often as victims and more often as criminals. Confinement is therefore justified, and the focus shifted to the flaws of the criminal and away from flaws in the criminal justice system. Although many of this era's films revolve around violence—riots, escapes, and inmate and guard hostility—individual offender rehabilitation was seen as a possibility.

The third era, **authority and control correctional films** (1963 to 1980), is exemplified by films such as *Cool Hand Luke* and *Escape from Alcatraz*. This era reintroduced a pessimistic view of corrections against a continuing backdrop of riot and escape stories. Offender confinement is still justified, but it occurs for less serious offenses. This era is most significant for immortalizing the "smug hack" portrait of correctional officers as the evil foil of the inmate heroes. In these films correctional officers are vaguely crazy, insensitive, and ineffective. Officer corruption is portrayed as universal. The world of corrections is constructed as a freestanding social ecosystem with corrupt correctional officers as just one of the system's species. Like the Galapagos Islands, correctional institutions are painted as strange primitive islands, long separated from the mainland, where bizarre species have evolved to fill unique local niches. Within this isolated ecosystem, all facets of prison life became subject to exploitation, producing the first, if unrealistic media portrayals of real prison problems—rape, racism, and drugs.

The fourth and current prison film era, **freedom and release correctional films**, is represented by futuristic science fiction films about prison colonies and prisoner transportation systems, exemplified by the films *Escape from New York, The Fortress*, and *Aliens 3* or throwback renditions of early era portraits represented by films like *Holes* and *The Shawshank Redemption*. Extreme violence appears for the first time in prison movies, and the prison action film appears. The ambiguity and confusion about the function and role of prisons in society is reflected in these films, which finalize the process of humanizing the inmates and dehumanizing the guards. In the current era, the keepers are certifiably crazy and are sometimes inhuman part-machine creatures or simply holographic projections. The correctional world as constructed in these films reflects the fantasy world of comics more than any recognizable social reality.

With this sometimes bizarre, always myopic, long-running cinematic base of information, the public is more disadvantaged in constructing an alternate worldview of corrections than it is in constructing prior components of the criminal justice system. The true issues and needs of corrections are absent or perversely distorted in these constructions. In these movies the kept are the heroes and the keepers are the villains. In film, correctional institutions are as removed from their real-world counterparts as most science fiction films are from the NASA space program. Unfortunately, when the other sources of correctional information available to the public are examined and added in, their contribution does little to correct the dominant prison film constructions of a world sprinkled with a few good men among a population of violent, crazed, sex-driven individuals. True to form in getting it backwards, in the media, more often than not, the good men are wearing the inmate jumpsuits; the crazed, violent, evil ones are wearing the correctional officer uniforms.

## Correctional Television and Infotainment

In television entertainment programming, corrections is the least shown component of the criminal justice system—and therefore by extension the least important. Television has had fewer shows focused on corrections and they have been shorter lived than any other aspect of the criminal justice system.[9] The few television programs that have featured jails or prisons have either been slapstick comedy or featured inmates rather than staff. More often, television information about corrections is communicated through indirect negative allusions to the correctional alumni, recidivist offenders found in law enforcement shows. With habitual criminals outnumbering first offenders by more than four to one on television, media indirectly constructs corrections as ill equipped and unable to rehabilitate offenders. Instead, media imply that the corrections system is simply a way station for criminals from which they frequently return to society as worse criminals than when they were sentenced. With the scarcity of television programming that looks directly at corrections, perhaps the greatest impact of television on the social construction of corrections is as a means of extending the life and reach of commercial prison films. Television's recycling of the more than one hundred corrections movies made since the 1920s provides a continuous, negative media loop in which corrections is constructed negatively anew for each succeeding generation.

The infotainment genre has yet to significantly discover corrections. There are no shows yet with titles like "The People's Parole Board" or "Guards" to match the popular court and police counterparts. The lack of correctional infotainment programming is partly due to the fact that, as noted, prison entertainment films already market themselves as accurate portraits of correctional life. The public is told that it is already getting reality programming about corrections in the movie theaters. Even if there were greater interest by media to create correctional infotainment products, correctional administrators have little incentive to cooperate. Due to the entertainment criteria that drive the infotainment programming creation process, correctional infotainment, if it existed, is not likely to result in greater public support for corrections or a better image of correctional personnel. The historical impact of film documentaries that have focused on corrections substantiates this conclusion. The few correctional documentaries that have received widespread public play have ultimately resulted in negative attention and criticism for their subject institutions. For example, the documentary film *Titticut Follies,* which shows life in an institution for the criminally insane, and *Scared Straight,* which describes a popular shock incarceration program for juveniles, both resulted in criticisms of the correctional administrators and personnel and lawsuits against the institutions.

## Corrections in the News

Contrary to television entertainment and common impressions, there is not a lack of attention about corrections in the news. In an extensive study of television and newspaper news, Steven Chermak found that 17 percent of crime-and-justice stories involved correctional institutions in some manner.[10] This is still substantively less than the level of attention given to law enforcement or courts, but corrections is not as off-the-radar in the news as it is in television entertainment programming.[11] Most references to

© AFP/Getty Images

The coverage of Iraqi prisoner abuse by the U.S. military is an example of negative correctional news. Negative content about corrections far outweighs positive content in the media.

corrections, however, are found inside stories focused on a different component of the criminal justice system or are found within stories that trace an individual offender or case as it progresses through the system. Still about one-fifth of the crime-and-justice news at least acknowledges the existence of corrections.

Concerning the mainstay of news coverage, the coverage of individual cases, Table 6.1 reports Chermak's findings and shows how corrections fares compared with law enforcement and the courts in terms of news coverage. Individually based correctional stories are usually presented through a reference to an offender's commitment to prison, behavior on parole, or execution.[12] The operation of the front-end focus of the news media on law enforcement is clearly shown. News reports that concentrate on law enforcement activities (discovery of crimes through the formal charging of suspects) comprise more than 50 percent of news stories, court proceedings (pretrial motions through Supreme Court decisions) about 30 percent, and corrections (probation to execution) less than 5 percent.

| TABLE 6.1 | Newspaper and Television Crime Incident Stories by Stage of Criminal Justice Process |
|---|---|

| Stage of Process | Percent of Cases |
|---|---|
| Discovery of crime | 18.7 |
| Investigation | 4.2 |
| Arrest | 15.4 |
| Arraignment | 13.1 |
| **Cumulative Law Enforcement** | **51.6** |
| Pretrial motions | 3.7 |
| Plea agreement | 2.7 |
| Trial | 9.1 |
| Jury deliberation | 0.4 |
| Verdict | 3.9 |
| Sentence | 7.3 |
| Appeal | 2.3 |
| Supreme Court decision | 0.8 |
| **Cumulative Courts** | **30.2** |
| Probation behavior | 0.1 |
| Commitment to prison | 0.4 |
| Parole behavior | 1.8 |
| Pardon request | 0.3 |
| Release from prison | 1.1 |
| Execution | 0.5 |
| **Cumulative Corrections** | **4.2** |
| Follow-ups* | 12.7 |
| Other† | 1.4 |

Note: N = 1,979 stories.

*Follow-ups include either victim, defendant, or crime follow-ups (for example, a story about the impact that a crime has had on a victim's family).

†Other stories include other court settlements.

Source: Chermak, "Police, Courts, and Corrections in the Media," 92.

As far as individual cases and offenders are concerned, what happens in corrections is not the typical news story focus. Once an offender leaves the courtroom, the offender usually disappear from the news unless he or she violates parole or probation, is released from prison, or is executed. News stories that discuss correctional institutions are found either inside stories about other criminal justice topics or within lengthy special reports, usually produced by the print media. In television news coverage of corrections, extraordinary events dominate. The more mundane aspects of prison management, legislation, and litigation are unlikely to appear on national televised news.[13] More developed and contextualized issue-focused news stories that discuss the daily operation of prisons, how inmates adapt to the conditions of incarceration, and institutional programs do exist. Unfortunately, they are rare. In contrast, many news stories incorporate day-to-day police and court operations such as arrests, charging, verdicts, and sentencing. Nonincarceration elements of corrections, such as probation or community corrections, receive even less media attention.

Why do corrections fare so poorly in the news? A number of factors determine the quantity of correctional news coverage. First, compared to other crime-and-justice stories, corrections has a relative low newsworthiness value. News personnel do not think a defendant's correctional behavior is interesting to the public. Once a newsworthy individual enters a correctional institution and settles into the routines of correctional life, unless he or she does something noteworthy in prison, such as dying, the individual is not often seen as particularly newsworthy. Second, corrections stories are difficult to produce because news media traditionally have only limited access to corrections sources. There is no corrections newsbeat that matches the police and court beats in journalism, so corrections stories are time consuming to produce because a preexisting journalism–corrections link does not exist. The information channels and public information officers commonly found in police stations and courthouses are absent in many correctional institutions. Third, reporters usually have limited prior knowledge of corrections and likely need to be newly introduced to the field during a breaking news story, almost always a negative one involving an escape, assault, or riot. Reporters do not maintain relationships with correctional officials as they often do with police or court officials. The weak news media–correctional personnel relationship is reflected by the fact that correctional personnel are the least likely of all sources to be quoted in news stories, accounting for less than 1 percent of the total.

On the corrections side of the news creation process, the closed environment of correctional programs helps to shield officials from external scrutiny. Correctional officials are more able to control information because media access to inmates is limited by law to a much greater extent than in the other components of the criminal justice system. For corrections administrators, controlling information frequently translates into releasing no information. Prison administrators have a large number of justifications and mechanisms available to limit media access. Claims of institutional security needs; ongoing investigations; prisoner confidentiality, privacy, and rehabilitation considerations; and bureaucratic red tape (especially in arranging interviews) are common justifications to deny access. Delaying mechanisms include using uninformed personnel to slow the release of information to the media (corrections are the least likely criminal justice agencies to employ trained public information officers and to seek positive coverage so that the large majority of prison news stories remain media initiated), directing staff to present themselves as apolitical and inappropriate to comment on political decisions such as punishment policies, and simply being geographically isolated.[14] Ironically, the net result of these information blocks and delaying tactics is that newsworthy offenders are often pilloried by the media before trial, when they are still presumed innocent, and shielded from the media afterwards, when they have been deemed guilty.[15]

Despite the limitations on media access, prison officials are not able to significantly influence the coverage that does occur because a number of alternate sources of information about correctional conditions are available to the media. These include inside leaked information provided by correctional officers (this source is limited though by the historic media portrait of correctional officers as "hacks" and the resultant officer distrust of the media, job loss if their identity is revealed, and confidentiality agreements many institutions require correctional officers to sign); inmates (limitations on interview access is often severe); inmate families, elected officials, defense attorneys, researchers and academics, and prison support and prisoner rights groups. In addition, because administrators are less likely to have the media competing for access, they cannot use a need for access to influence the content of coverage. Aaron Doyle and Richard Ericson describe this relationship:

> Prison officials are less able to offer "exclusives" or "scoops." Unlike the situations with police, the routine operations of prisons seldom offer news items for which media outlets will compete. As interviews with correctional officials responsible for public relations show, the chief messages they are trying to mobilize consist of "good news" about the system, such as stories about Christmas in prison or prisoners doing woodwork or growing flowers. These represent puny coin in the currency of crime news, compared to accounts featuring more dramatic fare such as official deviance and mayhem within the walls.[16]

Media do not need to fill a daily corrections news hole, which gives the media more control over correctional news creation and provides less leverage to correctional administrations to influence content. In that there is no media need to maintain access to correctional authorities, the news media need not worry about burning their bridges to corrections; there is no continuous bridge traffic.

The cumulative effect of these factors is that access to the criminal justice system as well as the resulting media content remains front-end loaded. Compared with the police, who are sometimes eager to interact with the media and who work on the public streets, and the courts, whose main events are usually open to the public and press, the daily lives of prisons are far more shrouded. The pressrooms and available documents such as police blotters and court dockets have no equivalents in corrections. Therefore, most of the news of corrections that is produced is dominated by riots, escapes, and the release or death of newsworthy individuals—just like in the movies. In the end, three types of negative stories typify correctional news. The first are stories about correctional failures to protect the public. These include prison escapes, staff negligence in supervising inmates, and failure to control prisoners. Second are stories of corrections pursuing inappropriate goals in which punishment is absent while amenities are highlighted. The description of prison partying by inmates, plush recreation rooms with color television, and air-conditioned cells are the stock of these stories. Third are stories of **correctional horrors**, which are exemplified by corruption and misconduct exposés. These can be either individual bad-apple stories (the sadistic guard) or systemic corruption stories (the corrupt warden and administration), and they often employ the death of an inmate as the symbolic crime of the correctional system's failure. As Box 6.1 highlights, when presented with a story that fills one of these niches, the media are willing to expend considerable effort and resources, at least for a short time.

In sum, the news construction of corrections is scanty, and when covered, corrections are marketed in a manner that emphasizes predators and criminogenic institutions. The day-to-day administration of punishment and attempt to rehabilitate do not fit common media narratives. The prison sentence as a long tedious block of time where nothing changes is absolute anathema to the dramatic event that is typical of a "hard news" item. There are few dramatic rituals or events involved in prison life, and those that do occur are negative and involve death and violence.

Finally, just as in the entertainment media, news of corrections focuses on the inmates and ignores the staff. After a content study of 1,546 newspaper articles, criminologist Robert Freeman reports that negative stories about corrections significantly outnumber positive ones, and the positive ones tend to focus on inmates, not staff.[17] Thus, as also found in news of crime, law enforcement, and the courts, corrections is covered more often as an act connected to an individual than as an issue connected to a system. Even so, corrections news does focus on policy questions more often than do police and court news. Release policies, institutional conditions (usually as follow-up to riot, death, and escape stories), execution

## 6.1   Media Resources and Correctional Bad News

An Atlanta police source called a veteran police reporter of the *Journal and Constitution* with a blockbuster: The Atlanta Federal Penitentiary was under siege. "He said the [Cuban] detainees had taken over part of the prison and they might have hostages." The tip was passed to the day city editor. Within minutes, amid the normal pressure of an early dead-line, the newsroom kicked into high gear. During the eleven-day crisis, the assistant managing editor would assign more than a hundred staffers to the story:

> We had constant updates for all seven editions. The Staff produced nine to 12 new stories daily. In 48 hours we did mini-profiles on 65 of the hostages plus nine others who had been released. And a 5,000 word history of the Marielitos and a 2,500 word piece about what life is like inside the prison.

Four extra open pages provided prison news each day. Photographers were stationed in helicopters, in cherry pickers, in trees, and on rooftops around the clock. Reporters worked shifts at the prison, and each shift included one person who was fluent in Spanish. A Spanish-speaking copyeditor was sent with a news team to Oakdale, Louisiana, to cover events at the federal detention center there, where rioting had begun two days before the Atlanta uprising. A Hispanic copy clerk monitored radio transmissions in the newsroom. Suburban reporters maintained a twenty-four-hour vigil at Dobbins Air Force Base near Atlanta to alert editors if federal troops arrived. (They didn't.) The Washington bureau covered angles at the Immigration and Naturalization service and the Justice Department.

---

*Source:* Frederick Talbott, "Reporting from Behind the Walls." *The Quill* 76 (1988): 16.

coverage (which sometimes incorporates the debate over the death penalty and the issue of the racial composition of death row), and the incarceration of juveniles and mentally retarded offenders all receive periodic coverage. In addition, news stories periodically appear concerning innovative cor-rectional projects such as intermediate sanctions, shock incarceration, or electronic home monitoring. A final irony of correctional news coverage emerges. Although corrections is the least covered component of the criminal justice system, it is the most likely to have its policies, missions, and basic functions discussed in the news. Corrections is comparatively ignored by the media, but at least it is ignored in depth.

## CORRECTIONS PORTRAITS AND STEREOTYPES

What are the portraits of corrections that are constructed from these information sources? The three most important ones involve the social construction of prisoners, correctional institutions, and correctional officers. The construction of incarcerated prisoners together with the construction of freed offenders discussed in Chapter 3 provide the public with its cumulative picture of criminality, its nature, and most important, its amenability to rehabilitation. If inmates are constructed as incorrigible and innately evil, this logically leads toward correctional policies of incapacitation and capital punishment. On the other hand, if inmates are shown as victimized—basically good but misled—then policies of rehabilitation and resocialization make more sense. In essence, the more inmates are constructed as similar to the rest of us, the more it makes sense to offer more help and less punishment. The more they are constructed as different, as predatory and inhuman, the more sensible it is to permanently remove, punish, and execute them.

In the same vein, the manner in which correctional institutions are constructed is important for the correctional policies and programs that make sense to society. If the institutions are violent madhouses filled with irrational predators (inmates or staff), money for work, education, or counseling programs will appear to be wasted. However, if the institutions are constructed as understaffed, underfunded places where humane correctional officers are trying to supervise large numbers of offenders, some of whom are redeemable, then public monies for these institutions and their programs will make more sense. Again, the more inmates are seen as like the rest of us—if there is a "there but for the grace of God" reaction to the way they are portrayed—the more palatable improvements to conditions and programs in these institutions will be.

Finally, the social construction of correctional officers is important, particularly if they are villainized. The more violent and predatory the staff is shown to be, the less attractive these positions appear to recruits as possible careers and the more the public is led away from putting money into corrections. Why give money to innately corrupt vile administrations or raise the salary of brutal guards? In contrast, a social construction of a humane staff striving to help salvageable inmates brings an opposite reaction. In that frame of mind, steering public resources into corrections would be sensible. With these implications in mind, the portraits and stereotypes of prisoners, correctional institutions, and correctional officers are described.

## Prisoners

Two popular constructions of inmates are found in the mass media. One is for male prisoners and the other is for females. The dominant construction of male prisoners derives from the role reversal of offenders and criminal justice system workers where those in authority are portrayed as predators and those caught up in the system are shown as victims. A minor portrait in the total media picture of law enforcement and court personnel, in the social construction of corrections such role reversals are common and result in a portrait that frequently sides with the kept rather than the keepers. Tapping into the American cultural tendency to root for underdogs, the irony of the media construction of male prisoners is that most of the predator criminals who terrorized society in the crime-fighting media are reconstructed in the correctional media as victims. The predatory offenders who remain and appear in corrections media constructions are there to threaten the **heroic inmates** and to create an atmosphere of constant menace within the institutions.

If the male prisoners appear within narrow stereotypes, female inmates fare even worse. With remarkably few exceptions, female inmates are found in constructions containing high levels of gratuitous sex (primarily lesbianism and rape) and correctional officer dominance and sadism. Female prisoners are portrayed in a number of bad-girl, low-budget "B" movies that have been described as squalid mixtures of sex and violence. Criminologist Robert Freeman argues that these images are powerful elements of the popular image of female corrections, especially for young males.[18] Their construction of women offenders and female correctional institutions is so juvenile and ridiculous that it could be dismissed if there were an alternate information source to counter them. Unfortunately there is not.

Collectively then, male and female prisoners are often portrayed as victims rather than as offenders. The more normal and similar to law-abiding people they appear, the more they are constructed as victims of corrupt correctional systems. Victimization of offenders can come from other predatory, violent, psychotic inmates or predatory, violent, psychotic correctional officers. Both clearly are more dangerous than the struggling inmate heroes. The message is that both need to be removed from the correctional institutions they are terrorizing. The constructed portrait of these institutions reflects the paradoxical construction of their populations—that reform must begin not with the prisoners but with the institutions and staff. Prisoners are either incorrigible and beyond rehabilitation and need to be separated from the redeemable or are the moral superiors to staff and administration and must not be brought down to their level.

## Correctional Institutions

The media-constructed universe of corrections contains a galaxy of institutions in which the most sensational and dramatic correctional stereotypes are emphasized. The complex political, social, and economic realities of correctional facilities are ignored, and a corrections template that is stark and bleak is presented instead. **Smug hack corrections**, described as seven interwoven portraits of negative correctional imagery, make up the media-constructed correctional world.[19]

Physical brutality in the name of inmate discipline is common. Control is maintained with corporal punishment and severe infliction of pain, often for trivial rule violations. This physical brutality is often linked with the exploitation of inmates as a cheap source of labor and profit. Staff incompetence, corruption, and cruelty are common, ingrained, and unchallenged. Under the thumb of a despotic staff, the prisoners suffer systemic racial prejudice, homosexual rape, and institutionalized violence. If female, the inmates suffer further degradation, sexual assaults, and harassments. Ironically, although the inmates are often shown sympathetically, the overall construction of corrections does not result in public support for correctional programs. The largely negative portraits of correctional officers and staff and the violent institutions they inhabit promotes a nonsupportive public image of corrections. Not only is this negative media image of correctional institutions the historical portrait found in film, but recent media depictions on cable television and in popular literature show little progress.

## Correctional Officers

As pointed out, correctional media usually focus on the inmates, frequently ignoring the staff and administration totally, or when they are portrayed, showing them negatively. The **smug hack** portrayal of correctional officers—caricatures of brutality, incompetence, low intelligence, and indifference to human suffering—dominates. This negative correctional officer construction creates a perception of modern corrections that remains locked in a pre-1960s frame of punitive human warehousing. The media promulgated imagery provides the baseline for the public's construction of corrections and correctional officers. Whereas the police are heroic rescuers and the attorneys (at least sometimes) are the preservers of truth and justice, media-constructed correctional officers are, more often than not, oppressive villains. If not oppressive, they are irrelevant. In the media, incarceration turns criminal predators into imprisoned prey and villainous criminals into inmate heroes. These inmate heroes need villains to defeat, and the

# The Orange County Jail has
# OFFICERS

## NOT

**Guard:** minimally trained person who watches over property (not a Certified Corrections Officer).

**Muckraker:** negative term from the 1800's for journalists who accused large companies of exploitation and corruption but based their stories mostly on fiction rather than fact.

**Hack:** someone working for hire especially with mediocre professional standards.

**Shyster:** one who is professionally unscrupulous especially in the practice of law or politics.

**Pig:** slang, usually disparaging law enforcement personnel.

**Deadbeat:** one who persistently fails to pay personal debts or expenses.

**Quack:** a pretender to medical skill.

**Charlatan:** one making usually showy pretenses to knowledge or ability.

**Flack:** a derogatory term used to describe public relations practitioners.

## Guards
## Jailers
## Screws
## Turnkeys
## Fuzz
## Hacks
## Pigs
## Lackeys
## Keepers

Courtesy Orange County, Florida, Corrections Department

Some correction agencies recognize the harm that results from a media-generated negative public image of correctional officers and try to counteract that image.

correctional staff members are enlisted to fill that role. The end result is that the inmates often end up as more sympathetic characters than the correctional officers. The accompanying role reversal makes good theater and escapism, but it paints a particularly onerous portrait of the correctional officer.

# THE PRIMITIVE "LOST WORLD" OF CORRECTIONS

In the novel *The Lost World,* by Arthur Conan Doyle, an isolated primitive environment filled with prehistoric beasts is found to secretly exist. The media-constructed portrait of corrections shares similarities with Doyle's fictional lost world: primitive predators, bizarre rituals and tribes, a society ruled by the law of the jungle, hidden but existing near our own—there but invisible. The impact of the media on the public's constructed portrait of corrections is due to its primacy effect. That is, like the adage about "making your first impressions count," the first set of information about a person, group, or organization that is received has greater weight than later information because it creates an initial resilient perception. In constructionist terms, once a construction takes root, it is resistant to change. If the first information is negative, the unflattering initial impression created by that information will tend to dominate and persist even if later information is positive. For corrections, the first impressions are usually picked up from prison films and other entertainment media and are likely to be negative. They also are likely to be reinforced rather than challenged by information provided in the news and infotainment media. The impact of the initial negative messages is compounded for the public through its repeated exposure to the continually rerun prison films and recycled news footage of past prison riots and escapes. It is highly unlikely for the typical media consumer to have positive perceptions of corrections or to have their negative perceptions of corrections challenged in the current media environment.

Prison films, tabloid-style crime reporting, television programming, the focus on prison riots and brutal attacks by paroled assailants, and the less-than-flattering portrait of correctional staff and administrators comprise the foundation for the social construction of corrections. This construction has been blamed for helping to heighten the public's fear of crime; for eroding public confidence in the ability of corrections to deter, rehabilitate, or even retain criminals; and for increasing the public's desire to make the system more punitive for all offenders regardless of their offense history or forecast dangerousness.[20] Reflecting on these media images, Laura Zaner comments, "the bad rap corrections takes in the [media] may translate into a lack of public support for real-life correctional institutions."[21] It is difficult to imagine any other effect.

To this point the tour of the media-constructed world of criminal justice has made its way from the crimes and criminals, to the crime fighters, through the courts, and into the correctional system. In general, neither the criminal justice system nor its employees are well presented in the media, and the further one moves into the system, the less information is available and the worse the constructed image is. How does this portrait of criminality and criminal justice translate into criminal justice policy? What public attitudes about crime and justice are associated with these constructions? Which steps to deal with crime are encouraged and which ones are discouraged? In answer, Chapter 7 examines crime control efforts based on media communication campaigns and media technologies. Chapter 8 looks at the media's influence on the public's support for various criminal justice policies.

## DISCUSSION QUESTIONS

1. Why is bad news about corrections more newsworthy than good news?
2. Can correctional personnel do anything to significantly change the public image of corrections?
3. Who is most responsible for the content and nature of news about corrections—correctional administrators, journalists, news agency administrators, or the public?

## IN-CLASS ACTIVITIES

1. Compare real correctional officer duties to the media portrait of them, similar to the Chapter 4 comparison of media and street police.
2. Watch *The Shawshank Redemption* and discuss the use of correctional stereotypes. If this film was all someone knew about corrections, what correctional policies would he or she likely support and oppose?
3. Invite a local probation officer or representative of a prisoner support group to speak to the class about the differences between media images of prison and prisoners and actual incarceration experiences.

## ASSIGNMENT

Watch crime shows for a week and note how many criminals are also ex-cons. Note how deterrence and rehabilitation are portrayed as likely outcomes of incarceration.

## Suggested Readings

Robert Freeman. 2000. *Popular Culture and Corrections*. Lanham, MD: American Correctional Association.

Frankie Bailey and Donna Hale. 1998. *Popular Culture, Crime, and Justice*. Belmont, CA: West/Wadsworth.

## Notes

1.  Freeman, *Popular Culture and Corrections*, 208.
2.  Graber, *Crime News and the Public*; and Roberts and Stalans, *Public Opinion, Crime, and Criminal Justice*.
3.  Marsh, "A Comparative Analysis of Crime Coverage in Newspapers," 76.
4.  Freeman, *Popular Culture and Corrections*.
5.  Mason, "The Screen Machine," 279–280; and Wilson and O'Sullivan, *Images of Incarceration*.
6.  Cheatwood, "Prison Movies"; and Freeman "Public Perception and Corrections."
7.  Rafter, *Shots in the Mirror*, 127.
8.  Cheatwood, "Prison Movies." For a critique of Cheatwood's typology, see Mason, "The Screen Machine," 284–288.
9.  For a discussion of British television programs about corrections, see Mason, "Watching the Invisible"; and Wilson and O'Sullivan, *Images of Incarceration*.
10. Chermak "Police Courts and Corrections in the Media," 96.
11. Doyle and Ericson, "Breaking into Prison." See also Lotz, *Crime and the American Press*.
12. For example, Andrew Hochstetler ("Reporting of Executions in U.S. Newspapers," 8) provides evidence that the backwards law of media content extends to coverage of death row so that the more sensational cases receive the most coverage.
13. This was found to be true for the 1970s by Jacobs and Brooks, "The Mass Media and Prison News"; and for the 1990s by Doyle and Ericson, "Breaking into Prison," 157–158.
14. Doyle and Ericson, "Breaking into Prison," 167.
15. Ibid., 183.
16. Ibid., 183–184.
17. Freeman, *Popular Culture and Corrections*, 114–115.
18. Ibid., 46.
19. Ibid.
20. Mathiesen, "Television, Public Space and Prison Population," 39.
21. Zaner, "The Screen Test," 64; see also Getty, "Media Wise," 126–131.

# CRIME CONTROL

## CHAPTER OBJECTIVES

After completing this chapter, you will be able to discuss the use of Madison Avenue style anticrime ads aimed at victims, offenders, and witnesses and the increased use of media technology to process criminal cases from arrest to court proceedings through jury deliberations. You will also have an understanding of the growth of surveillance of the public and the issues and controversies associated with this practice.

## MEDIA AND CRIME CONTROL

It's rude to stare. We all have heard this common admonition. Violation of this and other taken-for-granted clauses of the social contract underlie the concerns discussed in this chapter. Much has been written concerning the media as a cause of crime. This chapter examines the increasing use of media and media technology to control crime and to administer justice. These efforts are historically rooted in the success of prosocial entertainment programs and public information campaigns beginning in the 1960s. More recently media techno-logical advances, which allow easy recording, transmittal, storage, and review of moving images, further spurred criminal justice interest. Beginning in the 1970s these factors resulted in development of a number of media-based anticrime programs and the widespread adoption of media technology in the criminal justice field. Now common, these programs and applications can be divided into three areas: anticrime advertising, case processing using media technology, and police surveillance systems. Can media and media technology be used effectively to enforce laws, administer justice, and patrol society? This

**171**

chapter examines how the adoption of media technology has changed the reality of criminal justice.

Media-based anticrime efforts are targeted at two audiences, criminals and citizens. Programs targeting criminals are mass media public information and communication campaigns geared to deter offenders from future offending. Programs targeting citizens include mass media public information campaigns aimed at reducing victimization and solving crimes. Both types of programming are designed to reduce crime, so media anticrime programs are usually driven by crime control values. Critiques of these programs raise due process and civil liberty concerns.

## Public Service Announcements Join the War on Crime

Efforts to use the media to reduce and solve crimes are not new. The "Wanted Dead or Alive" posters on the Western frontier and the FBI's "Most Wanted" list are two long-standing examples of fugitive searches that used available media. What is new is the rapid increase in the number of media-based anticrime efforts since the 1980s. With broad-based support, these efforts use the media to attempt to construct a social reality with less crime. The original projects in this area were prosocial public information campaigns aimed at influencing public attitudes in the 1930s.[1] With the ability of media to negatively affect social attitudes established through research and government propaganda campaigns, social planners and politicians set out to employ the media to effect planned positive changes in public attitudes and perceptions.

During the 1950s, media campaigns aimed at changing general social practices in health and other areas began to appear. For a time during the 1960s, negative research findings led to widespread pessimism about the media's ability to influence audiences, and it was not until the late 1960s that attempts were again made to use the media to purposely influence the public. Evaluations of **prosocial television** programming such as *Mr. Rogers' Neighborhood* and *Sesame Street* found that children cooperate more and display other positive social behaviors after watching prosocial television episodes. The evaluations of these and similar shows revealed that programs of various types (animated, adventure, comedy, and fantasy) all have the ability to elicit socially valued behaviors from children and adolescent viewers. In contrast to the bulk of negative assessments of commercial television programming, it was concluded that properly designed television programs can have beneficial effects.[2] Encouraged by this, newfound enthusiasm for mass media developed in the 1970s with the expectation that media-generated positive social effects could be gained in a number of social areas—including crime reduction.

Media-based anticrime efforts have a long history as shown by the 1930s U.S. government-produced film *Reefer Madness*.

From this foundation, media-based anticrime programs proliferated. The current renditions all utilize brief advertisement-like media messages and collectively separate into three groups. The first group—aimed at offenders—employs ads designed to deter people from committing crimes. These anticrime messages are deployed in existing mass media advertising avenues as **public service announcements** (or **PSAs**). A second group of

| TABLE 7.1 | Three Basic Types of Media Anticrime Ad Programs | | |
|---|---|---|---|
| **Program Type** | **Behavior Change Sought** | **Mechanism** | **Example** |
| *Targeting Offenders* | | | |
| Deterrence | Voluntary reduction of criminal behavior by criminals | Deterrence | Antidrug public ad campaigns |
| *Targeting Citizens* | | | |
| Victimization reduction programs | Adoption of self-protective, crime preventive behavior by citizens | Target hardening | The McGruff "Take a Bite Out of Crime" campaign |
| Citizen participation programs | Increased public cooperation and involvement with law enforcement efforts | Monetary rewards and anonymity | Crime Stoppers |

PSAs—these aimed at citizens—are victimization reduction messages. Similar in form to the deterrence messages, victim-targeted PSAs use existing mass media outlets to distribute crime-reducing information and work to reduce opportunities for crime by inducing citizens to better protect themselves. The third set of anticrime ads is aimed at eliciting citizen cooperation. These ads are designed to increase crime clearance and arrest rates by encouraging citizen cooperation with law enforcement investigations. Table 7.1 summarizes these three approaches and their basic designs.

Both the earliest and some of the most recent mass media efforts to reduce crime involve public communication campaigns aimed at drug abusers. Antidrug media campaigns have a historical tie to *Reefer Madness* and similar films produced by the Federal Bureau of Narcotics in the 1930s. Laughable, cumbersome, and today's college campus cult movies, these films and the associated media campaign nevertheless facilitated the criminalization of marijuana in the United States.[3]

These early campaigns never generated the hoped for deterrent effect, however. While they seemed able to influence public opinion, they didn't influence offender behavior. Evaluations of media-based antidrug projects during the 1970s first offered an explanation for the difficulties in using media to induce deterrence. The failure in using the media to deter was blamed on the inability to make drug abuse a salient social issue and the irrelevance of the campaign messages to the target audience. To be effective, it was found that a media campaign must tailor its content to a specific population, and that population cannot be simultaneously receiving competing conflicting information. In that these early antidrug campaigns were diffuse efforts and the general mass media content was ripe with prodrug images, they were fatally flawed and doomed to failure. Successful lobbying efforts have reduced the levels of prodrug information in the media, and more recent media antidrug campaigns are better designed and marketed. Their evaluations indicate that specifically designed media campaigns can significantly affect attitudes toward drugs among preteens, teenagers, and adults. Whether behavioral changes and reduced drug use follow as a result has not been substantiated.[4] As in other areas where the media are seen to influence perceptions more easily than they do behaviors, antidrug media messages are more likely to affect the attitudes of non–drug users than the behaviors of drug abusers. Currently available information indicates that the media appear best able to deter offenders involved in victimless crimes such as drug abuse by increasing their fear of health and social consequences rather than through increasing their fear of punishment.[5]

Another problem in using the media to deter crime is that offenders also sometimes display a type of anticipatory reaction, termed an **announcement effect**, to the media campaign. Evoked in offender populations, this effect occurs when media publicity causes offender behavior changes in anticipation of a new criminal justice policy or program that has been publicized in the media. This media-induced behavior effect will occur with or without an actual criminal justice change. For example, a jurisdiction can reduce DUIs for a short time just by publicizing that they are instituting an aggressive, special anti-DUI enforcement effort. They do not have to actually have an anti-DUI unit to gain the reduction; publicity about a phantom unit will suffice. Such announcement effects decline and dissipate over time though.

Announcement effects generated from the publicity surrounding the implementation of new criminal justice policies and programs also interweave with any effects from actual criminal justice changes. This makes separating the media announcement effects from those of the criminal justice programs difficult. New criminal justice policies have been acclaimed as successful by too quickly ascribing the media-induced change in offender behavior to a new criminal justice policy when it is only the announcement effect that has reduced offenses.[6] The entrenchment of an ineffective criminal justice program or policy can result. Because offenders think that enforcement has significantly changed, they are more cautious for a while, and the new policy gets credit and is termed a success. Eventually offenders realize that the new policy or program is not meaningful and resume their offending.

## Victimization Reduction Ads

Programs aimed at reducing victimization, usually by teaching and encouraging crime prevention techniques, obviously differ from offender

(MUSIC UNDER)

SONG: Where have all the children gone.

Long time passing.

Where have all the children gone.

Long time ago.

Where have all the children gone.

Gone to graveyards, one by one.
Oh, when will we ever learn?
Oh, when will we ever learn?

ANNCR VO: Every day, ten children are killed by gunfire. The killing won't stop, unless you help stop it.

1-800-WE-PREVENT
TAKE A BITE OUT OF CRIME
Ad Council
U.S. Department of Justice
Crime Prevention Coalition of America

Call 1-800-WE PREVENT, to find out what you can do.

Not one more lost life, not one more grieving family.

NOT ONE MORE

Not One More.

SONG: Oh, when will we ever learn?

The storyboard of a televised PSA from the McGruff "Take a Bite Out of Crime" campaign displays elements needed for a media-based anticrime campaign to have a chance at success: raising the salience of the issue to viewers by showing danger to loved ones (children are being killed by guns); aiming at a specific target audience (parents and family members of children); and providing a simple response to deal with the fear and concern raised by the PSA (call the number provided).

deterrence programs. Victimization reduction campaigns strive to increase the use of personal crime prevention techniques by citizens. Crime prevention falls under the umbrella of self-protective behaviors, which include avoiding health risks and other hazards. Identified as key for triggering self-protective behaviors are people's beliefs about their likelihood of being harmed (What are my chances of being robbed?), the likely severity of an injury or illness (Will a robbery be fatal?), the efficacy of recommended precautions (Will doing this prevent a robbery?), and the costs of taking action when compared with inaction (How much time and money is involved?). Persuading people to adopt more self-protective behaviors is difficult because of the complex interactions among these four factors.

Programs advocating the adoption of behaviors to prevent possible unpleasant future events, such as crime, tend to be less successful than those that encourage actions with an immediate recognizable reward, such as an increase in health from exercising or dieting.[7] In general, unless individuals are recent victims of crime, they do not see crime as a likely event, do not feel that they will be injured, see precautions as not particularly useful, and see better uses for their time and money. In addition, perceptions of the importance of crime and the effectiveness of preventive behavior vary considerably among groups. Like campaigns aimed at offenders, messages must be carefully matched to target populations to have any impact. Adding to the difficulty of determining which campaigns actually work, victimization reduction programs have rarely been adequately evaluated. The McGruff "Take a Bite Out of Crime" campaign in the United States has received the most extensive study.[8]

Victimization reduction campaigns are considered useful means of disseminating anticrime information to the public and sometimes influencing related attitudes, but they appear to affect behavior only marginally. More significant effects may be beyond their reach. That is, people will change how they feel about crime prevention and more will see it as a good thing, but few will actually begin to take additional precautions. To be effective, programs should tailor their message to their audience; focus their efforts on television, which seems to have the greatest impact; present simple messages; and directly and clearly instruct audiences on crime prevention behavior. Most important, additional local community follow-up and the creation of community support organizations such as citizen crime watch groups are necessary to achieve lasting effects. Similar to the media's deterrent effect on offenders, based on the available data, media campaigns appear able to affect people's attitudes toward crime prevention more easily than their actual behavior.

## Citizen Cooperation Ads

Citizen cooperation ads aim to increase the level of crime-related information made available to law enforcement by the public. These programs (commonly known by the name Crime Stoppers) use reenactments of crimes to obtain information (tips) through anonymous phone calls and reward money.[9] The logic is the same as the "Most Wanted" reward posters of the nineteenth century and the FBI's "Ten Most Wanted" posters displayed in post offices in the twentieth century. Getting images and descriptions of wanted suspects and unsolved crimes out to as many people as possible and enticing reluctant citizens with monetary rewards increases the prospects for solving crimes and apprehending suspects. The innovation is using electronic mass media to distribute posters and portraits, thereby enormously increasing the audience.

Development of these efforts raises a number of issues. The first and most obvious is the effectiveness of these programs. Do they result in more arrests and solutions of crimes, and are they an efficient means of gathering information? Second is the question of the image of criminality that such programs project. Do they perpetuate stereotypes of criminals, victims, and crime? Third, what is the proper role of the media in law enforcement efforts?

First, no one knows if citizen cooperation programs affect the crime rate. The number of cases cleared is not great enough to expect an effect on the overall crime rate in a community unless one assumes a general deterrent effect from the mass media coverage. Neither effect has been reported. But anecdotal evidence does suggest that the programs solve felony cases that are unlikely to be solved otherwise.[10] They appear especially effective in solving cases involving fugitives, bank robberies, and narcotics and may be useful in antiterrorist efforts. The visibility of these programs also increases their effectiveness by attracting secondary tips for unadvertised crimes. Indeed, given the large amount of unsolicited information received regarding unadvertised crimes, crime reenactments shown in the media appear to be more important as vehicles for obtaining tips regarding other crimes than as a means of solving the crimes actually publicized. Bolstered by supportive court rulings and by low operational costs, these programs are generally viewed as cost-effective and their continuance currently assured. Despite their support and successes, critics argue that their gains against crime are outweighed by other negative social effects. Paying for information from anonymous sources is the crux of the uneasiness felt toward these programs. The fear is that paying rewards and providing anonymity for informants will reduce voluntary citizen cooperation and encourage malicious retributive snitching by citizens on their neighbors, family, and friends.

Second, because citizen cooperation ads are presented as representative of the actual crime in a community, the image they portray has great potential to influence the social construction of criminality. Presented in news-like segments akin to reality programming, these anticrime ads focus on unsolved cases in the community committed by dangerous-looking suspects. The image of criminality shown in these ads is similar to that portrayed in the general entertainment media—that of a dangerous, crime-ridden world where violent attacks are common.[11] In addition, these ads are often produced in infotainment programming styles, with mood music, voice-overs, and heightened dramatic elements.[12] Furthermore, by emphasizing predatory violent crimes that appear to be due to greed or irrationality, individual explanations for crime and crime control-based punitive crime-and-justice policies are emphasized while broader structural, social, and economic factors are downplayed.

Finally, what is the proper role of the mass media in law enforcement efforts? Should the media restrict themselves to basic reporting of events or become involved in their resolution? Citizen cooperation ads shift the media from their traditional roles as watchdog observers and reporters to active infotainment participants in investigating crimes and hunting fugitives. Some argue that the media should cooperate because it is their civic duty. Many media agencies do not cooperate, however, apparently because they perceive involvement as contrary to the philosophy of separation of press and government.[13] How these concerns are to be resolved is unclear. Unfortunately, we have little independent data to support or lay to rest the expressed fears. We simply do not know at this time if the hypothesized negative consequences of citizen cooperation programs counteract their positive anticrime effects. For one thing, we don't know how much of an anticrime effect they actually have.

Collectively, PSAs, victimization ads, and citizen cooperation ads are popular, have demonstrated limited positive effects, but have also encountered unanticipated problems. Success has not been as direct or as simple to achieve as first envisioned. Despite their current popularity, their actual impact on crime levels is ambiguous. All of these efforts aim for behavioral changes in the audience to reduce crime, but most are actually designed to influence attitudes and perceptions about the reality of crime under the belief that attitude changes will subsequently lead to changes in behavior. All three of these media campaign types accordingly rest on a questionable premise, and they have not been able to show the initially hoped for crime reductions.

The technology of the mass media has also migrated into the criminal justice system as a tool for case processing in both law enforcement and judicial efforts. This is the subject of the next section.

## CASE PROCESSING USING MEDIA TECHNOLOGY

In general, the ultimate goal in using media technology in criminal justice case processing is to simulate a traditional, live, face-to-face judicial proceeding. Unlike face-to-face encounters, however, participants must

# Fonda Speaks To Vietnam Veterans At Anti-War Rally

Actress And Anti-War Activist Jane Fonda Speaks to a crowd of Vietnam Veterans as Activist and former Vietnam Vet John Kerry (LEFT) listens and prepares to speak next concerning the war in Vietnam (AP Photo)

Separate images of John Kerry and Jane Fonda were joined digitally in this fake newspaper clipping that circulated widely on the Internet during Kerry's presidential run. The photo appears undoctored and "real" and illustrates the difficulty in deciphering the truthfulness of photos in an age of digital imagery discussed on page 182.

interact through the equipment, often testifying directly into a camera or participating in their processing by watching a television screen. In contrast to the use of media equipment in news coverage, here the technology has changed from a tangential, temporary visitor to an unavoidable, permanent judicial tool. Media technology has been embraced as a means to efficiently process cases, and cost and speed are the usual factors considered in these applications.

Though the use of media technology has come to be widely accepted in the presentation of physical evidence and testimony, using the technology to create permanent records and conduct live proceedings currently enjoys only limited support. Expanded applications such as prerecording entire trials have been experimented with but generally have been rejected. The acceptability of media technology in the courtroom seems to rest on how much the media-constructed judicial reality is seen as different from the traditional judicial reality. For preliminary and short procedural steps, most participants, including defendants, appear to feel that the integrity of the process is unaffected. With regard to longer, more significant, and more symbolic steps such as trials, concerns and resistance arise.

## Law Enforcement Use

After the development and widespread acceptance of videotaped evidence and testimony in the 1970s, **videotaped interrogations** were one of the first expanded uses of video technology into law enforcement practices. A videotape record is felt to provide more objective, fuller accounts of interactions between police, witnesses, and suspects, as well as evidence regarding the voluntariness of statements, suspects' understanding of their rights, police coercion and interrogation practices, and the physical and mental condition of suspects. Following pilot projects, most have embraced this law enforcement use of media technology. For example, a two-year evaluation of a Canadian experiment in videotaping police interrogations by Alan Grant showed that the expected advantages of protection against unwarranted allegations of misconduct, the introduction of accountability in interrogation procedures, and the reduction in challenges to the admissibility of suspect statements were all realized.[14]

Grant further reported that suspects did not appear inhibited by the cameras and that the suspect confession rate remained the same. In fact, police, prosecutors, and defense counsel all came to support continuation and expansion of the project—police because it relieves them of the need to take written notes during interrogations and reduces their court appearances, prosecutors because it usually disposes of all legal questions surrounding the police–suspect interview, and defense counsel because it ensures that police more strictly follow legal procedures and because the defense often can use the tapes to demonstrate their client's intent and remorse for sentencing purposes. The interrogation tapes provide a record of the frame of mind and emotional reaction of a suspect much nearer in time to the actual commission of a crime than was previously available.

An increasing number of police departments also use media technology to record the booking of their arrests. These video mug shots provide a pictorial record of arrestees that includes voice, accent, and a continuous front-to-profile view. These video records have also allowed changes in two other common law enforcement practices—identification of a suspect from a traditional lineup and identification of a suspect from a set of photographs (a mug book) of known offenders. In a **video lineup**, a crime witness is shown a series of video bookings selected for their similarity. The witness chooses from this video lineup the individual he or she feels is the offender. This process is felt to be fairer than the old practices in that the individuals in video lineups more closely resemble one another than the groups usually assembled for a live lineup, and it provides a permanent record of the lineup for later review should questions arise. In **video mug books**, a computer searches a pictorial file for specific characteristics (for example, tattoo, bald, heavy, white, and male) and displays the pictures that match.

## Judicial System Use

In the judicial system, video recording of arraignments, first appearances, bond hearings, and pleas have proven inexpensive and useful.[15] A single videotape of hundreds of cases can be stored as a permanent record that can be consulted should the state of mind of a defendant, his or her comprehension of rights or instructions, or the voluntary nature of a plea later be questioned. As with videotaping interrogations by police, once instituted these systems gain support from both crime control and due process advocates. Crime control proponents like the savings of time and money. Due process adherents feel the knowledge that a permanent record is being created makes law enforcement and judicial personnel more conscientious in following due process rules. Videotaping these procedural steps also provides a means not previously available of resolving any subsequent due process concerns. Furthermore, the same technology used in creating video records and testimony also allows, if desired, the physical separation of the participants, thus allowing a judicial proceeding to be conducted in a new way—in live media-linked sessions. Judges and attorneys can now be in a courtroom, defendants in a jail, and witnesses in another state, all simultaneously participating in a live hearing.

Recent computer technology advances have brought new issues to the table, however, including the **digital manipulation of visual images**. The same tools that can be used to crop, retouch, and edit images can be used just as easily to distort, alter, and fabricate them. This ability undermines the previously unquestioned validity that pictures of an event gave to a social construction and associated factual claims. The use of obviously faked but realistic looking photos in advertising and entertainment—the destruction of the White House by invading aliens, for example—repeatedly demonstrates the commonness and sophistication of visual deception. The uncertain validity of visual images has implications for the evaluation of visual evidence in the criminal justice system. As Gary Marx reflects, "In this sense, *seeing is believing*," his point being that the public is constantly reminded that it should not automatically believe what it is shown.[16] Clearly a potential future problem is that jurors may begin to reject photographic evidence as innately untrustworthy in a manner similar to how jurors now sometimes reject scientific evidence if it doesn't meet entertainment media standards. Ironically, technological advances may ultimately result in questioning all technologically processed information, and eyewitness and human testimony may again dominate the criminal justice process.

In addition, when the traditional, familiar reality of the judicial system is drastically changed by the use of media technology, resistance to the new reality rises. Even for the now common procedural applications of media technology, the alteration of the reality of the judicial system is connected to three concerns: the effect of media technology on working relationships among courtroom personnel, concerns about depersonalization of the criminal justice system, and the impact of media technology on the legitimacy of the judicial system.

Comments from attorneys (especially public defenders) and judges indicate that the relationships among courtroom personnel can be upset by the introduction of media equipment.[17] It is significant that in a number of pilot projects public defenders remain largely skeptical of the advantages of media technology. Do attorneys deliver equivalent representation if they feel legally and organizationally disadvantaged in media-constructed proceedings? If their morale suffers, does their subsequent effort on behalf of clients also suffer? These questions remain unanswered.

A second concern is that expanded use of media technology within the judiciary will almost certainly lead to further depersonalization of criminal justice proceedings. Adjudication within the criminal justice system is based on face-to-face interaction, particularly that the accused are entitled to face their accusers. Extended use of media technology, however, will reduce live, face-to-face encounters between witnesses and defendants, police and the public, attorneys and clients, judges and defendants, and jurors and all the previous groups. These media-mediated interactions will seriously alter the nature of the personal relationships within the criminal justice system. Technological advances that make this equipment more economical, less obtrusive, and more like a live meeting are likely to further this depersonalization.

A third unresolved concern is what is lost in legitimacy and the public image of justice when media technology is employed. In addition to being a means of adjudicating guilt and administering punishment, the judicial system is also a means of legitimizing the whole social system—its rules, laws, and government. Accordingly, the judicial system and its personnel have a symbolic value. Loss of these symbolic qualities may diminish the aura of legitimacy sustaining the entire system. From the social construction perspective, how the system is seen as treating individuals is crucial. If people become alienated from the system or if they feel intimidated or dehumanized by it, the benefits from using media technologies in the courtroom will be canceled out. If these technologies ultimately result in the further isolation and separation of the police from the policed and the courts from the public, the social costs of such losses would outweigh any administrative benefits that accrue from their use. As crime control values become more popular, there is considerable desire, especially on the part of crime-and-justice administrators, to make the system more efficient. Nevertheless, the criminal justice system must remain legitimate in the public eye if it is to remain a viable system of justice.

The visuals created by this technology are frequently used in news reports, contributing directly to the social construction of the public's image of justice. The criminal justice system will become, for good or ill, a less arcane, more open system as its procedures become more visible. The myriad applications of media technology have changed the reality of justice on many levels and have opened previous backstage judicial activities to public scrutiny. Ironically, although the courts are still wary of the news media, the criminal justice system's adoption of media technology has had many of the same effects that were feared from news coverage. The main concern remains whether this new reality of justice is ultimately seen as an impersonal, unfair, and unacceptable substitute.

The greatest concerns are not associated with the use of media technology in case processing, however. The greatest concerns for the increased use of media technology in criminal justice revolve around the enhancement of law enforcement surveillance capabilities.

## SURVEILLANCE

Media's enhanced technical capabilities, coupled with immense concerns about possible terrorism, have created a strong impetus for surveillance programs. Taking advantage of the **surveillance effect**—the psychological effect of fearing that you might be under observation—surveillance programs have expanded the traditional police use of the stakeout and hidden camera to encompass more applications in public spaces. Reduced equipment costs have given more agencies surveillance capabilities, and concerns with terrorism have increased public acceptance of their implementation. Media technology has made constant surveillance of broad public areas possible, and surveillance cameras permanently mounted on street corners,

A typical video surveillance system monitors a sixteen-block stretch in the downtown business district of Baltimore. The cameras, which are mounted on existing light poles at intersections, fifteen feet above street level, use zoom lenses to detect crime. Both hidden and open systems take advantage of a surveillance effect, using the psychological impact of the belief that one might be under surveillance.

in patrol cars, and within and without various buildings are common today. Not surprisingly, the use of this potentially powerful and intrusive technology has raised fears concerning its ultimate impact on a free society.

"You watched TV. Now it watches you"[18] neatly summarizes the expected future and inherent concerns regarding modern police surveillance systems. Surveillance, or the stakeout, by law enforcement agencies has a long history and has traditionally been an accepted part of police investigations. Surveillance applications based on media technology have been in use for a number of years—for example, surveillance cameras in banks, subways, and department stores—and have recently been expanded to include public schools, airports, highway toll booths, and other locales. The police have also traditionally used temporary camera surveillance of specific locations after obtaining a court order.

These traditional uses differ from newer applications in that the areas surveyed are small, and public domain areas are not involved. In contrast, the new surveillance programs use media technology in large public areas such as outdoor malls, downtown centers, parks, and residential streets. Traditional surveillance was aimed at gathering evidence for a specific case

© AP Photo/PA

The abduction of James Bulger in 1993 by his murderers was caught on video. This crime and its symbolic images subsequently served as a thrust for the expanded use of public surveillance systems in the United Kingdom.

or deterring crime at one specific point such as a ticket booth, but today the prime justifications for public surveillance systems are couched in broad-scale public safety and antiterrorism goals.

Contemporary media technology has also changed the nature of surveillance from on-scene, limited human observers and whatever notes they might produce to the automated technological interception, recording, and transmittal of immense amounts of information. The reality of police surveillance has shifted from a rare, narrow, activity determined by a need related to a specific criminal case to a common, pervasive, constant presence. The historical idea that you have to have done something to be brought under surveillance is no longer the case with broadly targeted, automatic, continuous surveillance systems. This potential surveillance of everyone whenever they appear in public places is the prime cause of unease.

## Wiretaps and Camera-based Systems

The use of telephone wiretaps in the 1900s first raised the specter of surveillance abuse. Writing before the era of electronic eavesdropping and other modern technology, Earl Warren and William Brandeis predicted that "mechanical devices threaten to make good the prediction that 'what is whispered in the closet shall be proclaimed from the house-tops.'"[19] Today, the updated quote would be "whatever is done in the dark will be shown on the news." To understand the social impetus for these new surveillance systems and the likely future of police surveillance in the United States, one must look to England. No Western democracy has embraced police surveillance systems more than Britain (see Box 7.1). The electronic recording of images and pervasive, broad-scale, permanent surveillance systems in use in Britain have resulted in the English population being described as the most surveilled population on the planet.[20]

The rise of surveillance capabilities increased dramatically with the development of modern camera-based systems in the 1960s.[21] **CCTV**, or **closed circuit television**, was initially used both in the United States and Britain sparingly as an in-store means of apprehending and deterring shoplifters. Although the technology became less expensive and increased in its capabilities throughout the 1970s, the Western political environment remained hostile to expanded use. The Cold War discouraged the use of police surveillance systems that smacked of Communist style secret police tactics. Western politicians and police chiefs did not want to be viewed as advocates of systems that could in any way be described as "Big Brother" spying on the general population.

In the mid-1980s, as the Cold War dissipated, municipal police CCTV surveillance systems appeared across England. By the mid-1990s, a rapid increase in the number of systems was well under way, and today it is the rule rather than the exception for any reasonably sized British community to have police camera surveillance of its public spaces.[22] By May 1999, there were more than 500 operating CCTV systems in England. Beyond the defusing of the Cold War, rising local crime rates and a declining faith in the traditional criminal justice system's ability to deal with crime has been credited for increased public support for surveillance systems.[23] (Of course, the traditional criminal justice system's inability to deal with crime is a mainstay of the entertainment media's content.)

Capping the social construction of police surveillance systems as positive and necessary in England was a symbolic crime, the 1993 murder of two-year-old James Bulger.[24] The boy was recorded on a mall security camera system being taken away by his two teenage killers. The images gave an irresistible impetus to the introduction of CCTV systems, and the British media shifted from questioning whether surveillance is a good thing to asking why are cameras not everywhere. Once installed, logic inevitably calls for coverage of larger areas, and every murder or terrorist act intensifies the demand for expanded surveillance.

*(Continued on page 191)*

## 7.1 A United Kingdom Story of Everyday Video Surveillance

Thomas Kearns' day starts as usual. At 7.15 a.m. the sounds of BBC Radio Four, emanating from his clock radio, penetrate his slumbering consciousness. He wakes quickly, showers and dresses in his best sales-man suit which flatters his 38-year-old frame. His ten-year-old son and four-year-old daughter are washed and dressed by the time he joins them for breakfast. At 8:15 he kisses his wife goodbye and shuts the front door of his apartment behind him, children in tow, to dispatch them to school and nursery, before embarking on another office day. They head towards the lift along the concrete walkways and are captured on a covert video surveillance operation, set up by the local authority, aimed at identifying residents who are dealing in drugs from their premises (1) [The numbers in parentheses tally surveillance systems]. As they wait for the lift their presence is monitored on the concierge's video system twelve floors below, as is their descent for there is also a camera in the lift and their predictable daily routine is preserved on tape to be stored for twenty-eight days, or longer if necessary (2). As they walk from the lobby of their apartment block to the car, it is not only the concierge who monitors the Kearns' departure, but Mr. Adams on the fifteenth floor, who has tuned his television to receive output from the Housing Estate's cameras (3).

Thomas drives out of the estate on to the dual-carriage way and, although vaguely aware of the sign that declares reduce your speed now—video camera in operation—still drives at ten miles an hour over the speed limit and trips the automatic speed cameras (4). By 8.30 he has dropped his daughter off at the CCTV monitored nursery (5) and is heading towards his son's school. He stops at a red light, which is as well because had he jumped it, another picture would have been taken to be used as evidence in his prosecution (6). As they wait in the playground for the buzzer to signal the start of school, they are filmed by a covert camera secreted in the building opposite to monitor the playground for signs of drug dealing (7) and their goodbye kiss is also captured on the school's internal CCTV system which monitors every entrance and exit (8). Noticing that his fuel tank is nearly empty, he drives to the petrol station and fills up. He knows that he is being filmed as a large sign at the cash desk declares: "These premises are under 24 hour video surveillance" (9).

He leaves the garage and approaches the station, and quietly curses as he is stopped by the barriers at the railway level crossing. His location is caught on one of the four Railtrack cameras monitoring the crossing specifically to ensure that the intersection of road and track is clear when the train crosses (10). A few minutes later he is parked in the car park opposite the station under the watchful eye of another set of cameras (11).

As usual, Thomas buys a newspaper at the newsagents and is filmed by their in-store security cameras as he does so. No one is monitoring the images from the two cameras but they are taped on a multiplex video recorder which records the images from both cameras on one tape, and enables any incident to be reviewed should it be necessary (12). Before buying his ticket he makes a telephone call from the public call box on the station forecourt to remind his wife that he will be late home. Unbeknown to him he is filmed by a covert camera installed by British Telecom to try and catch those who vandalize their telephone boxes and hoax callers to the emergency services (13). His call made, he buys his ticket, walks to the platform and waits for his train all of which has been recorded and monitored by the thirty-two cameras operating at the station (14). On arrival at his destination, he walks the short distance to his office and smiles at the camera monitoring the reception area (15). He is, however, unaware that his movements are being recorded by a number of covert cameras hidden in the smoke detector housings as he walks along the corridor towards his office (16).

At lunchtime, he is going to visit his sister, who has just given birth to a healthy baby boy. He leaves his office and heads for the High Street. His movements along the streets are watched by three operatives in the town hall's CCTV control room (17). His first port of call is the street-side automatic cash dispenser, he makes his withdrawal and his face is captured by a covert camera hidden inside the cash machine (18). He crosses the road and enters Marks and Spencers to buy his sister some flowers and himself a new raincoat. Should the CCTV operative so wish, his every turn could be tracked on the 35 camera in-store security system. At the till he writes a check for $45.75 but he doesn't notice a camera zooming in on him to ensure that the store has good pictures of his face should he be touting a stolen check card (19).

Outside, he hails a taxi for the two-mile journey and, as they cross a major arterial road, the taxi's number plate is photographed by the Metropolitan Police's new CCTV based automatic license plate

*A United Kingdom Story of Everyday Video Surveillance (continued)*

recognition system (20). On arrival at the hospital he is photographed by two cameras covering the main entrance and again as he enters the maternity unit (21). Having carried out his family duties, he walks to the nearest Underground station; here his progress will be recorded on video from the moment he enters the station to the point he boards his train (22). He alights at Heathrow Airport to meet some prospective clients who have flown in for a meeting the following day and, of course, his movements are monitored by dozens of security cameras (23). He escorts his guests to the airport hotel, and then to the car park where a hire car is awaiting them. They drive out of the car park and the number plate is photographed automatically. It is then checked against the computerized database of all cars using the airport car parks (24).

They are heading to Chelsea Football Ground in South London where Thomas, as part of his sales routine, is treating them to a Premier League match. En route they are fleetingly caught by the town centre CCTV systems operating in Southall, Ealing and Hammersmith (25). They are photographed as they enter the stadium and while they are seated their faces are scanned and checked against a pictorial database of known hooligans (26). After the match they drive across the river to a bistro in Streatham. As they are unfamiliar with the area they drive slowly down Bedford Hill looking for the correct turn-off. They are filmed on a mobile camcorder, deployed by a detective from the local vice squad in an effort to prevent 'curb crawling' in this 'red light district' (27). The officer loses interest when they turn off.

Thomas is relieved when they find the restaurant and even more relieved when dinner is over and he awaits the 11:14 train from Clapham Junction Station where his presence is recorded on the station's cameras (28). He returns home just before midnight, pours himself a drink and sits down to check the post. His heart sinks as he opens an official-looking letter with an even more officious content. The local police, he is informed, have photographed his son associating with a teenage gang, and wish Mr. Kearns to come to the police station to view the video (29). Thomas downs his drink and, as he heads to bed, wonders what on earth his son can have done wrong to warrant being photographed by the police.

At the end of his day, Thomas had been filmed by over three hundred cameras on over thirty separate CCTV systems.

---

*Source:* This contrived but plausible day-in-the-surveilled-life of a British citizen was authored by Clive Norris and Gary Armstrong, *The Maximum Surveillance Society: The Rise of CCTV* (Oxford, UK: Berg, 1999), 40–42.

The result in England has been the normalization of police surveillance systems to the level that CCTV surveillance has been described by evaluator Stephen Graham as a public "fifth utility," along the lines of gas, water, electricity, and telephones.[25] Police CCTV surveillance is today perceived as an affordable and efficient technical fix for crime in England. One British Chief Constable describes his twenty-camera system as the equal to twenty full-time police officers on the beat twenty-four hours all taking notes without meal breaks, holidays, or sick leave.[26] In the aftermath of the September 11, 2001, terrorist attacks on the New York World Trade Centers and the Pentagon, it is safe to predict that the United States will be joining England as a heavily camera-surveilled society in the near future.

In the United States and elsewhere, camera surveillance programs today take one of two basic forms: completely hidden systems that give potential offenders no indication that they are being observed, and clearly marked, open systems. Although the first form functions more as a means of gathering evidence and aiding in apprehensions, both forms take advantage of the surveillance effect, using the psychological impact of the belief that one might be under surveillance.[27]

How effective are surveillance systems in reducing crime? Evidence based largely on interviews with offenders does suggest that offenders take into account the apparent level of surveillance and the likelihood of intervention when deciding whether to commit certain crimes,[28] and recent reviews of the available evaluations suggest that the systems are effective in reducing crime when combined with other interventions.[29] The literature also suggests that the impact of surveillance is related to the actual threat of intervention.[30] That is, unless surveillance actually leads to intervention, a surveillance-generated deterrent effect will soon wane.

## Benefits and Concerns of Increased Surveillance

The benefits usually cited for police camera surveillance systems also incorporate the concerns raised about these systems. Thus, a CCTV benefit is to be able to observe and react to previously unnoticed acts; the concern is that net-widening from police arresting more people, particularly juveniles, for minor offenses will result in more people with formal arrest records.[31] A benefit is to be able to expel actual and potential deviants from specific locations; the concern is that profiling and polarization will result as certain groups such as minority teenagers are targeted for exclusion from public spaces, especially commercial shopping districts. A benefit is to provide evidence against offenders; the concern is the development of databases to track and identify specific members of the population based on their prior labeling as individuals that "need to be watched" rather than being surveilled because of their current behavior. A benefit is the creation of quiet, disturbance-free streets; the concern is the suppression of public exuberance and uninhibited but lawful social or political expression. Finally, a benefit is the creation of crime-free surveillance zones; the concern is that displacement effects will push crime into adjacent communities without the money or political clout to obtain their own surveillance systems.

Of the concerns, **displacement** of crime to adjacent areas has been empirically examined along with the additional potential benefit of a diffusion of crime reduction impact. **Diffusion** of benefits is seen as a possible effect from surveillance systems because offenders might not be aware of the boundaries of the surveillance coverage and therefore reduce their offenses in adjacent nonsurveilled areas. In the field evaluations, evidence of both displacement and diffusion effects have been reported.[32] For example, United Kingdom evaluator Nick Tilley found local diffusion of benefits for theft of and from cars.[33] He also found evidence of significant displacement to outlying distant English towns, suggesting that diffusion of benefits may accrue nearby from these systems while crime displacement can be occurring simultaneously farther away.

The recent appearance of video cameras mounted on patrol car windshields in the United States represents another expanded, mobile use of video technology for surveillance. The mobility of the patrol car extends the practice of general law enforcement surveillance to virtually the entire society without the need for permanent fixed systems. Challenges to this practice based on privacy concerns have been rejected by the U.S. Supreme Court, which has stated that an invasion of privacy cannot result unless there is a reasonable expectation of privacy. Because there is no expectation of privacy in a traffic stop or on a public street, the use of in-car video cameras by police on patrol or on fixed mountings monitoring public streets is allowed under almost all circumstances.[34]

Resistance to even greater adoption within law enforcement agencies appears to arise when law enforcement officers perceive the cameras as an administrative tool, installed to watch them, more than as a law enforcement tool. In reality the cameras are both: the police on the surveilled street or in front of their patrol cars during a videotaped traffic stop are also under surveillance. In addition, the ubiquitous video cameras in citizens' hands means that a surveillance effect may have an impact on the police at least as much as on the public. Research has also indicated that citizen-videotaped arrests have a significant negative impact on the public's perception of police use of force.[35] In response, the police have been long advised to operate under the premise that cameras are everywhere and that any of their actions might be taped.[36]

Police surveillance video transforms the relationships between line police officers, their administration, and the public by providing a reviewable record of officers' street interactions. The benefits of having a visual record of a patrol are many; administrators and the courts can later review officers' and suspects' actions, and thereby decide liability, voluntary search consent, misconduct claims, and have more credible, objective evidence of behavior and statements for DUI and drug intoxication cases. In addition, the cameras are credited with deterring suspects from resisting arrest and deterring officers from mistreating suspects and engaging in other unprofessional acts.[37] In effect, the technology appears to protect police officers from frivolous charges of abuse and misconduct while protecting the public from actual abuse and misconduct by officers.

## Balancing Police Surveillance and Public Safety

All surveillance systems raise issues related to the use of media technology in the daily policing of our society. Surprisingly, concerns over "Big Brother" and "1984" are usually raised by the news media, law enforcement officers, and external observers, not by the citizens under surveillance, who appear quite ready to trade off a measure of personal privacy for a potential reduction in victimization and fear. The social acceptance of surveillance runs throughout our popular culture as shown by the songs listed in Box 7.2, and today the increased social tolerance for surveillance of public spaces is linked to the increased exposure of private, backstage behaviors in the news, entertainment, and infotainment media—if privacy is already rare, then surveillance is less offensive. Since the terrorist attacks of September 11, 2001, public support in the United States for surveillance systems has been strong, with close to 80 percent in one poll supporting the installation of surveillance cameras in public places to prevent terrorist attacks.[38]

Unresolved questions concern effects on the legitimacy, symbolic impact, and the public image of justice when surveillance technology is employed. The justice system is a mechanism for adjudicating guilt and administering punishment. It is also a means of legitimizing the whole social system. Accordingly, the police have a symbolic value. On the street, both the presence of a live police officer and the assurance of knowing when one is being observed by the police affirm the values of voluntary consent and public control of law enforcement. Loss of these symbols may diminish the aura of legitimacy sustaining the entire criminal justice system. Misuse or overuse of this technology will construct a social reality of mistrust and cynicism, where fear of crime is replaced by fear of authority. In addition, police surveillance systems may actually be ineffective over the long term, and their use could result in the neglect of broader approaches to crime control.

## 7.2  Popular Songs with Surveillance Themes

He's making a list and checking it twice
Gonna find out who's naughty and nice.
He sees you when you're sleeping
He knows when you're awake
He knows if you've been bad or good
So be good for goodness sake

Lyrics from
"Santa Claus Is Coming to Town" (1934) by Haven Gillespie,
     J. Fred Coots (EMI)
Other surveillance themed popular songs
"Slippin and Slidin" (1956) by Little Richard (Specialty)
"I've Got My Eyes on You" (1954) by The Clovers (Atlantic)
"The Night Has a Thousand Eyes" (1963) by Bobby Vee (Liberty)
"Subterranean Homesick Blues" (1965) by Bob Dylan (Sony)
"Miles and Miles" (1967) by The Who (TRO-Essex)
"Fingerprint File" (1974) by Rolling Stones (Rolling Stones)
"Private Eyes" (1981) by Hall and Oates (BMG)
"Electric Eye" (1982) by Judas Priest (CBS)
"Every Breath You Take" (1983) by The Police (A&M)

---

*Source:* Song list compiled by Gary Marx (1996), "Electric Eye in the Sky: Some Reflections on the New Surveillance and Popular Culture." In David Lyon and Elia Zureik, editors, *Computers, Surveillance, and Privacy* (pp. 193–233). Minneapolis: University of Minnesota Press.

Moreover it is feared that reliance on technological fixes for crime can have negative community effects, working against positive community participation, creating a siege mentality, and undermining natural community surveillance by residents. For example, the presence of a police surveillance system might result in fewer phone calls to the police if residents assume that the local police surveillance camera will observe incidents and alert the authorities. Police surveillance by means of technology may thereby undermine natural surveillance by encouraging people to have faith in the disembodied electronic eye and encourage a "why get involved" attitude. Instead of worrying about "Big Brother" watching them, the public may perceive that "Big Father" has sorted everything out.

The basic problem these programs present is how to balance police surveillance and public safety—how much safety is gained at what cost? The equation seems clearly to be that increased fear of crime and terror results in increased tolerance for surveillance. Citizens fearful of crime and terrorism are willing to open more social areas to observation, even when the observers are hidden. Orwell's *1984* society of total surveillance is less frightening than a local mugger or homicidal terrorist. The danger is that fear will drive citizens to glibly surrender personal privacy for an unknown measure of personal security. Whether these programs actually reduce crime or protect against terrorist attacks enough to warrant the loss in privacy is still an open question. They are capable of producing positive near-term effects for certain types of crime, with vehicle-related offenses appearing to be deterred most often. Whether the systems can maintain even such limited effects over the long term is not known. How surveillance power is held to account and what limits are placed on its operation are also unresolved issues. The impact of new computing and database technologies will increase the power of surveillance—facial recognition, vehicle and person tracking, and behavior recognition software are all a reality with the coupling of video cameras to fast, inexpensive processors to create computer-aided surveillance. Widespread police access to a real-time, computer-analyzed, media-augmented reality will soon be common.[39]

The camera unavoidably changes the nature of the relationship between those being watched and those doing the watching. Most of the time, the negative social consequences of increased surveillance dominate the debate. However, the latest applications have positive potentials also. When the actions of the law enforcers and the public are both monitored, stored, and subject to later review, surveillance cameras can restrain the actions of authorities as much as offenders. It remains to be seen whether the impact of these projects in democratic societies will be greater on the police than on the public. A significant effect on employees has already been reported in correctional settings where the behavior of both correctional officers and prisoners is monitored.[40] Like other two-edged swords, the dual nature of police camera surveillance is apparent. British criminologist Jock Young has observed that "in the wrong hands it can invade privacy and make Orwell's 1984 a reality. But it can also, in a different political context, be liberating and protective."[41] Which reality will emerge is yet to be determined.

## *1984:* AN ICON BEFORE ITS TIME

Today, the media can be used to influence people's attitudes about crime and make more crime-related information available to the police. Others uses can speed the processing of criminal cases. The technology of the media can be used to videotape police patrols, vehicle stops, and inter-rogations. And the technology is useful in the investigation, surveillance, and deterrence of crime. The administrative, mostly crime control, benefits associated with these uses follow quickly, and projects have consistently been evaluated as efficient and cost-effective. Increased social fears as well as technological advances that make the equipment more economical, more flexible, more capable, and less obtrusive are hastening wide use of media surveillance. However, there are concerns about potential social costs. If evidence of negative effects is found in future studies, the technological genie will be out of the bottle, and it will be difficult to curtail established practices.

Efforts that do not include surveillance show no behavioral effects, and it appears doubtful that the mass media can by themselves deter criminal behavior—much as they alone cannot criminalize individuals. Surveillance programs do show deterrence effects, but their ability to deter crime without displacement and without significant worrisome social effects remains unproven. Media efforts to reduce victimization by teaching crime preventive behaviors have high recognition levels among the general public and have increased public knowledge and changed public attitudes about crime prevention, but they have not yet shown an ability to significantly change crime prevention behavior. Finally, programs designed to increase public cooperation by advertising crimes are effective in gathering information and in solving specific types of crimes. Their effect on the overall crime rate is not known, but it is likely negligible.

With all of these caveats in mind, media technology is still an extremely useful tool, but social costs invariably accompany technological benefits. Costs include increased depersonalization of the criminal justice system; isolation of the police from the policed; increased citizen fear and suspicion of surveillance; polarization of society due to the creation of affluent, technologically secured garrison communities; and possible decreased citizen support and legitimization of the criminal justice system. Finally, when news media convey the message that these efforts are the answer for reducing crime rates and when this is coupled with the entertainment message of crime being generated through individually based causes, crime as a technological rather than a social problem becomes the logical end result. The belief that we can engineer our way out of the crime problem through more equipment and manpower is bolstered. The collective message is that media-based programs are indeed panaceas for the general crime problem. To the extent that the public believes this and policy makers act on it, resources for other equally needed approaches will be drained.

To solve crimes and deter criminals the government must intervene in its citizens' lives. The media and media technology provide a means to do so in new ways that are felt to be both more efficient and less obviously intrusive. In practice such applications cannot avoid opening up for view new areas of public life, of the criminal justice system, and of police–citizen interactions. In certain instances, such as in the use of patrol car cameras, which record police actions as much as citizen actions, this is clearly seen as a positive course. In other instances, such as in the use of hidden police surveillance systems, the desirability of doing so is not so clear. Still, with proper oversight the media and media technology can have both due process and crime control benefits. Media and their technology are a potentially positive but, it must be remembered, ultimately limited resource for criminal justice. The media should be an aspect of our total criminal justice policy, but media cannot be the mainstay of our policies. Connected to the question of how much of our criminal justice policy should be media based is the question of how many of our criminal justice policies are media generated. Chapter 8 looks at the broader relationship between the media and criminal justice policy.

## Discussion Questions

1. Why has media technology been so readily embraced as a solution for various criminal justice system tasks?
2. Why do you think some police unions have opposed the installation of video cameras in patrol cars?
3. Who should have access to the video records and images produced by a public agency surveillance system? Should surveillance video be released to news agencies, used in civil cases, or employed in infotainment programming?
4. Where and when are surveillance cameras acceptable? Does it matter if they are hidden or openly viewed? Does it matter who is watching? Do people have the right to be informed that they are within the view of a surveillance system? Rather than having a human monitor, would you feel more comfortable with computer-monitored surveillance systems?

## In-Class Activities

1. Watch the Film *Enemy of the State* and discuss the concerns of living in a high-surveillance society.

2. Listen to a selection of popular music with surveillance as a theme and discuss the lyrics and the phenomenon of the surveillance effect ("Every Breath You Take" by The Police is highly recommended).

## ASSIGNMENTS

1. Count and note the location of the surveillance cameras you notice over a seven-day period. Record what entity (government, business, or individual) is operating each camera system, whether you can determine the boundary of the surveilled area, whether there are signs announcing the presence of the surveillance cameras, and whether the cameras are difficult or easy to spot.
2. Find and watch five anticrime PSAs and note their target audiences, the crime problem they are addressing, their use of fear, and the behaviors they are trying to encourage and discourage.

## SUGGESTED READINGS

Benjamin Goold. 2004. *CCTV and Policing*. Oxford, UK: Oxford University Press.

Clive Norris and Gary Armstrong. 1999. *The Maximum Surveillance Society: The Rise of CCTV*. Oxford, UK: Berg.

Clive Norris, Jade Moran, and Gary Armstrong, editors. 1998. *Surveillance, Closed Circuit Television and Social Control*. London, UK: Ashgate.

Garrett O'Keefe, Dennis Rosenbaum, Paul Lavrakas, Kathaleen Reid, and Renee Botta. 1996. *Taking a Bite Out of Crime*. Thousand Oaks, CA: Sage.

## NOTES

1. Research on media effects on public attitudes began in the 1930s with a set of research projects collectively called the Payne Fund studies. Among other findings, this early research reported that films such as *Birth of a Nation*—a sympathetic and romantic portrayal of the creation of the Ku Klux Klan—could generate unfavorable attitudes toward blacks among viewers. Although the effects eventually wore off, they were found to persist for a significant period of time (up to eight months).
2. National Institute of Mental Health, *Television and Behavior*, 90.
3. Lindesmith, *The Addict and the Law*.
4. American Association of Advertising Agencies, *What We've Learned About Advertising*.

5.  Black, *Changing Attitudes toward Drug Use*; and O'Keefe et al., *Taking a Bite Out of Crime.*

6.  Surette, "Methodological Problems in Determining Media Effects on Criminal Justice."

7.  Weinstein, "Cross-Hazard Consistencies."

8.  See O'Keefe and Reid, "Media Public Information Campaigns and Criminal Justice Policy"; and O'Keefe et al., *Taking a Bite Out of Crime.*

9.  Rosenbaum, Lurigio, and Lavrakas, *Crime Stoppers,* 110.

10. Rosenbaum, Lurigio, and Lavrakas, "Enhancing Citizen Participation and Solving Serious Crime," 417.

11. An assessment of a Florida program's "crime of the week" and "most wanted" cases for the first two years of operation revealed that the types of crime portrayed most often were violent crimes: nonviolent crimes were rarely portrayed, and homicides were the single most popular crime shown. On the whole, the program portrayed criminality as an attribute of a young, violent, dangerous class of criminals composed mostly of minorities. Crime was portrayed as largely stranger-to-stranger, injurious or fatal encounters in which handguns had a dominant role. See Surette, "The Mass Media and Criminal Investigations." Yvonne Jewkes (*Media and Crime,* 155–161) found that in Britain nearly all of the crimes shown on *Crimewatch UK* conform to news values of predatory violence, particularly against women and children.

12. Pfuhl, "Crimestoppers," 519.

13. Lavrakas, Rosenbaum, and Lurigio, "Media Cooperation with Police."

14. Grant, "The Videotaping of Police Interrogations in Canada."

15. Surette and Terry, "Videotaped Misdemeanor First Appearances."

16. Marx, "Electric Eye in the Sky," 228.

17. Surette and Terry, "Video in the Misdemeanor Court."

18. Patton, "Caught," 125, quoted by Stephen Graham in "Toward the Fifth Utility?", 89.

19. Warren and Brandeis, "The Right to Privacy," 195: "Recent inventions and business methods call attention to the next step which must be taken for the protection of the person, and for securing to the individual what Judge Cooley calls the right 'to be let alone.' Instantaneous photographs and newspaper enterprise have invaded the sacred precincts of private and domestic life; and numerous mechanical devices threaten to make good the prediction that 'what is whispered in the closet shall be proclaimed from the house-tops.'"

20. Norris and Armstrong, *The Maximum Surveillance Society,* 39, quoting a 1997 assessment offered in an article in the British newspaper *The Economist:* "Britain is leading the world in CCTV technology and its use. Precise figures are not available, but it appears that Britain now has more electronic eyes per head of population than any other country in the world, one-party states included ("The All-Seeing Eye," 52). See also Wardell, "4.2 Million Cameras Keep Eye on British."

21. Chris Horne ("The Case for: CCTV Should be Introduced") states that one of the first systems was installed in 1961 in Cumbernauld, England. Norris and Armstrong (*The Maximum Surveillance Society,* 18) state that the first systems were launched in English retail stores in 1967. Chris Williams ("Police Surveillance and the

Emergence of CCTV in the 1960s," 14) places the first police use of a CCTV system in Liverpool, England, in 1964.

22. Borg, "The Structure of Social Monitoring in the Process of Social Control," 287–288.

23. Newburn and Hayman, *Policing, Surveillance and Social Control.*

24. For example, the use of security camera video of the child, Jamie Bulger, being led from the Bootle Strand Shopping Center near Liverpool, England, in 1993 by his two teenage killers resulted in demands for more camera systems following its widespread broadcast on news programs (Goold, *CCTV and Policing,* 34–35).

25. Graham, "The Eyes Have It."

26. "The All-Seeing Eye," 52.

27. Marx, *Undercover.*

28. Short and Ditton, *Does Closed Circuit Television Prevent Crime?* and "Seen and Now Heard."

29. Welsh and Farrington, "Evidence-Based Crime Prevention," 21.

30. For research reviews see Gill, *CCTV;* Goold, *CCTV and Policing;* and Welsh and Farrington, "Crime Prevention Effects of Closed Circuit Television."

31. Surette, "The Thinking Eye," 152.

32. Brown, *CCTV in Town Centres;* Burrows, "Closed Circuit Television and Crime on the London Underground"; and Welsh and Farrington, "Crime Prevention Effects of Closed Circuit Television."

33. Tilley, *Understanding Car Parks, Crime and CCTV.*

34. The Supreme Court's legal reasoning is summarized in *United States v. Knotts* 368 U.S. 276, 281–82 (1983): "A person traveling in an automobile on public thoroughfares has no reasonable expectation of privacy in his movements from one place to another. When [an individual] traveled over the public streets he voluntarily conveyed to anyone who wanted to look the fact that he was traveling over particular roads in a particular direction, and the fact of his final destination when he exited from public roads onto private property."

35. Jefferis, Kaminski, Holmes, and Hanley, "The Effect of a Videotaped Arrest on Public Perceptions of Police Use of Force," 381; Weitzer, "Incidents of Police Misconduct and Public Opinion."

36. Parrish, "Police and the Media," 25.

37. Sechrest, Liquori, and Perry, "Using Video Technology in Police Patrol."

38. "Americans OK with Video Scrutiny," CBS News Poll.

39. Surette, "The Thinking Eye," 152.

40. Newburn and Hayman, *Policing, Surveillance and Social Control.*

41. Young, *The Exclusive Society,* 192.

# THE MEDIA AND CRIMINAL JUSTICE POLICY

## CHAPTER OBJECTIVES

After reading Chapter 8, you will understand the link between media content and criminal justice policy. You will learn about the effects of the law of opposites, the media's crime-and-justice ecology, how immanent justice underlies media portrayals, and how technology is advanced as a crime-fighting tool. You will understand that the assessment of criminal justice policy is based on faulty information and that the public crime-and-justice agenda, beliefs about criminality, and attitudes about policy are all influenced by the media. The convoluted, not always straightforward relationship between the media and criminal justice policy creation is detailed, and you will understand the effects media can have on the formation of criminal justice policy.

## SLAYING MAKE-BELIEVE MONSTERS

The cumulative result of the media's construction of crime, crime fighters, courts, corrections, and crime control leads to punitive criminal justice policies as the media mainstay for dealing with crime. When the dominant media portrait is of predatory offenders committing violent crimes in continuous battle with the criminal justice system, nonpunitive policies come across as being simply naive. You don't need crime-fighting heroes to battle wayward citizens who have made mistakes they regret. Nor do you rehabilitate innate predators. In that you very rarely find the regretful offender and usually find the innate predator, the ultimate policy push from the overall media social construction of crime and justice is a no-brainer. What remains to be clarified are the pathways through which media content influences criminal justice policy.

# MEDIA CRIME-AND-JUSTICE TENETS

Two crime-and-justice tenets provide insight into the way criminal justice, as a social issue, is constructed. The first tenet is the "law of opposites," which is associated with a particular crime-and-justice "ecology." The second tenet is the "rule of immanent justice," which paradoxically is associated with an enhanced view of technological solutions to crime. The cumulative constructed reality has the police imbedded in a randomly violent and dangerous environment where they battle predators more than keep the peace; the courts deal with psychotic offenders and conduct investigations more than dispense justice; corrections exist as a bizarre, primitive lost world of frequent brutality; surveillance of the public all the time is prudent, and the entire criminal justice system points unwaveringly toward the need for swift, sure, and increased punishment. In this Darwinian media-generated crime-and-justice reality, survival of the violent emerges as the operative selective rule.

## *The Law of Opposites*

The law of opposites or **backwards law** can be summarized as follows: The media's crime and justice portraits will be the opposite of what is true. In every subject category—crimes, criminals, crime fighters, attorneys, correctional officers, and inmates; the investigation of crimes and making of arrests; the processing and disposition of cases; and the experience of incarceration—the media construct and present a crime-and-justice world that is not found in reality. Whatever the truth about crime and the criminal justice system in America, the entertainment, news, and infotainment media seem determined to project the opposite. The wildly inaccurate and inevitably fragmentary images and facts found in the entertainment and infotainment media reflect this law most clearly. They provide a distorted reflection of crime within society and an equally distorted reflection of the criminal justice system's response to crime. Basic to this process is a front-end loaded portrait that concentrates on the activities of law enforcement and crime fighters. The further into the criminal justice system one looks, the more the activities of other components of the criminal justice system are ignored. The lack of information and the unreality of the information that is available mystify the criminal justice system, exacerbating the public's lack of understanding of it while constructing a perverse topsy-turvy portrait of criminal justice reality.

The backwards law also applies to crime-and-justice news content. First, the criminal justice system and its component parts are seldom the subject of news reports. The criminal justice system serves as a background setting for a news story more often than it appears as the subject. When the justice system is explicitly referred to, it is usually the courts that are portrayed, not as institutions but as backdrops to present information about individual cases. Seldom are broader system issues covered. For example, the broader policy issue of sentencing as a range of options incorporating fines, community supervision, and incarceration is not often discussed. Instead, references to sentencing are reported within stories about an individual receiving a sentence, most often prison. Nonincarceration sentencing options such as fines appear in less than 10 percent of news stories.[1] Alternate sentences, such as restitution or community service, almost never appear. Similarly, crime prevention stories are rare when compared to the number of stories about individual violent crimes—and when crime prevention does get covered, the coverage is usually negative. The end result is news that approaches criminal justice policy from the bottom up; that is, as the piecemeal, cumulative result of a focus on individual crimes and individuals rather than as a coherent, system of justice.

This bottom-up perspective can be found in the way news stories are formatted, either as episodic or thematic.[2] The more common **episodic format** treats stories as discrete events: a crime is described and a resulting case is followed. The rarer **thematic format** highlights trends, persistent problems, or other systemic phenomena: a crime-and-justice issue or a category of crimes is explored. Episodic formatted stories encourage viewers to place responsibility for social problems totally on individuals and to ignore possible societal forces—an individual committed a crime, why did he do it? Stories told in the thematic format take the opposite approach and effect—a set of problems have developed, what changed in society? The entertainment media reflects the same dichotomy, concentrating on events more than issues—the big heist, the murders, the investigation, the trial, the riot, and so on. By being episodic rather than thematic, the media reinforce the popular wisdom that says crime is caused solely by individual choices and that punitive, harsh deterrent-based policies are the only effective response.

The media supply a large amount of information about specific crimes and convey the impression that criminals threaten the social order and its institutions with imminent collapse. Media provide little explicit information to help the public comprehend the larger society-wide phenomena that underlie individual crimes and cases. Rare is the thematic interpretive analysis that places criminal justice information in historical, sociological, or political context. In the absence of system-wide information, the public is left to build its own picture of the effectiveness of current criminal justice policies and the desirability of newly offered ones.

Most media evaluations of the criminal justice system are implicit rather than explicit, indirectly conveyed through countless episodic references to the ability or inability of the system to apprehend specific criminals, to convict and punish them when they are apprehended, and to return them to society reformed and deterred. Concerning the main components of the criminal justice system—the police, courts, and corrections—in sociologist Doris Graber's assessment, the media portray the police as doing a fair job, and the courts and the correctional system as doing poor jobs.[3] When she queried a sample of the public, the system's components did only slightly better in the same order—police being rated as good to fair, the courts as fair to poor, and corrections as poor. The media's construction of the criminal justice system appears to lead the public to evaluate the overall system poorly while paradoxically leading the same public to increase support for crime-and-justice policies so long as they are crime control and law enforcement oriented.

Katherine Beckett and Ted Sasson attribute this paradox to the public's adherence to an image of a street criminal and to media depictions that show curable deficiencies in the justice system and personality defects in individuals as the main causes of apparently rampant crime.[4] Overall, the faulty system frame does the best in the media. Not surprisingly, researchers have found that most people who pay regular attention to the media support as their first policy choice criminal justice reforms that would toughen and strengthen the existing system.[5] This is true even though these same people place a large share of the blame for current crime levels on the existing criminal justice system. Despite the media presentation and public acceptance of the criminal justice system as ineffective, the media implicitly suggest that improving it, at least as a law enforcement and punitive system, is the best hope against the many violent crimes and predatory criminals that are portrayed. From the law of opposites emerges a recurrent picture of social reality that disparages social structure solutions while constructing a particular social structure regarding crime and justice. This constructed social reality incorporates a unique crime and justice ecology.

## Media's Crime-and-Justice Ecology

The social dynamic underlying the media image of crime—an image that has not substantively changed over the hundred plus year history of the modern media—is of a trisected society composed of wolves, sheep, and sheepdogs. In the media vision of society, evil and cunning predator criminal wolves create general mayhem and prey on weak, defenseless— and often stupid—victim sheep (women, the elderly, the general public),

## MEET 10-YEAR-OLD BECKY'S 12-YEAR-OLD INTERNET FRIEND.

The internet is a great place to buy cars, sell collectibles and stay informed. But for child molesters, it's a new, effective and more anonymous way to sexually exploit children. To reduce the risks, you need to know the potential dangers and report them. At the National Center for Missing & Exploited Children, we've created the CyberTipline to help fight back. And it works. Since 1998, we've dealt with more than 120,000 leads and we've worked tirelessly with law enforcement to help bring these predators to justice. To report child sexual exploitation, call the police. Then call us at 1-800-843-5678 or contact us at www.cybertipline.com. Child molesters may hide behind cute screen names. But together we can expose them for what they really are.

NATIONAL CENTER FOR **MISSING & EXPLOITED** C H I L D R E N
1-800-THE-LOST
www.cybertipline.com

**WE'RE HERE BECAUSE THEY'RE OUT THERE.**

Courtesy of the National Center for Missing and Exploited Children

The icon of the difficult to recognize and combat predator criminal extends to the social construction of Internet predators.

while good crime-fighting hero sheepdogs (usually middle class, white, and male) intervene and protect the sheep in the name of retributive justice. Over the course of the last century, characters in this ecological landscape have darkened. Media criminals have become more animalistic, irrational, and predatory—as have media crime fighters—and media crimes more violent, random, senseless, and sensational. In parallel, media victims have become more innocent. Differences between the general public and criminals have thus widened. In a subtle shift, the earlier predatory but rational criminal wolves have become unpredictable, irrational mad dogs, while over the years the protective noble sheepdogs have become wolf-like rogues and vigilantes for whom the law is an impediment to stopping crime. Heroes and villains have become more alike and less human. Today's media-constructed crime-and-justice ecology is populated with ideal offenders, victims, and heroes.[6] The **ideal offenders** are the outsiders, strangers, foreigners, aliens, and intruders who lack essential human qualities. Offenders have become generic others and as such can never be rehabilitated or resocialized. The **ideal victim**, on the other hand, is the innocent, naïve, trusting, obviously in need of protection true human. Children are the archetypal innocent victims and key symbols in the media's social construction of crime.[7] Finally, although capable of great violence similar to the ideal offender, the **ideal hero** displays the additional admirable human qualities of sacrifice, nobleness, and strength.

By depicting this predatory violent social environment, the media project messages to the audience, both criminal and law-abiding, concerning whom to trust, whom to victimize, and how victims and criminals should act. The consistent message is that crime is caused by predatory individuals who are inherently different from the rest of us—more ruthless, greedy, violent, or psychotic. Combating these predators requires a special person, an equally tough, predatory, and most important, unfettered crime fighter. Criminality is an individual choice and other social, economic, or structural explanations are irrelevant and can be ignored. Limited to this simplistic, incomplete picture of crime as mostly individual, socially isolated acts, the public is shown that counterviolence is the most effective means of combating crime, that due process considerations hamper the police, and that, in most cases, the law works in the criminal's favor. The public is further instructed to fear others because criminals are not always easily recognized and often are rich, powerful, and in positions of trust.

This constructed social environment, combined with the emphasis on investigations and arrests—the front end of the criminal justice system—ultimately promotes pro-law enforcement and crime control policies. When the public relies on infotainment formatted media and avoids media that present criminality as a complex social problem, punitive "quick fixes" are supported over preventive long-term approaches to crime.[8] Paradoxically, although the media frequently portray the criminal justice system unfavorably, the solutions they depict as being the most effective—harsher punishments and more law enforcement—entail expansion of the existing criminal justice system. Underlying this construction is a persistent, if often unstated, explanation of crime. The media consistently point to individual personality traits as the cause of crime and to violent interdiction as its solution. If one accepts the media's explanation of crime as being caused by predatory personality traits—by innate greed and violence—then the only valid approach to stopping crime is to hold individual offenders responsible for their past crimes and forcibly deter them from committing future ones. In the media's simplistic notion of crime, the most effective solution is dramatic, individual action that emphasizes violence and aggression, with a preference for weapons and sophisticated technology. By portraying criminality as innate and crime as an act of nature, the logical response is found in God-like revenge and punishment. Justice in the media has a uniquely divine twist.

## Immanent Justice Rules the Media

In this media-constructed crime-and-justice ecology, immanent justice rules. **Immanent justice** is the belief that a divine higher power will intervene and reveal and punish the guilty while protecting the innocent. The operation of divine intervention in the media becomes most clear in entertainment gunplay. Weapon accuracy and killing power are unequally held by the evil criminals and the good crime fighters. Their aim apparently guided by the moral imperatives of right and wrong, sinful, evil criminals

An evil Nazi who is ultimately destroyed by the ark in the film *Raiders of the Lost Ark*. Evil criminals and their ordained defeat are inherent in the portrayals of immanent justice found in crime and justice media.

© Paramount/The Kobal Collection/Picture Desk

miss or inflict benign flesh wounds while blessed, good crime fighters hit and kill. Similar to the medieval socially constructed reality that made trial by combat logical, the modern media reality relies on the moral superiority of the crime fighter to ultimately defeat criminality. No longer a social problem, criminality is reduced to an individual moral battle of good versus evil. The idea that criminals personify evil, which is exemplified by the proverbial "dangerous criminal underclass," has deep historical roots. A dangerous, immoral, underclass, in turn, justifies the wide use of violence and punishment. Sin must be resisted and sinners punished.

This good versus evil perspective on crime and justice is also reflected in the common media crime fighter who is motivated by personal injury and revenge. This media portrait ties into an overall emphasis on individualism and personal action as the appropriate solution to crime and victimization. These constructed crime-and-justice images gain support from our basic cultural values of free will, individualism, and personal responsibility. The result is that an individualized, revenge-oriented justice dominates where, God willing, the good guys win despite heavy odds. This pursuit of individualized immanent justice in the media tends to crowd out other competing constructions of crime and justice and their associated policies. In this fashion, crime is further removed as a social problem. Instead, it becomes a theological one, albeit not without a role for technology.

## Technology Enhances Crime Fighting

In contrast to their focus on individual factors as the cause of crime, the media do portray some collective responses to crime as effective if they are technology based. Immanent justice is often helped along in the media's crime-and-justice environment by technology and gadgets. If God is not handy, then a good engineer or scientist (not a social scientist though) will do. In this way, criminal justice is reduced in the media to controlling crime and is analogous to traffic control. Crime-and-justice issues are seen as a technological engineering problem. As a data and analysis driven dilemma, crime in the media argues for a technological solution. Within this portrait, it makes sense to ignore social and structural sources of conflict such as racism, sexism, and economic inequality and focus on solutions requiring more equipment, manpower, and resources. It suggests that we can engineer our way out of crime. Such an approach works well for true technological problems like reaching the moon, and the money and resources poured into NASA in the 1960s and 1970s successfully accomplished that goal. Unfortunately, for true social problems like crime and poverty, technology-based moon-shot solutions do not work.

## Real-World Criminal Justice Problems

In the real world, social problems come bundled together—crime is found with poverty, unemployment, poor health, poor schools, high divorce rates, high out-of-wedlock pregnancy rates, community decay and deterioration, drug use, illiteracy, high school dropout rates, and so on. Communities and societies that experience one of these problems tend to experience most if not all of them together. The media present crime as largely autonomous from other social problems and not as linked to them in any serious way. With its individually rooted causes, crime is constructed as an autonomous plague on society, its genesis not associated with other historical, social, or structural conditions. It follows that criminological theories that are individually focused gain more support from the media's construction of crime and justice than do group or culturally focused theories. Retribution and deterrence are trumpeted; rehabilitation and social reform are belittled.

The end product from a constructed backwards world of immanent justice, where policy is steered by divine intervention and derived from contests between good and evil individuals is, ironically, a preference for high-tech policy solutions. Crime is ultimately painted as a technological problem imbedded in a randomly violent, socially impersonal landscape that can only be tamed by more manpower and equipment. But does the public make the connection between the content they see and the policies they support? Do they even pay attention to the implicit policy messages?

## CRIMINAL JUSTICE POLICY AND MEDIA RESEARCH

While the content of the media certainly leads toward some policies and away from others, it is worthwhile to examine the research evidence of the media's ability to influence crime-and-justice policy. This section looks at the media and criminal justice policy relationship, examining the pathways that connect the media and criminal justice policy: the effects on crime's rank on the list of social problems; attitudes about the world as mean and dangerous; fear of crime; and echo, counterproductive, and anticipatory influences.

### Crime on the Public Agenda

Can the media, by emphasizing or ignoring topics, influence the ranking of issues that are important to the public—that is, what the public thinks about rather than what the public thinks? The hypothesis is that people will tend to judge a social issue such as crime as significant to the extent that the media emphasize it. If true, in time the media will construct the **public agenda**. When a correlation is looked for between media attention and public concern, a weak to moderate relationship is found.[9] Encouraged by this association, the agenda-setting research has concentrated on the media's effects on the public's ranking of issues with the idea that the issues that receive government attention are chosen from the public's list. A key early assumption in agenda setting is that the media influence public policy through a linear process. Crime stories appear, crime as an issue increases in importance to the public, the public becomes alarmed about crime, neighborhood and other public interest groups mobilize and rally for action, and crime-and-justice policy makers respond. Consistent evidence of such a linear process has not emerged from the research, however. The media's influence is seldom direct; more often media's influence is modified through multiple personal social networks.

As the research now stands, a media effect on the public's agenda is generally acknowledged, but unless the effect also appears among policy makers, it is usually regarded as unimportant. The research to date indicates that media effects are variable; appear to increase with exposure (those who are exposed to the media content mirror the media ranking of issues more closely); are more significant the less direct experience people have with an issue; are more significant for newer, concrete issues than for older abstract ones; diminish quickly; and are nonlinear, sometimes reciprocal, and highly interactive with other social and individual processes.[10] Specifically regarding crime and justice, the media emphasis on crime and associated claims about the nature of crime have been credited with raising the public's fear of being victimized and giving crime an inappropriately high ranking on the public agenda. It is felt that crime's high ranking also encourages moral crusades against specific crime issues, heightens public anxiety about crime, and pushes or blocks other serious social problems such as hunger or health care down or off the public agenda.

## Beliefs and Attitudes about Crime

The second question is whether exposure to crime and justice claims in the media affect a person's beliefs and attitudes about crime—the statements about crime a person accepts as true, and the feelings about crime a person believes to be justified. George Gerbner and his colleagues investigated the association between watching large amounts of television and general perceptions about the world, with the idea that television creates a particularly pernicious social reality for its audience.[11] This process, first described as **worldview cultivation**, was felt to be directly related to the

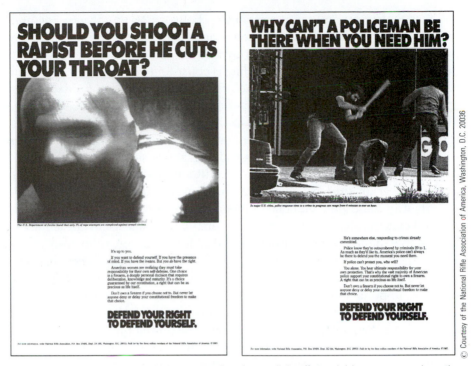

Despite the lack of clear conclusions regarding the media's effects, lobby groups such as the National Rifle Association commonly use the media to try to influence the public's views.

number of hours of television viewed. The researchers hypothesized that through exposure to television's content most everyone comes to have a similar media-constructed view of the world. Over time the repetitive themes and content of the mass media homogenize the viewpoints and perspectives of the public. People would come to think like the media and, consequently, to think alike. Prodded by critiques of their initial research,[12] Gerbner and his colleagues amended their initial hypothesis from one of "worldview cultivation," which stated that all media viewers would be affected, to the current one termed "mainstreaming." **Mainstreaming** posits that the media affect some viewers more than others regardless of exposure level. Gerbner and his colleagues now argue that the media are homogenizing society, influencing those heavy television consumers who are currently not in the mainstream to move toward it, while not affecting those already in the mainstream. The significance and extent of a media mainstreaming effect has yet to be determined.

One factor that has emerged as important in determining the impact of the media is the local environment of the media consumer. Local conditions influence the acceptance or rejection of media-based claims about crime and justice. For example, the relationship between television viewing and one's attitudes tends to diminish when actual neighborhood crime levels are taken into account. If one's world truly is mean, the media have less effect on one's view of the world. This finding is consistent with the general social construction proposition that media effects are most powerful for issues that are outside a subject's personal experiences or their experienced reality. Thus, media-based claims would be expected to have less impact on beliefs about crime among those who have had direct neighborhood experience with crime and thereby have a powerful alternative source of information.

The most relevant crime-and-justice attitude that has been linked to the media is fear of criminal victimization. Fear-of-crime levels are socially important because they influence support for punitive criminal justice policies and encourage increased social isolation. Viewing television crime shows, for example, has been found to be related to fear of crime, perceived police effectiveness, and opposition to gun control.[13] As the most accessible and pervasive potential source of fear, the role of the media in generating fear is therefore important—but that role is not clear. Currently, research suggests that media exposure to crime content is more strongly related to fear about distant places than to fear about local personal victimization. Not surprisingly, the public is more likely to accept fear-generating claims about places known only via the media than about local, directly experienced communities. It also follows that media consumption is more strongly related to fear of general social violence than to fear of personal risk,[14] fear of nonlocal more than local communities,[15] and fear of urban areas more than fear of nonurban areas.[16]

What does this research say about the media and people's beliefs and attitudes about crime? At the least, heavy media consumers do share certain beliefs about high societal crime and victimization levels and live in a socially constructed world that is seen as more violent and dangerous—and to be feared—than the socially constructed world of those who consume less media. The most common effects are increased belief in the prevalence and spread of crime, victimization, and violence, and increasingly cynical, distrustful social attitudes. The media provide the individual social construction "bricks" in the form of individual criminal events and associated crime-and-justice claims to create a crime-and-justice reality foundation. Together with attitudes about crime and justice as mortar, the public blends all of its media knowledge with personal experiences into a final crime-and-justice social reality. The media's portrayal of crime and justice thus defines a broad public reality of crime, which helps shape the public's final beliefs and attitudes. In that the media tend to construct a particular crime-and-justice reality for their consumers, the logical next question is whether these beliefs and attitudes translate into support for specific crime-and-justice policies.

## Crime-and-Justice Policies

The relationship between the mass media and the formation of criminal justice policies is important because media effects on criminal justice policy translate into how limited tax monies are spent and what actually happens to offenders and victims. Effects on crime-and-justice policy are the ultimate prize in the competition over the construction of crime-and-justice reality (see Box 8.1). Victorious, policy-influencing claims makers gain power, resources, and social construction ownership of a core social issue. Recognizing this, they work diligently to garner media attention and favor.

At the same time, researchers continue to explore the nature of the media–criminal justice policy relationship, and they have been able to report clear connections between the two. The results of the research have established that the media can directly affect what actors in the criminal justice system do without having to first change the public's attitudes or agenda. The idiosyncratic nature of the media–justice policy relationship, however, makes predicting the direction and magnitude of media influence in specific situations difficult. The difficulty arises because the media may themselves be claims makers or serve as the voice of nonmedia claims makers, and because the media are as likely to affect criminal justice decision making indirectly as they are to directly influence the formation of crime-and-justice policy. For example, it has been discovered that among criminal justice system officials, responses to the media can be either reactive or proactive—that is, they may react to what they have seen and heard in the media or act in anticipation of what they expect to find in the media. As the source of much news information, criminal justice policy makers also strongly influence the content of crime-and-justice news. This ability has expanded as criminal justice agencies have become more adept at dealing with the media, developing public information and public relations offices, and employing Madison Avenue style marketing strategies.

The available information indicates that among criminal justice officials, even more than among the public, the media significantly influence both policy development and support. Effects are multidirectional, and media content, the timing and presentation of the claims, and the characteristics and concerns of the general public, claims makers, and the criminal justice policy makers interact to determine the media's influence on criminal justice policies. Effects have been shown to range from broad, far-reaching policy crusades and criminal legislation to specific narrow influences on decisions in individual cases. The difficulty is not in the media's lack of significant policy effects but in determining when these effects occur and the form they will take.

## 8.1   *Three Strikes and You're Out*

In the Three Strikes and You're Out legislation, serious crime was rede-
fined and part of the faulty criminal justice system was "fixed." In 1988,
Diane Ballasiotes was abducted and stabbed to death in Washington state
by a convicted rapist who had been released from prison. In reaction to this
crime, a group called *Friends of Diane* formed to seek harsher penalties for
sex crimes. This group eventually joined forces with another Washington
state policy lobby group that was advocating for Three Strikes legislation.
Despite their combined efforts, however, through 1992 there was little
legislative or criminal justice professional interest in Three Strikes legislation in Washington. The proposed legislation was perceived as similar to
a habitual offender law already on the books, and a petition drive to get
three strikes on a statewide ballot failed. Although there was some media
coverage, up to that time the Friends of Diane and the Three Strikes
groups did not find a receptive social and media environment. As a result,
they were unable to be successful claims makers and forward a new
dominant construction of criminal justice policy.

In 1993 the Three Strikes group (renamed the Washington Citizens for
Justice) allied with the National Rifle Association and succeeded in getting
the proposition on the November ballot. This time, despite some

As the models in Box 8.2 show, the media may actually be the cause of a
criminal justice policy change (model A). Conversely, an external event may
be the cause, while the media simply covers the event prior to the policy
change, which would have occurred without media attention (model B). Or
the media's coverage of an external event and the event may both be influencing criminal justice policy (model C). The task of sorting out the effects of
the media from the effects of external events is difficult. Compounding these
problems, another set of unexpected effects arise from the novel manner in
which the media relate to criminal justice policy. Three types appear: echo
effects, counterproductive results, and anticipatory reactions.

An **echo effect** (first discussed in Chapter 5) refers to the tendency for
officials to treat defendants in unpublicized cases harshly if the press has
been demanding such treatment for defendants in publicized cases. For
example, a study of the processing of criminal cases prior to, during, and
following a highly publicized case involving the sexual abuse of toddlers at a

opposition from elements of the criminal justice professional community, 77 percent of Washingtonians approved the Three Strikes law. The catalyst for this shift was a tragic "symbolic crime" in California. As the Washington vote approached, a young California girl, Polly Klaas, was abducted and murdered. Coupled to this crime, and unlike prior years, media coverage of Three Strikes was extensive, and politicians and citizens across the nation and the political spectrum embraced the new policy panacea.

A number of social construction concepts clearly come into play in the Three Strikes saga. With the alliance of the NRA, Friends of Diane was able to become a much more powerful claims maker—the NRA was a preestablished group that the media would readily contact. Also, with the kidnapping and murder of Polly Klaas, the Three Strikes and You're Out claims makers had a tragic and powerful symbolic crime that they were able to use to reconstruct the crime problem. Symbolic crimes are crucial as they ensure media access for claims makers while providing dramatic stories, visuals, and evidence of policies that must be implemented. In Three Strikes, the Polly Klaas murder became the symbolic event that focused the media's attention and lifted the new crime-defining legislation to become a new social reality.

*Sources:* David Shichor and Dale Sechrest, editors, *Three Strikes and You're Out: Vengeance as Public Policy* (Thousand Oaks, CA: Sage, 1996); Ted Gest, *Crime and Politics* (London, UK: Oxford University Press, 2001); Valerie Callanan, *Feeding the Fear of Crime: Crime-related Media and Support for Three Strikes* (New York: LFB Scholarly Publishing LLC, 2005).

private day care center demonstrated that an echo effect was in operation.[17] Initial analysis showed marked increases in the number of filings of cases involving child victimization following the publicized case and an increase in the sentences of defendants adjudicated guilty. The existence of echo effects portends an influence spillover from the coverage of newsworthy criminal cases onto nonpublicized ones. Diffused but pervasive systemic media effects on a large number of unpublicized cases are likely.

The second unexpected result, **counterproductive effects**, occurs in situations where media attention results in unanticipated consequences, usually involving a crime reduction program. In this effect, media-based anticrime campaigns have sometimes been found to have effects opposite to the campaign goals. A massive multimedia Canadian anticrime campaign was found to actually result in fewer people taking personal anticrime measures.[18] This negative effect was credited to the campaign, which raised concern about crime to a fatalistic acceptance

## 8.2 *Media Criminal Justice Policy Relationship Models*

### A. Direct Media Influence

Media Coverage → Criminal Justice Policy Change

An investigative news report of ticket fixing leads to a new department policy regarding tickets.

### B. No Media Influence

External Event ⟶ ┌→ Criminal Justice Policy Change
                  └→ Media Coverage

An external evaluation reveals that low-income defendants are less likely to be offered alternatives to jail sentences. The review and selection process is adjusted as part of a preplanned program refinement cycle at the same time as local media report on the existence of program bias.

### C. Simultaneous Media Influence

External Event ┌→ Media Coverage ┐→ Criminal Justice
               └──────────────────→ Policy Change

A prisoner on a furlough program commits a violent rape. As a result, the corrections department reviews and alters the furlough program. Due to media publicity of the rape, the program is also suspended for a number of months and more severe restrictions than otherwise considered are instituted.

---

level among the target population. Together, echo and counterproductive effects underscore the idiosyncratic nature of the media–criminal justice policy construction relationship. The unpredictability makes it difficult to determine the direction and magnitude of influence or to specify the mechanism through which the media's influence is being exerted.

In addition to systemic and counterproductive effects, a final unique effect also makes such determinations difficult. Rare for other social research areas, but not uncommon for the media, **anticipatory effects** seem to reverse the causal order of media attention and criminal justice policy change. In these situations, the effect on policy occurs before any observable change in media content. The policy changes occur because criminal justice system officials respond in a proactive manner to anticipated local media coverage, perhaps due to seeing negative media coverage of a criminal justice practice in a distant jurisdiction.[19] In these cases, even if the media pay no attention to an issue, an official still acts on the idea that attention might be forthcoming and initiates a new policy or fails to implement a requested policy to avoid the expected negative media attention. In the first instance, a successful policy change cancels the potential coverage, and in the second, the proactive policy change is in anticipation of coverage that might never have occurred. In either case, because the media influence policy without any tangible coverage, the task of determining and studying a media policy effect is daunting. The problem is similar to determining how many crimes were not committed as a result of the possible deterrent effect of a new punishment-based program. Not impossible, but more difficult than measuring events that do occur.

Counterproductive, echo, and anticipatory effects add a unique level of difficulty to deciphering the relationship of the media and the criminal justice system. These media-related effects interweave with any criminal justice policy effects. Observed changes can be in anticipation of the media attention (as when prosecutors decide to increase DUI prosecutions to head off potential negative publicity), in anticipation of a policy being changed (as when prosecutors decide to pursue harsher sentences for drunk drivers due to the echo effect from a highly publicized DUI case), or due to a criminal justice policy change directly lobbied for by the media (as when DUI prosecutions increase due to an investigatory media series suggesting that lenient treatment for DUI offenders is common).

There is the real possibility of one effect occurring to prevent a second. In such a case, a preemptive decision to not change an established policy in favor of a new policy might occur so as to avoid the anticipated negative media coverage generated by the appearance and subsequent waning of an announcement effect of the (now rejected) new criminal justice policy. For example, a prosecutor sensitive to media dynamics may decide against launching a tougher but expensive DUI policy to avoid the problem of future negative coverage of the apparent loss of initial prosecutorial effectiveness that will occur when the media-generated announcement effect wanes. At that point, the new DUI policy, cast as suddenly failing to maintain its initial successful deterrent impact, results in the prosecutor being called to task. Sensing this pitfall, the prosecutor might well decide to forgo this or other new policies. The recognition and delineation of the media's role in such a scenario would be Herculean. Indeed, based on the discussion thus far, confidently comprehending any effect of the media appears daunting, and it is perhaps surprising that knowledge has progressed as far as it has.

# THE SOCIAL CONSTRUCTION OF CRIME-AND-JUSTICE POLICY

The media are not the most important factor in the construction of crime-and justice policy, but their influence cannot be ignored. Perceptions of crime and justice appear to be intertwined with other social perceptions, and crime-related attitudes are not determined solely by one's perception of the crime problem. Instead, perceptions of crime and justice are part of a larger construction of the nature and health of society and not a unique, separate component. And if perceptions of crime are intricately related to broader perceptions of the world, it is unrealistic to expect that they would change solely in accordance with media presentations of crime. That being said, if there is a general media effect on criminal justice policy, it is to increase its punitiveness.

The impact of the media on crime-and-justice policy follows from the media's construction of crime and justice. This is true for the entertainment, news, and infotainment elements of the media, for it is no coincidence that similar crimes and criminals appear in each. The goals and needs of each are to assemble the largest audience possible to maximize readership, ratings, and revenue. Therefore, the image of justice that most people find the most palatable and popular is the image that the media have historically projected. The repeated message in the media is that crime is largely perpetrated by predatory individuals who are basically different from the rest of us; that criminality is predominantly the result of individual problems; and that crimes are acts freely committed by individuals who have a wide range of alternate choices. This image locates the causes of crime solely in the individual criminal and supports existing social arrangements and approaches to crime control. The media-constructed reality of crime also allows crime to be more easily divorced from other social problems and highlighted as society's greatest threat.

In the end, crime-and-justice media advances system-enhancing crime control policies. The media do not provide the public with enough knowledge to directly evaluate the criminal justice system's performance, but media content steers people toward particular policies and assessments. It has been reported, for example, that the public learns as much information about punishment and sentencing from televised dramas and soaps as from factual media.[20] Not surprisingly, the overriding concern involves the image of the criminal justice system that the media constructs and the public receives. Learning about the criminal justice system from the media is analogous to learning geology from volcanic eruptions. You will surely be impressed and entertained, but the information you receive will not accurately reflect the real world, whether you're looking at volcanoes or at the criminal justice system. The media-constructed reality of predatory crimes, high-stakes trials, and violent riots contrasts starkly with the criminal justice system's daily reality of property crime, plea bargains, and order maintenance. Ironically, the public is shown that the traditional criminal justice system is not effective and simultaneously told that its improvement remains the best solution to crime. Hence, while critical and analytic pieces on criminal justice have increased in frequency, the tendency is to portray police misconduct within a "bad apple" framework and to preserve the overall portrait of the police and the criminal justice system as the sole solution to crime.[21] These messages translate into support for order over law, punitive crime policies, and enhanced criminal justice agencies. This portrait of crime and justice has naturally led to concern. As David Altheide observes: "The only response we seem to have is to wait and to prepare (get armed, lock doors, build walls, and avoid strangers and public places). This may be a good formula for cinema thrillers, but it is lousy for everyday life."[22] Fear and fatalistic acceptance of crime, mystification of the criminal justice system, monopolistic support for punitive criminal justice policies, and increased tolerance for illegal law enforcement practices are all concerns.

How could the media portray crime and justice better? They have the experience and a coverage model to adopt if they wanted to improve. The media are able to provide comprehensive, contextual coverage for sporting events on a daily basis. Sports coverage stands as a model for reporting on individual events, supplemented by statistics, trend analysis, forecasts, commentary, and discussion. Sporting events are consistently placed by the media in their larger social context (the world of sports in this case) and constructed in a way that provides historical understanding and current comprehension. Covering justice like sports would provide the public with a counterbalance to the widely distorted and currently unchallenged entertainment and infotainment constructions. In that manner, crime could be removed from the realm of the bizarre, grotesque, and sinister and placed in the social world of poverty, loss of community, alienation, group conflict, and psychological disorders.[23]

Sports, however, are covered in breadth and depth because there is a strong public demand and interest. Lacking a similar incentive regarding criminal justice, there is no reason to expect the commercial media to direct their limited resources to delivering an expanding justice portrait. It's not that they cannot do it, but lacking a large enough market they cannot afford to do it. In the social construction of crime and justice we won't get what too few of us are willing to pay for. The crime-and-justice media that will be delivered will be that which can be produced profitably.

*Inside: Homeland Security Act debated—See B3 for coverage*

# Crime & Justice

Tuesday, February 2, 2006

SECTION **B**

## Resurrected: Executions take off

By Carole Boyd
The Mirror

Once looking to be completely shut out, executions in the U.S. have made a dramatic comeback, surging to

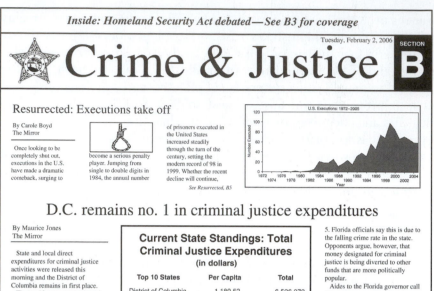

become a serious penalty player. Jumping from single to double digits in 1984, the annual number

of prisoners executed in the United States increased steadily through the turn of the century, setting the modern record of 98 in 1999. Whether the recent decline will continue,

*See Resurrected, B5*

U.S. Executions: 1972–2005

## D.C. remains no. 1 in criminal justice expenditures

By Maurice Jones
The Mirror

State and local direct expenditures for criminal justice activities were released this morning and the District of Columbia remains in first place.

The top 10 states were released by the government with standings broken down into state, local municipalities, and counties. Standings are calculated based on statistics published by the National Institute of Justice.

For the first time in the 20-year history of the State Expenditure Report, Florida fell out of the top

| Current State Standings: Total Criminal Justice Expenditures (in dollars) | | |
|---|---|---|
| **Top 10 States** | **Per Capita** | **Total** |
| District of Columbia | 1,189.52 | 6,526,972 |
| Alaska | 768.27 | 8,515,351 |
| New York | 651.96 | 171,232,216 |
| Nevada | 630.05 | 11,223,671 |
| Delaware | 618.73 | 5,152,073 |
| New Jersey | 553.80 | 54,511,830 |
| Florida | 526.05 | 84,300,913 |
| Oregon | 525.90 | 24,086,300 |
| Maryland | 512.37 | 30,598,125 |
| Wyoming | 500.70 | 3,741,777 |

5. Florida officials say this is due to the falling crime rate in the state. Opponents argue, however, that money designated for criminal justice is being diverted to other funds that are more politically popular.

Aides to the Florida governor call this outrageous and say that the governor fully supports all available monies going toward state criminal justice programs.

"The governor personally oversees bills that put money into correction programs, boot camps, and juvenile halfway houses," said a top aide. "She would never divert money for political gains."

*See Expenditures, B7*

## Local Highlights

By Piper Chilus
The Mirror

**WEEKEND TERRORIST THREAT: ORANGE**

**HOME INVASIONS**
❒ Two this weekend: 1 in Pine Hills, 1 in Goldenrod.
❒ Orange County ranks third in state.
❒ Florida ranks first in nation, inching above California. New Hampshire claims 5th.

**DOMESTIC VIOLENCE**
❒ 196 this weekend, 63 involving guns.
❒ Orange County ranks seventh in state.
❒ Florida moves up to 6th place, replacing New Jersey, which falls into 3rd.

**DRUG OVERDOSES**
❒ Three this weekend; 2 minors are dead.
❒ Orange County still steady at 1st in the state.
❒ Florida moves up to 1st in nation, edging out New York.

**CONSUMER FRAUD**
❒ Twenty-seven reported this week at a total cost to the public of $172,000.
❒ Orange County ranks 11th in state.
❒ Florida ranks 9th in the county, falling two spaces from last week.

*See Crime Stats, B6.*

## Video games cause crime—Okay or no way?

### PRO

By Dianne Berrie

Juvenile crime is on the rise and video games are a cause. Teenagers should not be allowed access to violent, misogynistic games for their own and society's good.

*See Pro, B7*

### CON

By Brett Pocock

To strip the rights of America's young people to play the games of their choice is as unfair as past practices not allowing women to vote. Thousands of teenagers who

*See Con, B7*

### State Prison gets 3 in trade with city jail

Name: Mike Ros
Stats: 5'10", 159 lbs.
County: Orange
MO: Strong arm robbery
Release date: 3-15-2012
Habitual offender: Yes
Other: Also has battery on LEO, cocaine addict.

Name: Joe Johnson
Stats: 6'1", 205 lbs.
County: Seminole
MO: Home invasion
Release date: 12-28-2012
Habitual offender: Yes
Other: Third trade; first 8 years in military prison.

Name: Derek Boyd
Stats: 5'9", 185 lbs.
County: Dade
MO: first-degree murder
Release date: 10-15-2012
Habitual offender: No
Other: Has ties to domestic terrorism groups.

Covering justice like sports would provide the public with a counter balance to the widely distorted and currently unchallenged entertainment and infotainment constructions.

The most profitable content follows entertainment narratives, formatting, and frames. This profitable and entertaining content carries imbedded messages about criminal justice polices and encourages public support for policies that will fix and enhance the apparently "faulty" criminal justice system while discouraging support for all other approaches.

## DISCUSSION QUESTIONS

1. Discuss a recent local crime or criminal justice event that resulted in heavy media coverage and calls for a change in a criminal justice policy. Discuss how the competing constructions of the issue are being framed, whether the event is becoming a symbolic crime, and whether a policy change is likely to occur.
2. Which component of the criminal justice system adheres most to the law of opposites (is portrayed in the media least like its actual reality)?
3. Discuss the use of immanent justice ideas in the social construction of terrorism.
4. What recent crime-and-justice events have become or have the potential to become the basis for memorial criminal justice policy changes? What features of the events make them more or less likely to generate a memorial policy?

## IN-CLASS ACTIVITIES

1. Invite a local journalist who has a byline associated with a recent thematic story of a criminal justice policy issue to speak to the class.
2. Watch the film *Bonfires of the Vanities* (1990) or *Natural Born Killers* (1994) and discuss the media's construction of the news media's role in crime and justice.

## ASSIGNMENT

Follow the media content regarding a local criminal justice policy debate. Note the references to crime-and-justice events by politicians and other policy makers and how the policy alternatives are socially constructed and framed by the media and by claims makers.

# SUGGESTED READINGS

David Shichor and Dale Sechrest, editors. 1996. *Three Strikes and You're Out: Vengeance as Public Policy*. Thousand Oaks, CA: Sage.

Katherine Beckett and Theodore Sasson. 2000. *The Politics of Injustice*. Thousand Oaks, CA: Pine Forge Press.

Ted Gest. 2001. *Crime and Politics*. London, UK: Oxford University Press.

Valerie Callanan. 2005. *Feeding the Fear of Crime: Crime-related Media and Support for Three Strikes*. New York: LFB Scholarly Publishing LLC.

# NOTES

1.  Roberts and Doob, "News Media Influences on Public Views on Sentencing," citing Canadian Sentencing Commission, *Sentencing in the Media*.

2.  Iyengar, *Is Anyone Responsible?*

3.  Graber, *Crime News and the Public*.

4.  Beckett and Sasson, *The Politics of Injustice*.

5.  Barrile, "Television and Attitudes about Crime"; Graber, *Crime News and the Public*, 73; and Sasson, *Crime Talk*.

6.  Christie, "The Ideal Victim."

7.  Altheide, *Creating Fear*, 146.

8.  Sotirovic, "Affective and Cognitive Processes as Mediators of Media Influences on Crime-Policy Preferences," 311.

9.  Lasorsa and Wanta, "Effects of Personal, Interpersonal and Media Experiences on Issue Saliences"; and Protess et al., *The Journalism of Outrage*.

10. Rogers and Dearing, "Agenda-Setting Research."

11. Gerbner, Gross, Morgan, and Signorielli, "Growing Up with Television"; and Morgan and Shanahan, "Two Decades of Cultivation Research."

12. See, for example, Hirsch, "The "Scary World," and "On Not Learning from One's Own Mistakes."

13. Dowler, "Media Consumption and Public Attitudes toward Crime and Justice," 116. Valerie Callanan (*Feeding the Fear of Crime*), for example, found that in California heavy consumers of crime-related media are more fearful of crime, more likely to believe crime is increasing, more likely to rate crime seriously, more likely to believe the world is "just," less likely to support rehabilitation, and much more likely to support three strikes sentencing.

14. Sparks and Ogles, "The Difference between Fear of Victimization and the Probability of Being Victimized."

15. Heath and Petraitis, "Television Viewing and Fear of Crime." Specific media effects are discussed by Weitzer and Kubrin ("Breaking News," 516–518).

16. See Ditton et al., "From Imitation to Intimidation"; Eschholz, Chiricos, and Gertz, "Television and Fear of Crime"; and Lane and Meeker, "Ethnicity, Information Sources, and Fear of Crime."

17. Surette, "Media Echoes."

18. Sacco and Silverman, "Selling Crime Prevention."

19. For example, Snell, Bailey, Carona, and Mebane ("School Crime Policy Changes," 208) report that highly publicized school crimes impact school policy decisions to install metal detectors and video cameras in distant states.

20. Reiner, "Media Made Criminality," 387; and Gillespie and McLaughlin, "Media and the Shaping of Public Attitudes," 8.

21. Reiner, "Media Made Criminality," 403.

22. Altheide, *Creating Fear*, 137.

23. Bennett, *News*, 96.

# MEDIA AND CRIME AND JUSTICE IN THE TWENTY-FIRST CENTURY

CHAPTER

*9*

## CHAPTER OBJECTIVES

Chapter 9 summarizes many of the issues previously addressed and provides an overview of the relationship between media and crime and justice. You will learn two postulates that encapsulate the media crime-and-justice relationship and that will steer the media crime-and-justice world and criminal justice policy in the twenty-first century. You will also learn two scenarios that describe alternative futures for the media's role in the relationship that forms between the public and the criminal justice system.

## CRIME-AND-JUSTICE MEDIA MESSAGES

By the late nineteenth century, early print-based mass media contained the same criminal stereotypes and causal explanations of crime found in today's media. Narratives of individually focused crime and retributive justice have been common story lines for more than a hundred years. Composed of ever-multiplying outlets, today media weave a pervasive web of social reality and construct a distorted, erroneous crime-and-justice portrait. The merging of news and entertainment media and the constant looping of crime-and-justice content means that the portraits of crime and justice in each will continue to be more alike than different and that infotainment media presentations will continue unabated.

Crime-and-justice media messages conform to a law of opposites, and the media consistently reverse the real world of crime and justice in their media-constructed world. As a basic rule of thumb, news, entertainment, and infotainment media take the least common crime or justice event and make it the most common crime or justice image. Crime constitutes a constant, significant portion of the total content; criminals are normally constructed as either predatory street criminals or dishonest business-people and professionals; and the criminal justice system is shown as an ineffective, often counterproductive means of dealing with crime. In this media-made reality, traditional criminal justice system personnel and standard practices suffer, but alternatives to the criminal justice system approach fare even worse.

The lack of realistic information in the media further mystifies and obscures criminality and the criminal justice system.[1] The media emphasize individual personality traits as the cause of crime and violent interdiction as its solution, showing a preference for crimes involving weapons and solutions involving violence and sophisticated technology. Media present criminality as an individual choice and imply that other social, economic, or structural explanations are irrelevant. The "crime-fighter" and "war-on-crime" icons suggest to the public that crime must be fought rather than solved or prevented.[2] Media portraits further instruct the public to fear others, for the criminal is not easily recognizable and is often found among the rich, powerful, and seemingly trustworthy. These images tilt public perceptions toward law enforcement and crime control policies. The result is that although the criminal justice system is not shown favorably, the solutions to crime suggested by the media involve expansion of the existing criminal justice system through harsher punishments and more law enforcement. Increasing the punitiveness of the real criminal justice system appears to be the only reasonable policy course. And in a looping cycle, the actions of the real criminal justice system are evaluated by the public against the expectations and desires raised by the media-constructed criminal justice system.

Cumulatively, the media's crime-and-justice content support the following derived claims:

1. Crime fighters must use any means to catch criminals.
2. Corruption runs rampant throughout criminal justice agencies.
3. Bureaucratic red tape and due process protections hinder crime fighters and make it difficult to successfully conclude investigations.
4. Crime fighters need more training and resources because they are not capable of solving crimes legally.
5. Crime is a result of individual characteristics and is not related to social structure, racism, or poverty.
6. Criminals cannot be rehabilitated and, if given a chance, will recidivate.
7. Specific deterrence combined with incapacitation is the only punishment that will stop criminals from recidivating.
8. The courts allow dangerous offenders to avoid guilt.
9. Probation and parole allow dangerous offenders to go free.
10. Prisons make dangerous offenders more dangerous.

The dominant crime-and-justice portrait shows people outside of the criminal justice system and unburdened by due process considerations to be the most effective crime fighters. At the same time, media bolster the existing criminal justice system as being the best policy course. This media-constructed, ineffective, last resort criminal justice system sits within a portrait of a stark society of predatory criminals, violent crime fighters, and helpless victims.

The media's influence on criminality, independent of its effect on criminal justice, has not been adequately explored, and the specter of media-oriented terrorism is an issue of immediate concern. The available evidence suggests, and most researchers agree, that the media do affect crime rates and motivate terrorists. Aggregate crime rate studies further suggest that the media affect crime independently of their violent content. In addition, the media likely have more of a copycat effect on property crime than on violent crime. The more heavily the potential copycat criminal relies on the media for information about the world, and the more predisposed the individual is to commit similar crimes, the more likely is a copycat effect. Violence-prone children and individuals who have difficulty distinguishing fact from fantasy are particularly at risk for aping media violence. When sexual and violent content are yoked, hypermasculine males are most influenced. When the news media sensationalize crimes and make celebrities of criminals, people seeking notoriety imitate those crimes. And when successful crimes, in particular property crimes, are detailed, criminals emulate them.

## Media Anticrime Efforts

On the other side of the media social construction equation are media-based anticrime efforts. These efforts appear to be an effective means of disseminating information and influencing attitudes, but their ability to significantly affect behavior has not been established. Although useful in specific areas, media-based anticrime programs are not likely to significantly reduce the overall crime rate. No program has empirically demonstrated a significant long-term and displacement-free effect on crime. Single-handedly, the media and media technology are as unable to deter criminal behavior as they are to criminalize individuals, and they should not be looked to as panaceas for crime. Even so, media-based anticrime programs can have significant immediate effects, and their careful utilization is warranted.

By constructing crime-and-justice reality, the media also subtly but significantly affect crime-and-justice policies. To varying degrees, media influence the agenda, perceptions, and policies of consumers with regard to crime and justice. These media effects interact with other factors, are not easy to

**FIGURE 9.1**

**Competing Models of the Media's Relationship to Sex Crimes, Aggression, and Support for Punitive Criminal Justice Policies**

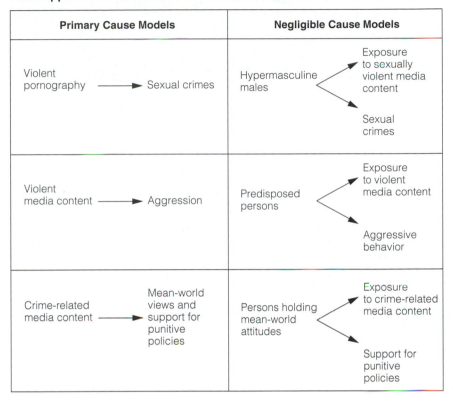

| Primary Cause Models | Negligible Cause Models |
|---|---|
| Violent pornography ⟶ Sexual crimes | Hypermasculine males ⟨ Exposure to sexually violent media content / Sexual crimes |
| Violent media content ⟶ Aggression | Predisposed persons ⟨ Exposure to violent media content / Aggressive behavior |
| Crime-related media content ⟶ Mean-world views and support for punitive policies | Persons holding mean-world attitudes ⟨ Exposure to crime-related media content / Support for punitive policies |

discern, and are difficult to counteract. Perceptions of crime and justice appear to be intertwined with other, broader perceptions of social conditions. Therefore, it is not surprising that consistent relationships have not been found between the media and public attitudes or policies on crime and justice.

As reflected in Figure 9.1, the conflicting arguments of the media as a primary cause versus a negligible cause of crime, aggression, terrorism, and other behaviors not only posit differing causal relations between the media and behavior but imply vastly different public policies as well. The *primary cause models* argue that a significant, direct linear relationship exists between media content and consumer behavior. The media, independent of other factors, directly cause varied social behaviors. If valid, these models indicate that strong intervention is necessary in the creation, content, and distribution of media.

The *negligible cause models* concede a statistical association between the media and some negative behaviors but argue that the connection is due not to

FIGURE 9.2
**A Reciprocal Feedback Model of the Media, Crime, and Justice Relationship**

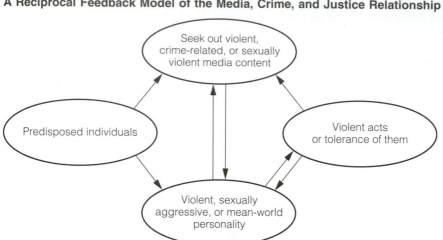

a causal relationship but to persons predisposed to certain behaviors seeking out particular types of media and concurrently behaving in ways similar to the behavior displayed in the media. As the relationship is associative and not causal, if these models are correct, policies targeted at the media will have no effect on social behavior and the media can safely be ignored.

Neither of these models is felt to inaccurately describe the media–social behavior relationship. As shown in Figure 9.2, the actual relationship is believed to be bi-directional and cyclical. In addition to people acting out their predispositions while seeking out supportive media and media causing behavior to be modeled, the media play a role in the generation of people predisposed to crime. As the made-for-TV movie industry exemplifies, real-world violence sometimes results in the creation of violent media. Providing live models of violence and creating community and home environments that are more inured to and tolerant of violence results in more violently predisposed individuals in society. Therefore, although the direct effect of media content on social behavior may not be large, its influence loops, recycles, and accumulates.[3]

## Two Postulates of Media and Crime and Justice

Overall, the media are constant, subtle, and unpredictable crime-and-justice agents—beneficial if carefully used, but neither the magic cure nor the potent demon they are sometimes cast as. Media cannot be ignored but should not be seen as omnipotent. Where then do we stand in terms of a broad understanding of media and the social construction of a crime-and-justice reality? To address this question, we begin with two postulates of media, crime, and justice that are distilled from earlier chapters and that will drive expectations about future media, crime, and justice interactions.

> *Postulate 1:* The media more often than not construct the criminal justice system and its people negatively and as ineffective. Yet the cumulative effect is support for more police, more prisons, and more money for the criminal justice system.

The media-constructed reality argues that the criminal justice system does not work well but remains the best hope against crime.

> *Postulate 2:* Media organizations have increasingly blurred the line between news and entertainment, and between fact and fiction. In the process, crime stories have become the mainstay of hybrid infotainment programs.

Led by the electronic visual media, the media have become more able and willing to portray events previously considered private and to expose and distribute new information previously considered out-of-bounds and sensitive. Spurred by competition, media present these events and information in an entertainment context to maximize revenues. The result is that all information that goes into and comes out of the media is processed through an entertainment lens.[4]

Together these postulates result in the continuing disparity between the media-constructed reality of crime and justice and the actual social reality of crime and justice. This disparity has developed because the media converge on a single image of crime and justice—an image of rampant, predatory criminality ineffectively checked by traditional criminal justice system methods. Commercial, organizational, and cultural forces drive the media to construct and perpetuate this predatory crime-centered image. The media are commercial businesses and must show a profit. Therefore they must compete for consumers while keeping their production costs low. This makes them socially aggressive and fiscally conservative. They are not particularly sensitive about their content's social effects and will copy any successful content ideas from their competitors. The result is media that are both redundant and boundary pushing. The media are redundant in that a successful type of content will rapidly spawn imitations and spinoffs (for example, the success of the reality show *Survivor* resulted in a spate of copycat reality shows). They are boundary pushing in that they are constantly trying to lure new, larger audiences through provocative, titillating content.

This dual process of similar types of media vehicles trying to out-compete each other for consumers is emphasized in crime-and-justice news, entertainment, and infotainment programming. And though the media have increased their capability to discover and deliver information about the world, they have also moved toward greater reliance on pre-packaged information, stereotypes, and entertainment-style content. As a result, the public receives an image of crime and justice that is not only distorted but that basically supports only one anticrime policy. Enhanced crime control mechanisms are advanced at the expense of due process protections and social policies that do not rely on the criminal justice system. Guarding against the violent predator criminal becomes the main message and policy focus.

Long-established cultural forces come into play in the wide-scale social acceptance of the media-generated predator criminal icon. As a culture, depictions of predatory criminals both entertain and comfort us. They entertain because they frighten and provide glimpses of realities we are not likely to encounter. They comfort because they relieve our social conscience of personal responsibility for crime and violence by constructing crime as not in any way connected to social inequities, racism, or poverty—things society could be held responsible for and might address. The media's maddened, greedy predators are criminals by their own will, or maybe God's will, but certainly not society's will. Such criminals can, therefore, be guiltlessly battled and eliminated. Together, the commercial, organizational, and cultural forces create a constructed reality that is resistant to alternative broader constructions of crime and justice. The media resist because they cannot commercially afford to seriously challenge the popular construction, and we resist as consumers because we are more comfortable with the narrower, entertaining, and guilt-free picture.

## Expanded Public Access to Criminal Justice Procedures

Running counter to the narrow construction of crime is the modern media's ability to expand our access to previously hidden criminal justice realms and thus to expand our crime-and-justice reality. Phrases such as "government in the sunshine" and "freedom of information" reflect responses to a media-driven social trend toward more open public institutions and enhanced scrutiny of public officials. Two dominant social institutions, the media and the criminal justice system, play critical roles in this process, which can be understood as part of the general process of exposing more of the previously private backstage areas of society to the public.[5] In our hypermedia society, closed institutions and proceedings and secret information and sources are automatically viewed with suspicion and challenged. Ironically, the criminal justice system and the mass media are among only a handful of social institutions that resist full, open access and struggle to keep their realities closed. As a result of this trend toward greater access, previously low-visibility criminal justice events are now revealed, more graphic news and entertainment programs are presented, the public's tolerance for surveillance devices has increased, judicial steps and interactions between the police and citizens are often recorded, media trials proliferate, and there is increased acceptance of media technology and entertainment formatting in criminal justice and social situations.

## Mass Media Reality

With regard to crime and justice, the critical issue is ultimately the media's role in the social construction of reality. Evidence is building that the media alter reality by affecting the ways in which the audience perceives, interprets, and behaves toward it. The question is no longer whether the media have a substantial impact but how their impact will be felt. These effects cycle through the media in loops where content is extracted from one context or medium, is reframed, and used in another, often resulting in new, ambiguous media realities. These looping effects are observed in both real events that are massively mediated, such as the traffic stop and beating of Rodney King and the World Trade Center attacks, and in the created-for-media pseudoevents found in crime-and-justice reality shows. The ultimate effect these media-reality loops will have on crime and justice is unknown. The availability of video and new media technologies has already created the genre of reality programming, which relies heavily on images of real crimes, criminal investigations, and criminal justice agency activities for fodder. It will be interesting to see what effect the common use of video recorders by the public will have on the reporting of citizen and authority violence and other types of crime news—as pictures invariably increase the newsworthiness of events and move the public debate from arguments about factual claims to interpretative ones. Perhaps this will have the positive benefit of moving the criminal justice debate to discussions about alternate policies and beyond the current focus on how to best implement a single policy.

The development of interactive media further changes the relationship between media and users and has steadily moved the media experience closer to direct personal experience. It has also changed the way people interact with each other, with less direct, face-to-face conversation but more face-to-face-like communication via media technology. Today people interact less with those physically near them such as neighbors and more with distant people via videophones, digital cameras, home computers, and other "being there" technology. The full effects of interactive media, both in games that emulate the experiences of crime and violence and as a means to carry on personal relationships on the social construction of crime-and-justice reality, will be significant.

A hybrid reality is in the making in which media-generated reality loops and interweaves with nonmediated reality. Many children today already spend more time in a media-constructed reality than in a directly experienced reality.[6] Across the United States a web of media-linked technology and products gives media reality enormous reach and impact. Unfortunately, we cannot have some of the media forces for social change without having other unwanted forces. As a result, we cannot use the media to educate without altering the functions of reading and the structure of the family and the school.[7] By the same token, we cannot use the media for fighting crime and processing criminal cases or providing media access to criminal justice proceedings without also changing the reality of the criminal justice system. Mixing and remixing media-constructed and real-world events harbingers a future where media constructions of other media constructions will dominate the social construction of reality. Directly experienced reality will lose its social significance, and only mediated knowledge will be important. Then crime and justice will be understood and experienced only through the mass media reality mixing bowl.

## THE FUTURE OF CRIME-AND-JUSTICE REALITY

What might the future media crime-and-justice reality look like? Let's look at two possible extreme scenarios for the future.

### SCENARIO 1

### Unrestrained Infotainment

In the first scenario, a free-wheeling infotainment media dominates the culture in a technologically resplendent journalism driven by an intrusive, near sadistic voyeurism. In this world, the media push the boundaries of taste and decency without constraints. In such an environment, a host of crime-and-justice programs are possible. Live executions would be a natural, with the modern version of the gallows speech again prominent. Following the last meal and hours of life, imbedded retrospective segments of the condemned prisoner's life and crimes, behind-the-scenes interviews with the executioner and other participants, close-ups of the family of the condemned and the victim's relatives at the moment of death, and of course the execution itself would all be compiled into dramatic, entertaining

Fights and violence would be a mainstay in unrestrained crime-and-justice infotainment.

productions. A Jerry Springer-like *Death Row Talk Show* with inmates, attorneys, victim families, and other commentators also has marketing possibilities. Numerous other reality TV programs would also be explored. *The Halfway House,* a show based on the activities of various offenders in an urban community corrections home that has been fitted throughout with cameras, would show the lives of drug abusers, prostitutes, and other offenders on probation and living in a court ordered group home. Driven by the drama of "caught-on-camera" rule breaking resulting in probation revocation and imprisonment, the show would allow audience input into who should be revoked and who given additional chances. *Hostage,* a show where a traveling media production crew is alerted beforehand by a hostage taker or cohort, and provides camera coverage of hostage situations, could be another venue. Each episode would be edited and formatted into an hour-long production containing interviews with hostages and hostage takers, film of law enforcement efforts and conditions inside the hostage site, and entertaining background information on participants. The show would also provide telegenic negotiators to move the incident along to its conclusion. The list of possible infotainment shows based on the entertainmentized stories of persons caught up in crime and justice is endless. Graphic shocking media constructions and shows with titles like *Rape Victim, Drug Dealer, Pedophile,* and so on would compete for audience shares.

Scott Adams offers a satirical take on unrestrained infotainment in his Dilbert comic strip.

Aggressive, proactive news will take off with news agencies staging their own sting operations aimed at offenders, politicians, police officers, and citizens. Catching people committing illegal acts will be a primary journalistic aim. Journalists will ride along not just with the police but with offenders, filming crimes as they happen and editing the material into entertaining news stories. In the criminal justice system, policy changes will be fast tracked and enacted without public debate due to massive media attention and the emotional impact of widely publicized symbolic tragic crimes. For the general public, expectations of privacy will be all but eliminated. Images taken through a bedroom window, for example, would be legally publishable as the courts rule that if couples don't want their sexual encounters filmed they should not have relations near open windows. Similarly, conversations, files, and information obtained by any means can be utilized by the media as the courts advance the position that media possession of information in whatever form and however obtained is usable under the First Amendment. Prior arrests, personal activities, past marriages, romances, illnesses, and indiscretions great and small all become open to media scrutiny. A new television reality show, *What's Your Neighbor Hiding?*, that randomly picks families with solid reputations and investigates and broadcasts embarrassing details of their lives is a big hit.

---

Besides the loss of privacy, another effect of the widespread use of surveillance cameras is to feed the infotainment industry with programming.

"Warning Anything Recorded" by Chris Slane. From CartoonStock.com Reprinted with permission.

## SCENARIO 2

### Restricted Commercial Media and Extensive Media Anticrime Efforts

In the second scenario, the commercial media operates under heavy restrictions, and their ability to cover, comment on, and portray crime-and-justice issues and cases is tightly restrained. At the same time, media technology is applied to its full capabilities in crime control efforts. Combined, these two trends create a society where the watchdog function of the media is disabled while the surveillance and control capabilities of the media and media technology are maximized.

Regarding the elimination of the media's constitutionally mandated government watchdog function, criminal cases would be processed absent media coverage, and verdicts would be announced only after trials are concluded and any sentences imposed. Filming and coverage of police operations, courtroom proceedings, and correctional facilities would not be allowed. Police chiefs, court officers, and correctional administrators could deny without explanation or appeal media access to their agency personnel, records, and meetings. Access to suspects and prisoners would never be granted.

Computerized face-mapping software matches a fugitive to a booking photo in a law-enforcement data base.

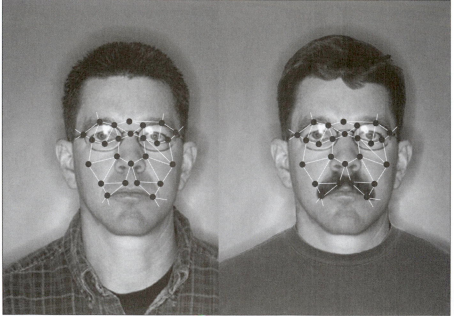

© Identix

Concerning the commercial media, all TV's will be equipped with sensors that identify viewers so that all "inappropriate" content can be automatically blocked. VCRs and other recording devices would be blocked from making copies of all but approved, prepaid materials. All print, visual, and audio entertainment media must be processed, reviewed, and approved by the new Federal Bureau of Media before marketing. Media programmers must prove "no harm" and provide evidence that content will not result in negative social effects on consumers before marketing approval is granted. Media liability is assumed by the courts for any copying by consumers of stunts, crimes, and other injury-causing behaviors contained in the media. Successful damage suits against the media need only show a similarity in the behavior shown in a media product to subsequent consumer behaviors resulting in harm or injury. To avoid paying compensation, media companies would have to prove that there is no significant relationship between their media content and consumer actions.

Finally, media-based anticrime efforts utilizing the full capabilities of the mass media and media technologies proliferate. Information about wanted suspects is continually run as crawl lines across the bottom of all TV programs. All print, visual, and audio media products are required to carry crime prevention public service announcements, reenactments of unsolved crimes, and Most Wanted fugitive descriptions as 25 percent of their advertising allotment and to give these messages prominent times and placement. Most dramatic, all streets and public spaces in communities with 50,000 or more people and the transportation links between them are under the continuous gaze of a national camera surveillance system. In addition, commercial and corporate camera security systems are tied into the overarching government camera matrix. Each of the millions of separate cameras analyzes its video output, automatically recognizing and flagging behaviors such as assaults, break-ins, fires, injuries, vandalism, speeding, reckless driving, loitering in shopping malls, and unauthorized work breaks in corporate areas. The video streams are linked to allow tracking of individual vehicles and persons from one location to another within a single city or from one city to another across the nation. Face recognition programs notify authorities when people are deemed "out-of-place" and when fugitives or terrorist suspects appear. They also allow retroactive searches for specific individuals and reconstruction of any individual's movements and actions that have occurred in a camera's field of view. Alibis and adherence to probation conditions are frequently checked using the video data files generated by the camera matrix. Augmenting the camera surveillance systems are web and communication tracking software programs accessible by government agencies and private corporations. Although everyone is not watched all the time, it is now possible to determine where the majority of Americans are at any particular time and date.

---

Obviously, neither scenario is attractive. Fortunately neither is likely to come to full fruition, but both are composed of elements and capabilities already available on a smaller scale in the United States and other Western democracies. Neither scenario contains outcomes that cannot be achieved today. The point they make is that it is vital that we understand how the media and crime and justice interact and plan for the type of media crime-and-justice relationship we desire.

## PIXEL POLICY AND CRIMINAL JUSTICE

Half a century ago W. I. Thomas stated that "if actors define situations as real they are real in their consequences."[8] What it is like to live in a society, how its citizens feel about their government, authorities, and neighbors, and the daily social expectations of people are all strongly influenced by what people see, hear, and read about crime and justice. The social construction of crime and justice loops back to influence the entire social reality of a nation.

Therefore, despite being only one of many factors rather than a stand-alone cause, the media cannot be ignored. Exactly how and to what extent the media cause long-term changes in social behavior remains unknown, but it is clear that they play an important, but not autonomous role. The media are one engine in the crime production process, working in combination with other more significant engines, increasing and exacerbating the crime production thrust of other social engines. Ethnic violence, racial strife, oppressive living conditions, violent cultural history, economic disparities, family destruction, and interpersonal violence are all more important for crime levels and all are subject to enhancement by the media. As with individuals, it seems that the media alone cannot criminalize a country—but once a country criminalizes its media through an emphasis on predatory and unrealistic portraits, a slow spiral of increased crime and tolerance for crime begins.[9] For modern societies, the media set the expectations and moral boundaries for crime, guide the public policies, and steer the social construction of crime-and-justice reality.

It must be emphasized that the single most significant social effect of media crime-and-justice content is not its direct generation of crime or other behavioral effects but its effect on criminal justice policies. The fear and loathing we feel toward criminals is tied to our media-generated image of criminality. We see numerous portraits about atypical occurrences near and far, and we see them day after day. The media portray criminals as typically animalistic, vicious predators. The public debate is flooded with dire warnings and sensational crime stories imbedded in a burlesque media, which is predominantly characterized by the demands of the marketplace. This image translates into a more violent society by influencing the way we react to all crime in America. We imprison at a much greater rate and make reentry into law-abiding society, even for our nonviolent offenders, more difficult than other advanced but less violent nations. The predator criminal image results in crime-and-justice policy being based on our worst-case criminals with a constant ratcheting up of punishments for all offenders. In its cumulative effect, media constructions provide both violent models to emulate and justification for a myopic, harshly punitive public reaction to all offenders.

The most important lesson running through this book is that a social construction competition is ongoing. The media are both reflections of reality and engines in the reality production process. If media prominence and a society imbedded in a multimedia web is a description of the present, we can expect the media to remain architectural agents of the future and an important social construction engine. Although not the sole or even the most powerful cause, the media are tied into the other crime-generating social engines and their influence is recycled, enhanced, and compounded. The result is a national character and crime-and-justice reality that is individualistic, materialistic, and violence prone. The media's enhancing role does not go totally unrecognized, however. Stuart Poyntz, discussing the problem of illegal drugs, clearly describes the link:

> American's popular commercial media—television, daily newspapers, music videos and movies—sets the stage for how we understand the symptoms, the people, the setting in which the War on Drugs takes place. It constructs or represents the layers of images which, over the course of time, have become the taken-for-granted stories we associate with the phrase, "the War on Drugs." But the way this whole process of representation works is not simple. The images we associate with the War on Drugs are part of a social construction—images assembled together which tell us what a particular social issue is about—but a social construction with a paradox: there is now so much media attention around drugs that the end result has not been an advance in the level of understanding or debate around this issue, but an obfuscation of debate. Hysteria reigns and a sensible, rational discussion of how illegal drugs are to be dealt with in society seems almost impossible, even as we see more movies and more television programs, and spend more money trying to deal with the problem.[10]

The phrase "War on Crime" could be substituted for "War on Drugs" in the above comments without any loss of validity. An obscuring flood of

Balancing the reality of crime-and-justice media and traditional
American values will be a 21st-century dilemma.

media information about crime and justice flows unabated today. Perhaps
wider recognition of the media, crime, and justice relationship will lessen
its policy impact in the future. As it now stands, by encouraging the public
to ignore the actual sources of crime-and-justice reality and not to question
the media-constructed crime-and-justice reality, the media continue to
function as much as a means of avoiding the reality of crime and justice as a
means of constructing it.

## DISCUSSION QUESTIONS

1.  Discuss which scenario is most disturbing and what steps you would
    support (increased censorship, for example) or what social conditions
    you might tolerate (less privacy, for example) to prevent either
    scenario from becoming reality.
2.  Discuss the social forces and trends that encourage and discourage
    development of the two scenarios presented in this chapter. How
    might technological changes in the media affect each scenario's like-
    lihood of becoming reality?

## In-Class Activity

With the class playing the role of network producers, present and pitch the new reality crime-and-justice program and the anticrime PSA you have created in the assignment below. Have the class rate program proposals on costs, ratings potential, accuracy, and social impact. Rate the PSAs on their potential to reach target audiences and to reduce targeted behaviors, costs, unplanned consequences such as increased fear, and likelihood of obtaining funding and sponsorship. Discuss which proposed programs and PSAs would have the best chance of actually being created in today's media and social environment.

## Assignments

1.  Create a crime-and-justice television program for Scenario 1 (unrestrained infotainment) complete with a target audience, celebrity guests, likely sponsors, and a script for a thirty-second promo for the new program.
2.  Develop a new line of anticrime advertisements and script out a thirty-second PSA (public service announcement) complete with a marketing plan, mascot, celebrity spokespersons, funding potential and sponsors, and target crime and offender audience.

## Suggested Readings

David Croteau and William Hoynes. 2001. *The Business of Media*. Thousand Oaks, CA: Pine Forge Press.

Vincent Sacco. 2005. *When Crime Waves*. Thousand Oaks, CA: Sage.

Gabriel Weimann. 2000. *Communicating Unreality: Modern Media and the Reconstruction of Reality*. Thousand Oaks, CA: Sage.

Michael Wolf. 1999. *The Entertainment Economy*. New York: Random House.

## Notes

1.  Sotirovic, "Affective and Cognitive Processes as Mediators of Media Influences on Crime-Policy Preferences," 313.
2.  Gorelick, "Join Our War," 429.

3.    Manning, "Media Loops."

4.    Penfold, "The Star's Image, Victimization and Celebrity Culture," 289.

5.    Mathiesen, "The Eagle and the Sun."

6.    Rushkoff, "Media: It's the Real Thing."

7.    Meyrowitz, *No Sense of Place*, 319.

8.    Thomas, *Social Behavior and Personality*, 81.

9.    Rapping, *Law and Justice as Seen on TV*.

10.    Poyntz, "Homey, I Shot the Kids: Hollywood and the War on Drugs," 8.

# Glossary

**abuse of power media trials**   A trial in which the defendant occupies a position of trust, prestige, or authority. The general rule is the higher the rank, the more media interest in the case.

**announcement effect**   Media audience behavior changes in anticipation of a new criminal justice policy that has been heavily publicized in the media.

**anticipatory effects**   Policy changes made when criminal justice officials respond in a proactive manner to anticipated local media, reversing the usual order wherein media attention to an issue causes criminal justice policy changes.

**authority and control correctional films**   A pessimistic cinematic view of corrections against a backdrop of riots and escapes by offenders confined for less serious offenses; this genre is most significant for immortalizing the "smug hack" portrait of correctional officers.

**backwards law**   The idea that media will present an image of criminality opposite that of crime-and-justice reality. In every subject category—crimes, criminals, crime fighters, attorneys, correctional officers, and inmates; the investigation of crimes and making of arrests; the processing and disposition of cases; and the experience of incarceration—the media construct and present a crime-and-justice world that is the opposite of the real world.

**biological theories of crime**   Crime is the result of innate genetic differences or the constitutional nature of criminals.

**business and professional criminals**   A media criminality frame is which criminals are characterized as shrewd, ruthless, often violent, ladies' men for whom crime is another form of work or business, similar to other careers but more exciting and rewarding.

**CCTV (closed circuit television)**   A limited access video system and the most common media technology used in surveillance systems. The term CCTV has become a common acronym for public safety surveillance systems regardless of the underlying technology employed.

**citizen crime fighters**   Two groups of crime fighters popular in the media: private investigators (PIs), who occupy the boundary between civilians and police officers as independent law enforcement contractors, and personally motivated private citizens who take on solving crimes as a hobby or due to some personal connection with a victim.

**claims makers**   The promoters, activists, professional experts, and spokespersons with a particular point of view who make specific claims about a social problem or condition.

**commodification**   The for-profit packaging and marketing of crime information for popular consumption.

**conversational reality**   Information people receive directly from people close to and similar to them, which is combined with personal experiences to make up the most influential social construction engine.

**cops**   A media law enforcement frame that constructs the local police as aggressive, crime fighting, take-no-prisoners, frontline soldiers in the war on crime.

**copycat crime**   A crime inspired by an earlier, media-publicized or portrayed crime that can be linked to the media attention.

**correctional horrors**   Negative correctional news stories often employing the death of an inmate as a symbol of the correctional system's failure and that are exemplified by corruption and misconduct exposés.

**corrections backwards law**   The backwards law applied to the media construction of corrections in which a role reversal derived from the media portrait of underdog, wrongly jailed inmate heroes are pitted against oppressive, smug hack correctional employees.

**counterproductive effects**   Media-based anticrime campaigns that have effects opposite to the campaign goal of crime reduction.

**criminogenic media**   Media content that is hypothesized as a direct cause of crime.

**diffusion effects**   Associated with surveillance systems, diffusion is a bonus benefit from the use of surveillance technology. Offenders are not aware of the boundaries of surveillance coverage and therefore reduce their offenses in adjacent nonsurveilled areas. See also *displacement effects*.

**digital manipulation of visual images**   Doctoring images through mixing real and nonexistent elements to distort, alter, or fabricate images of the world to produce realistic final images. Public knowledge of this capability undermines the previously unquestioned validity given to photographs as evidence and proof.

**displacement effects**   Associated with the use of surveillance systems, displacement pushes crime into adjacent communities without surveillance systems. See also *diffusion effects*.

**echo effects**   The tendency for criminal justice officials to treat defendants in unpublicized cases harshly if the press has been demanding such treatment for defendants in similar publicized cases.

**episodic format**   The most common crime news format—in which a particular crime is described and a resulting case is followed. Episodic formatted stories encourage viewers to place responsibility on the individual and to ignore societal forces by focusing on the question: Why did this individual commit this crime? See *thematic format*.

**evil strangers media trials**   Trials composed of two subgroups: non-American suspects or psychotic killers. Non-American evil stranger media trials involve ethnic and minority advocates of various unpopular causes. Psychotic killer media trials focus on bizarre murder cases in which the defendant is portrayed as a maddened, predatory killer.

**experienced reality**   Knowledge gained from one's directly experienced world; all of the events that have happened to you.

**factual and legal guilt**   The difference between having committed a criminal act (factual guilt) versus being legally responsible (legal guilt) and thus appropriate for punishment.

**factual claims**   Statements that purport to describe the world and "what" happened; they are put forth as objective, true "facts" about the world.

**frames**   Prepackaged constructions that include factual and interpretative claims and associated recommended policies. A frame is a fully developed social construction that allows the categorization, labeling, and conceptualization of new real-world events that fit into a preexisting frame.

**freedom and release correctional films**   A cinematic view of corrections that emphasizes extreme violence, such as prison action films. The ambiguity and confusion about the function and role of prisons in society is reflected in these films. The keepers are certifiably crazy or dehumanized and the constructed correctional world reflects the comics more than any recognizable social reality.

**Freedom of Information Act**   Legislation that states that information held by federal agencies must be available to the public unless the information falls within nine specific exempt categories.

**front-end loaded**   The media portrait of crime and justice that concentrates on crimes and their investigation and solution. The activities of criminals and law enforcement or citizen crime fighters are of primary interest, and criminal justice procedures are largely ignored.

**G-men**   A media law enforcement frame that originated in the 1930s and focuses on effective, professional, federal "crime busters."

**Government in Sunshine Act**   A federal law requiring that meetings of government agencies and departments be open to the public.

**hero inmate**   The dominant media construction of male prisoners, which employs the role reversal of offenders being caught up in a corrupt criminal justice system and shown as victims and heroes.

**ideal heroes**   Ideal heroes display the admirable qualities of sacrifice, nobleness, and strength. Sometimes they are traditional by-the-book police officers, but frequently they are rogue officers or civilians.

**ideal offenders**   The outsiders, strangers, foreigners, aliens, and intruders who lack essential humanity and rehabilitative potential.

**ideal victims**   The innocent, naïve, trusting, and protection-needing humans; children are the most ideal of the ideal victims in the media.

**immanent justice**   Belief that a divine power will intervene and reveal the guilty while protecting the innocent. Similar to the medieval socially constructed reality that made trial by combat logical, the modern media reality relies on the moral superiority of the crime fighter to ultimately defeat criminality. Criminality is reduced to an individual moral battle of good versus evil.

**infotainment**   Media content that delivers information about the world in an entertainment format.

**interactivity**   Media story lines and content that are influenced as they are created by consumer actions and decisions.

**interpretative claims**   Statements that focus on the meanings of events and either offer an explanation of why the world is as described in associated factual claims or offer a course of action and public policy that needs to be followed.

**lampooned police**   A popular media frame that satirizes law enforcement as foolish, slapstick police work.

**legal guilt**   See *factual and legal guilt*.

**linkage**   Association of one social construction effort with another previously accepted construction so that the significance of the first construction is connected to the latter.

**looping**    Reuse of media content in new contexts and media products.

**mainstreaming**    The idea that the media affect some viewers more than others regardless of exposure level, influencing heavy television consumers who are currently not in the mainstream to move toward it, while not affecting those already in the mainstream. In total effect, the media are hypothesized to be homogenizing society.

**media-oriented terrorism**    A terrorist strategy where the primary goal of a terror campaign is to attract media attention.

**media-oriented terrorist event (MOTE)**    A terrorist act designed and carried out in a manner that maximizes media attention. MOTEs are frequently characterized by the selection of high-visibility targets and locations, graphic dramatic terrorist acts, pre-event contact with media outlets, and postevent videos, interviews, and other media accommodations.

**media trials**    A regional or national crime or justice event in which the media co-opt the criminal justice system as a source of drama, entertainment, and profit. They involve the social construction of selected trials as infotainment products that are commodified and mass marketed. Coverage is live whenever possible, pictures are preferred over text, and content is characterized by conjecture and sensationalism. See *abuse of power media trials*, *evil strangers media trials*, and *sinful rich media trials*.

**media weapons cult**    The media portrait of weapons, especially handguns, that downplays their negative aspects (rarely is the pain of a gunshot realistically shown) and enhances their usefulness as problem solvers and crime-fighting tools. In the media, the people who get their way, both heroes and villains, are the ones who have the guns.

**mediated experience**    The comparative experience an individual has when he or she experiences an event via the media versus actually physically being at an event.

**memorial criminal justice policy**    Linking a criminal justice policy and legislation to an individual by name (such as the Brady law and Amber Alerts); the person is usually the victim of a violent, deadly crime.

**modeling personality**    An individual who looks to and sees other people and the media as profitable crime information sources; these individuals are hypothesized to be particularly susceptible to media copycat effects.

**multimedia web**    The interconnected and pervasive mix of contemporary media exemplified by the constant looping of media content.

**narratives**    Recurring preestablished social roles, characters, and story lines found throughout crime-and-justice media. Narratives are usually associated with a single individual or crime rather than with general criminality or a criminal justice issue.

**narrowcasting**    Marketing media content to small special interest self-selecting groups rather than to large, heterogeneous mass markets. Originally applied to television marketing with the introduction of cable networks, today the principle is applicable to all media.

**nature of confinement correctional films**    A cinematic view of corrections in which inmates are victims of injustice; a good man is either framed or accidentally imprisoned or pushed into crime by powerful societal forces. A recurrent message in this genre is the pervasive corruption of the correctional system and its administrators.

**on-demand**    Time and place access to media content is determined by the consumer rather than by the producer of the content.

**ownership**    Identification of a social condition with a particular set of claims makers who come to dominate the social construction of that issue. Claims makers own an issue when they are sought out by the media and others for information regarding its nature and policy solutions.

**pixel policy**   The fast-paced, media-driven development of contemporary public policy, especially noticeable in crime-and-justice policy formation.

**police procedurals**   A media law enforcement frame that concentrates on the dramatic backstage realities of police investigations. The crime fighters in these portraits normally rely heavily on teamwork and criminalistics to solve crimes.

**police reality programs**   Highly edited television productions in which viewers are invited to share a cop's point-of-view as a partner officer in voyeuristic ride-alongs.

**political theories of crime**   The idea that the political and economic structure of a society are the root causes of crime.

**predatory criminality**   The most common portrait of criminality found in the media, which is characterized by criminals who are animalistic, irrational, innate predators committing violent and senseless crimes.

**prejudicial publicity**   Dissemination by the media of either factual information that bears on the guilt of a defendant or emotional information without evidentiary relevance that simply arouses emotions against a defendant.

**priming**   When people read, hear about, or witness a criminal event via the mass media, priming influences them to hold similar ideas and results in related copycat acts.

**Privacy Act**   A federal or state statute that prohibits the invasion of a person's right to be left alone, restricts access to personal information, and prohibits interception of private communications. The federal Privacy Act permits an individual to access records containing personal information and to control the transfer of that information to other agencies.

**private investigator (PI)**   Nongovernmental independent contractors of law enforcement.

**privileged conversation**   A constitutionally based argument to protect journalists from having to divulge unpublished story information or to identify their sources. It is argued that a privileged conversation protection is needed so that journalists can fulfill their constitutional function as watchdogs of government activities and guarantee future access to story information and sources.

**proactive mechanisms**   Judicial measures such as closure, restrictive orders, and protective orders that are employed to counteract the production of news media publicity. The proactive approach to dealing with publicity directly clashes with the First Amendment protection of freedom of the press and has been vigorously resisted by the media.

**prosocial television**   Programs of various types (animated, adventure, comedy, fantasy) that have the ability to elicit socially valued behaviors and attitudes from viewers. *Sesame Street* is a well-known example.

**psychological theories of crime**   The idea that crime is caused by defective personality development.

**psychotic super-male criminals**   A popular media frame of criminality in which criminals possess an evil, cunning intelligence and superior strength, endurance, and stealth. Crimes committed by media psychotic super-males are generally acts of twisted, lustful revenge or random acts of irrational violence.

**public agenda**   The ranked list of social problems the public see as important and needing to be addressed.

**public service announcements (PSAs)**   Information disseminated in the media in ad-style messages. Anticrime PSAs are a common means of getting crime prevention information to the public.

**pursuit of justice correctional films**   A cinematic view of corrections where offenders are personally responsible for their actions and confinement is therefore justified. Although many of these films revolve around violence—riots, escapes, and assaults—individual offender rehabilitation is seen as possible.

**rational choice theories of crime**   The idea that crime is a rational, free-will decision that individuals will make when the gains from committing a crime outweigh the likelihood of punishment.

**reactive mechanisms**   Judicial procedures used to counteract the effects of news media publicity, which include expanding the jury selection (the voir dire), granting trial continuances, granting changes of venue, sequestering jurors, and giving special instructions to the jury.

**shield laws**   Legislation to prevent the forced divulgence of sources and testimony from journalists.

**sinful rich media trials**   Cases in which socially prominent defendants are involved in bizarre or sexually related crimes.

**smug hack**   The dominant media portrayal of correctional officers as caricatures of brutality, incompetence, low intelligence, and indifference to human suffering.

**smug hack corrections**   The dominant media construction of corrections that emphasizes physically brutal inmate discipline, corporal punishment and the infliction of pain, and the exploitation of inmates as a cheap source of labor and profit. Staff incompetence, corruption, and cruelty are common, ingrained, and unchallenged. Prisoners suffer systemic racial prejudice, homosexual rape, and between prisoner assaults.

**social constructionism**   A theoretical view that knowledge is socially created. Social constructionism focuses on human relationships and the way relationships affect how people perceive reality. Social constructionism studies the shared ideas, interpretations, and knowledge that groups of people agree to hold in common.

**socially constructed reality**   The reality perceived as the "real" world by each individual. It is constructed from knowledge each individual gains from his or her experienced and symbolic realities mixed together. The resulting constructed reality is what we individually believe the world to be like.

**sociological theories of crime**   The idea that criminal environments cause crime, and that people are criminals because of the people they associate with or share a neighborhood or culture with.

**surveillance effect**   The psychological effect of believing that you might be under observation.

**symbolic crimes**   Crimes and other criminal justice events that are selected and highlighted by claims makers as perfect examples to support a particular crime-and-justice construction.

**symbolic reality**   Knowledge of the world gained from other people, institutions, and the media that is shared via symbols, language being the most common symbolic system to share knowledge. Art, music, and mathematics are others.

**thematic format**   A crime news format that highlights trends, persistent problems, or other systemic phenomena. Stories told in the thematic format explore broader issues of causes and effects and focus on the question: A set of problems has developed, what changed in society? See *episodic format*.

**true crime**   A media law enforcement infotainment frame wherein the audience looks over the criminal's (frequently a killer) or cop's shoulder as they either commit crime or pursue criminals and solve murders.

**ultraviolence**   A media style popular since the 1960s that portrays violence using slow motion, detonating blood capsules, multiple camera views, and graphic visuals and special effects.

**victims and heroic criminals**   The least common media criminality frame, it presents criminals as either victims of injustice or unrecognized good guys. This frame often supports sociological and political explanations of crime.

**video lineups**   A crime witness is shown a series of videotaped images selected for their similarity.

**video mug books**   A computer searches a pictorial data file for specific characteristics (for example, tattoo, bald, heavy, white, and male) and displays matching pictures.

**videotaped interrogations**   Videotaped interactions between police and suspects that provide visual evidence regarding the physical and mental condition of suspects, the voluntariness of their statements, their understanding of their rights, and the use of coercion and adherence to standard interrogation practices by the police.

**worldview cultivation**   A media effect that hypothesizes that watching many hours of television will result in viewers holding general perceptions about the world as being a pernicious and dangerous place.

# References

Adoni, Hanna, and Sherrill Mane. 1984. "Media and the Social Construction of Reality." *Communication Research* 11, no. 3: 323–340.

Alexander, Yonah. 1979. "Terrorism and the Media: Some Considerations." In *Terrorism: Theory and Practice,* ed. Yonah Alexander, David Carlton, and Paul Wilkinson, 159–174. Boulder, CO: Westview Press.

Allen, Jesica, Sonia Livingstone, and Robert Reiner. 1998. "True Lies: Changing Images of Crime in British Postwar Cinema." *European Journal of Communication* 13, no. 1: 53–75.

"The All-Seeing Eye." 1997. *The Economist* 342, no. 7999 (January 11).

Altheide, David. 2002. *Creating Fear*. New York: Aldine de Gruyter.

Altheide, David, and Robert Snow. 1979. *Media Logic*. Thousand Oaks, CA: Sage.

Altheide, David, and Robert Snow. 1991. *Media Worlds in the Postjournalism Era*. Hawthorne, NY: Aldine de Gruyter.

Ambrose, Stephen. 2000. *Nothing Like It in the World*. New York: Simon & Schuster.

American Association of Advertising Agencies. 1990. *What We've Learned about Advertising from the Media-Advertising Partnership for a Drug-Free America*. New York: Author.

"Americans OK with Video Scrutiny." 2002. New York: CBS News Poll (April 21).

Armour, Robert. 1980. *Film*. Westport, CT: Greenwood Press.

Bailey, Frankie, Joycelyn M. Pollock, and Sherry Schroeder. 1998. "The Best Defense: Images of Female Attorneys in Popular Films." In *Popular Culture, Crime and Justice,* ed. Frankie Bailey and Donna Hale, 180–195. Belmont, CA: Wadsworth.

Ball, Milner. 1981. *The Promise of American Law*. Athens: University of Georgia Press.

Barber, Susanne. 1987. *News Cameras in the Courtroom*. Norwood, NJ: Ablex.

Barrile, Leo. 1984. "Television and Attitudes about Crime: Do Heavy Viewers Distort Criminality and Support Retributive Justice?" In *Justice and the Media,* ed. Ray Surette, 141–158. Springfield, IL: Thomas.

Beckett, Katherine, and Ted Sasson. 2000. *The Politics of Injustice: Crime and Punishment in America*. Thousand Oaks, CA: Pine Forge Press.

Bennett, W. Lance. 1996. *News: The Politics of Illusion*. New York: Longman.

Berkowitz, Leon. 1984. "Some Effects of Thoughts on Anti- and Prosocial Influences of Media Events: A Cognitive-Neoassociation Analysis." *Psychological Bulletin* 95: 410–417.

Berkowitz, Leon, and K. Rogers. 1986. "A Priming Effect Analysis of Media Influences." In *Perspectives on Media Effects*, ed. Jennings Bryant and Dolf Zillman, 57–81. Hillsdale, NJ: Erlbaum.

Best, Joel. 1991. *Images of Issues: Typifying Contemporary Social Problems*. New York: Aldine de Gruyter.

Best, Joel. 2001. "The Diffusion of Social Problems." In *How Claims Spread: Cross-National Diffusion of Social Problems*, ed. Joel Best, 1–18. New York: Aldine de Gruyter.

Best, Joel, and Mary Hutchinson. 1996. "The Gang Initiation Rite as a Motif in Contemporary Crime Discourse." *Justice Quarterly* 13: 383–404.

Black, Gordon. 1988. *Changing Attitudes toward Drug Use: Executive Summary and Statistical Report*. Rochester, NY: Partnership for a Drug-Free America.

Bleyer, Willard. 1927. *Main Currents in the History of American Journalism*. Boston: Houghton Mifflin.

Blumer, Herbert. 1933. *The Movies and Conduct*. New York: Macmillan.

Blumer, Herbert, and Paul Hauser. 1933. *Movies, Delinquency, and Crime*. New York: Macmillan.

Borg, Marian. 1997. "The Structure of Social Monitoring in the Process of Social Control." *Deviant Behavior* 18: 273–293.

Boyle, Karen. 2005. *Media and Violence: Gendering the Debates*. Thousand Oaks, CA: Sage.

Brants, Kees, and Peter Neijens. 1998. "The Infotainment of Politics." *Political Communication* 15: 149–164.

Broe, Dennis. 2003. "Class, Crime, and Film Noir." *Social Justice* 30, no. 1: 22–41.

Brown, Ben. 1995. *CCTV in Town Centres: Three Case Studies*. Police Research Group Crime Detection and Prevention Series, paper no 68. London, UK: Home Office Police Department.

Brown, Ben, and William Reed Benedict. 2002. "Perceptions of the Police." *Policing* 25, no. 3: 543–580.

Bruschke, Jon, and William Loges. 2004. *Free Press vs. Fair Trials*. Mahwah, NJ: Erlbaum.

Burrows, John. 1980. "Closed Circuit Television and Crime on the London Underground." In *Designing Out Crime*, ed. Ronald Clarke and Patricia Mayhew, 75–83. London: H. M. Stationery Office for Home Office Research Unit.

Callanan, Valerie. 2005. *Feeding the Fear of Crime: Crime-related Media and Support for Three Strikes*. New York: LFB Scholarly Publishing LLC.

Canter, Christopher, Peter Sheehan, Philip Alpers, and Paul Mullen. 1999. "Media and Mass Homicides." *Archives of Suicide Research* 5: 283–290.

Cavender, Gray 1998. "In the Shadow of Shadow: Television Reality Crime Programming." In *Entertaining Crime: Television Reality Programs*, ed. Mark Fishman and Gray Cavender, 79–94. New York: Aldine de Gruyter.

Cavender, Gray. 2004. "In Search of Community on Reality TV." In *Understanding Reality*, ed. Su Homes and Deborah Jermyn, 154–172. New York: Routledge.

Cavender, Gray, and Mark Fishman. 1998. "Television Reality Crime Programs: Context and History." In *Entertaining Crime: Television Reality Programs*, ed. Mark Fishman and Gray Cavender, 3–15. New York: Aldine De Gruyter.

*Chandler v. Florida,* 101 S. Ct (1981).

Charter, Werrett. 1933. *Motion Pictures and Youth: A Summary.* New York: Macmillan.

Cheatwood, Derral. 1998. "Prison Movies: Films about Adult, Male, Civilian Prisons; 1929–1995." In *Popular Culture, Crime, and Justice,* ed. Frankie Bailey and Donna Hale, 209–231. Belmont, CA: Wadsworth.

Cheatwood, Derrel. 2001. *Early Images of Crime and Criminal Justice: Commercial Radio from 1929 to 1962.* Paper presented at the American Society of Criminology, Atlanta, GA.

Chermak, Steven. 1995. *Victims in the News.* Boulder, CO: Westview Press.

Chermak, Steven. 1998. "Police, Courts, and Corrections in the Media." In *Popular Culture, Crime and Justice,* ed. Frankie Bailey and Donna Hale, 87–99. Belmont, CA: Wadsworth.

Chiasson, Lloyd. 1997. *The Press on Trial: Crimes and Trials as Media Events.* Westport, CT: Greenwood Press.

Christie, Nils. 1986. "The Ideal Victim." In *From Crime Policy to Victim Policy: Reorienting the Justice System,* ed. Essat A. Fattah, 17–30. New York: St. Martin's Press.

Cole, Jeffery. 1996. *The UCLA Television Violence Monitoring Report.* Los Angeles: UCLA Center for Communication Policy.

Conrich, Ian. 2003. "Mass Media/Mass Murder: Serial Killer Cinema and the Modern Violated Body." In *Criminal Visions: Media Representations of Crime and Justice,* ed. Paul Mason, 156–171. Devon, UK: Willan.

Cook, Thomas, Debra Kendzierski, and Steven Thomas. 1983. "The Implicit Assumptions of Television Research: An Analysis of the 1982 NIMH Report on Television and Behavior." *Public Opinion Quarterly* 47: 161–201.

Courtwright, David. 1996. *Violent Land: Single Men and Social Disorder from the Frontier to the Inner City.* Cambridge: Harvard University Press.

Curran, James. 1982. "Communications, Power and Social Order." In *Culture, Society and the Media,* ed. Michael Gurevitch, Tony Bennett, James Curran, and Janet Woollacott, 202–235. London: Methuen.

Dale, Edgar. 1935. *Children's Attendance at Motion Pictures.* New York: Macmillan.

DeFleur, Melvin, and Sandra Ball-Rokeach. 1975. *Theories of Mass Communication.* New York: McKay.

Ditton, Jason, Derek Chadee, Stephen Farrall, Elizabeth Gilchrist, and Jon Bannister. 2004. "From Imitation to Intimidation." *British Journal of Criminology* 44, no. 4: 595–610.

Dominick, Joseph. 1978. "Crime and Law Enforcement in the Mass Media." In *Deviance and Mass Media,* ed. Charles Winick, 105–128. Thousand Oaks, CA.: Sage.

Donovan, Pamela. 1998. "Armed with the Power of Television: Reality Crime Programming and the Reconstruction of Law and Order in the United States." In *Entertaining Crime,* ed. Mark Fishman and Gray Cavender, 117–140. New York: Aldine de Gruyter.

Dowler, Kenneth. 2003. "Media Consumption and Public Attitudes toward Crime and Justice: The Relationship between Fear of Crime, Punitive Attitudes, and Perceived Police Effectiveness." *Journal of Criminal Justice and Popular Culture* 10, no. 2: 109–126.

Dowler, Kenneth. 2004. "Comparing American and Canadian Local Television Crime Stories: A Content Analysis." *Canadian Journal of Criminology and Criminal Justice* 46, no. 5: 573–596.

Doyle, Aaron. 1998. "Cops: Television Policing as Policing Reality." In *Entertaining Crime*, ed. Mark Fishman and Gray Cavender, 95–116. New York: Aldine de Gruyter.

Doyle, Aaron. 2003. *Arresting Images: Crime and Policing in Front of the Television Camera.* Toronto: University of Toronto Press.

Doyle, Aaron, and Richard Ericson. 1996. "Breaking into Prison: News Sources and Correctional Institutions." *Canadian Journal of Criminology* (April): 155–190.

Drucker, Susan. 1989. "The Televised Mediated Trial: Formal and Substantive Characteristics." *Communication Quarterly* 37: 305–318.

Duwe, Grant. 2000. "Body-Count Journalism: The Presentation of Mass Murder in the News Media." *Homicide Studies* 4, no. 4: 364–399.

Eschholz, Sarah, Ted Chiricos, and Marc Gertz. Forthcoming. "Television and Fear of Crime: Program Types, Audience Traits and the Mediating Effect of Perceived Neighborhood Racial Composition." *Social Problems*.

Eschholz, Sarah, Matthew Mallard, and Stacey Flynn. 2004. "Images of Prime Time Justice." *Journal of Criminal Justice and Popular Culture* 10, no. 3: 161–180.

*Estes v. Texas*, 381 U.S. (1965).

Ferrel, Jeff. 1998. "Criminalizing Popular Culture." In *Popular Culture, Crime, and Justice*, ed. Frankie Bailey and Donna Hale, 71–83. Belmont, CA: Wadsworth.

Fishman, Mark, and Gray Cavender. 1998. *Entertaining Crime: Television Reality Programs.* New York: Aldine de Gruyter.

Freedman, Jonathan. 2002. *Media Violence and Its Effect on Aggression.* Toronto: University of Toronto Press.

Freeman, Robert. 1998. "Public Perception and Corrections: Correctional Officers as Smug Hacks." In *Popular Culture, Crime, and Justice*, ed. Frankie Bailey and Donna Hale, 196–208. Belmont, CA: Wadsworth.

Freeman, Robert. 2000. *Popular Culture and Corrections.* Lanham, MD: American Correctional Association.

Gerbner, George, Larry Gross, Michael Morgan, and Nancy Signorielli. 1994. "Growing Up with Television: The Cultivation Perspective." In *Media Effects*, ed. Jennings Bryant and Dolf Zillman, 17–41. Hillsdale, NJ: Erlbaum.

Gergen, Kenneth. 1985. "Social Constructionist Inquiry: Context and Implications." In *The Social Construction of the Person*, ed. Kenneth Gergen and K. Davis, 3–18. New York: Springer-Verlag.

Gest, Ted. 2001. *Crime and Politics.* London, UK: Oxford University Press.

Getty, Carol. 2001. "Media Wise." *Corrections Today* 63 (7): 126–131.

Gill, Martin. 2003. *CCTV.* Leicester: Perpetuity Press.

Gillespie, Marie, and Eugene McLaughlin. 2002. "Media and the Shaping of Public Attitudes." *Criminal Justice Matters* (Autumn): 8–9, 23.

Gilliam, Franklin, and Shanto Iyengar. 2000. "Prime Suspects: The Influence of Local Television News on the Viewing Public." *American Journal of Political Science* 44, no. 3: 560–573.

Goold, Benjamin. 2004. *CCTV and Policing.* Oxford, UK: Oxford University Press.

Gordon, Margaret, and Linda Heath. 1981. "The News Business, Crime, and Fear." In *Reactions to Crime,* ed. D. Lewis, 227–247. Thousand Oaks, CA: Sage.

Gorelick, Steven. 1989. "Join Our War: The Construction of Ideology in a Newspaper Crimefighting Campaign." *Crime and Delinquency* 35: 421–436.

Gorn, Elliott. 1992. "The Wicked World: The National Police Gazette and Gilded-Age America." *Media Studies Journal* 6: 3–4.

Graber, Doris. 1980. *Crime News and the Public.* New York: Praeger.

Graber, Doris. 1994. "The Infotainment Quotient in Routine Television News: A Director's Perspective." *Discourse and Society* 5: 483–509.

Graham, Stephen. 1998. "Toward the Fifth Utility? On the Extension and Normalization of Public CCTV." In *Surveillance, Closed Circuit Television and Social Control,* ed. Clive Norris, Jade Moran, and Gary Armstrong. Aldershot, UK: Ashgate.

Graham, Stephen. 1999. "The Eyes Have It—CCTV as the 'Fifth Utility'." *Town and Country Planning* 68: 312–315.

Grant, Alan. 1990. "The Videotaping of Police Interrogations in Canada." In *The Media and Criminal Justice Policy,* ed. Ray Surette, 265–276. Springfield, IL: Thomas.

Greenfield, Steve, and Guy Osborn. 2003. "Film Lawyers: Above and Beyond the Law." In *Criminal Visions: Media Representations of Crime and Justice,* ed. Paul Mason, 238–253. Devon, UK: Willan.

Gunter, Barrie. 1998. *The Effects of Video Games on Children: The Myth Unmasked.* Sheffield, UK: Sheffield Academic Press.

Gunter, Barrie, Jackie Harrison, and Maggie Wykes. 2003. *Violence on Television: Distribution, Form, Context, and Themes.* Mahwah, NJ: Erlbaum.

Hagell, Ann, and Tim Newburn. 1994. *Young Offenders and the Media: Viewing Habits and Preferences.* London: Policy Studies Institute.

Hallett, Michael, and Dennis Powell. 1995. "Backstage with *COPS:* The Dramaturgical Reification of Police Subculture in American Crime Infotainment." *American Journal of Police* 14, no. 1: 101–129.

Hariman, Robert. 1990. "Performing the Laws: Popular Trials and Social Knowledge." In *Popular Trials: Rhetoric, Mass Media, and the Law,* ed. Robert Hariman, 17–30. Tuscaloosa: University of Alabama Press.

Hayes, Mark. 2003. "Political Violence, Irish Republicanism and the British Media: Semantics, Symbosis and the State." In *Criminal Visions: Media Representations of Crime and Justice,* ed. Paul Mason, 133–155. Devon, UK: Willan.

Hays, Will H. 1932. *President's Report to the Motion Picture Producers and Distributors' Association.* Washington, DC: U.S. Government Printing Office.

Heath, Linda, Linda Bresolin, and Robert Rinaldi. 1989. "Effects of Media Violence on Children: A Review of the Literature." *Archives of General Psychiatry* 46: 376–379.

Heath, Linda, and John Petraitis. 1987. "Television Viewing and Fear of Crime: Where Is the Mean World?" *Basic and Applied Social Psychology* 8: 97–123.

Heller, Melvin, and Samuel Polsky. 1976. *Studies in Violence and Television.* New York: American Broadcasting Company.

Hennigan, Karen, Linda Heath, J. D. Wharton, Marlyn Del Rosario, Thomas Cook, and Bobby Calder. 1982. "Impact of the Introduction of Television on Crime in the United States." *Journal of Personality and Social Psychology* 42: 461–477.

Herbert, Rosemary. 1999. *Oxford Companion to Crime and Mystery Writing*. Oxford, UK: Oxford University Press.

Hickey, Eric. 2004. *Serial Murderers and Their Victims*. Belmont, CA: Wadsworth.

Hirsch, Paul. 1980. "The 'Scary World' of the Nonviewer and Other Anomalies." *Communications Research* 7: 403–456.

Hirsch, Paul. 1981. "On Not Learning from One's Own Mistakes: A Reanalysis of Gerbner et al.'s Findings on Cultivation Analysis, Part II." *Communications Research* 8: 3–37.

Hochstetler, Andrew. 2001. "Reporting of Executions in U.S. Newspapers." *Journal of Crime and Justice* 24, no. 1: 1–11.

Holaday, Perry, and George Stoddard. 1933. *Getting Ideas from the Movies*. New York: Macmillan.

Horne, Chris. 1996. "The Case for: CCTV Should Be Introduced." *International Journal of Risk, Security and Crime Prevention* 1, no. 4: 317–326.

Huesmann, L. Rowell, Jessica Moise-Titus, Cheryl-Lynn Podolski, and Leonard Eron. 2003. "Longitudinal Relations Between Children's Exposure to TV Violence and Their Aggressive and Violent Behavior in Young Adulthood: 1977–1992." *Developmental Psychology* 39, no. 1: 201–221.

Ibarra, Peter, and John Kitsuse. 1993. "Vernacular Constituents of Moral Discourse: An Interactionist Proposal for the Study of Social Problems." In *Reconsidering Social Construction*, ed. John Holstein and Gale Miller, 25–58. New York: Aldine de Gruyter.

Inciardi, James, and Juliet Dee. 1987. "From the Keystone Cops to Miami Vice: Images of Policing in American Popular Culture." *Journal of Popular Culture* 21: 84–102.

Iyengar, Shanto. 1991. *Is Anyone Responsible? How Television Frames Political Issues*. Chicago: University of Chicago Press.

Jacobs, James, and Helen Brooks. 1983. "The Mass Media and Prison News." In *New Perspectives on Prisons and Imprisonment*, ed. James B. Jacobs, 106–115. Ithaca, NY: Cornell University Press.

Jefferis, Eric, Robert Kaminski, Stephen Holmes, and Dena Hanley. 1997. "The Effect of a Videotaped Arrest on Public Perceptions of Police Use of Force." *Journal of Criminal Justice* 25, no. 5: 381–395.

Jenkins, Philip. 1998. *Moral Panic: Changing Concepts of the Child Molester in Modern America*. New Haven, CT: Yale University Press.

Jewkes, Yvonne. 2004. *Media and Crime*. London, UK: Sage.

Jo, Eunkyung, and Leon Berkowitz. 1994. "A Priming Effect Analysis of Media Influences: An Update." In *Media Effects Advances in Theory and Research*, ed. Jennings Bryant and Dolf Zillman. Hillsdale, NJ: Erlbaum.

Johnston, John, Darnell Hawkins, and Arthur Michner. 1994. "Homicide Reporting in Chicago Dailies." *Journalism Quarterly* 71: 860–872.

Kaplan, John, and Jerome Skolnick. 1982. *Criminal Justice*. Mineola, NY: Foundation Press.

Kirtley, Jane. 1990. "Shield Laws and Reporter's Privilege—A National Assessment." In *The Media and Criminal Justice Policy*, ed. Ray Surette, 163–176. Springfield, IL: Thomas.

Kirtley, Jane. 1995. "A Leap Not Supported by History: The Continuing Story of Cameras in the Federal Courts." *Government Information Quarterly* 12: 367–389.

Kooistra, Paul, John Mahoney, and Saundra Westervelt. 1998. "The World of Crime According to Cops." In *Entertaining Crime: Television Reality Programs,* ed. Mark Fishman and Gray Cavender, 141–158. New York: Aldine de Gruyter.

Lane, Jodi, and James Meeker. 2003. "Ethnicity, Information Sources, and Fear of Crime." *Deviant Behavior* 24: 1–26.

Langer, Gary. 2004. "Legacy of Suspicion." New York: ABC News Poll, July.

Lasorsa, Dominic, and Wayne Wanta. 1990. "Effects of Personal, Interpersonal and Media Experiences on Issue Saliences." *Journalism Quarterly* 67: 804–813.

Lavrakas, Paul, Dennis Rosenbaum, and Arthur Lurigio. 1990. "Media Cooperation with Police: The Case of Crime Stoppers." In *Media and Criminal Justice Policy,* ed. Ray Surette, 225–242. Springfield, IL: Thomas.

Lawrence, Regina. 2000. *The Politics of Force: Media and the Construction of Police Brutality*. Berkeley: University of California Press.

Leishman, Frank, and Paul Mason. 2003. *Policing and the Media: Facts, Fictions, and Factions.* Devon, UK: Willan.

Leitch, Thomas, and Barry Grant. 2002. *Crime Films.* Cambridge: Cambridge University Press.

Lichter, Linda S., and S. Robert Lichter. 1983. *Prime Time Crime*. Washington, DC: Media Institute.

Lichter, S. Robert, Linda S. Lichter, and Stanley Rothman. 1994. *Prime Time.* Washington, DC: Regnery.

Lindesmith, Alfred. 1965. *The Addict and the Law.* Bloomington: Indiana University Press.

Lindlof, Thomas. 1988. "Media Audiences as Interpretive Communities." In *Communication Yearbook 11,* ed. James Anderson, 81–107. Newbury Park, CA: Sage.

Lippmann, Walter. 1922. *Public Opinion.* New York: Macmillan.

Livingstone, Neil. 1982. *The War against Terrorism.* Lexington, MA: Heath.

Loften, John. 1966. *Justice and the Press.* Boston, MA: Beacon Press.

Lotz, Roy. 1991. *Crime and the American Press.* New York: Praeger.

Lowery, Sharon, and Melvin De Fleur. 1983. *Milestones in Mass Communication Research.* White Plains, NY: Longman.

Lynch, Michael, Paul Stretesky, and Paul Hammond. 2000. "Media Coverage of Chemical Crimes, Hillsborough County, Florida, 1987–97." *British Journal of Criminology,* 40: 112–126.

Manning, Peter. 1998. "Media Loops." In *Popular Culture, Crime and Justice,* ed. Frankie Bailey and Donna Hale, 25–39. Belmont, CA: Wadsworth.

Marcus, Paul. 1982. "The Media in the Courtroom: Attending, Reporting, Televising Criminal Cases." *Indiana Law Journal* (Spring): 235–287.

Marighella, Carlos. No date. Minimanual of the Urban Guerrilla. Havana: Tricontinental.

Marsh, Harry. 1991. "A Comparative Analysis of Crime Coverage in Newspapers in the United States and Other Countries from 1960 to 1989: A Review of the Literature." *Journal of Criminal Justice* 19: 67–80.

Marx, Gary. 1988. *Undercover: Police Surveillance in America.* Berkeley: University of California Press.

Marx, Gary. 1996. "Electric Eye in the Sky: Some Reflections on the New Surveillance and Popular Culture." In *Computers, Surveillance, and Privacy,* ed. David Lyon and Elia Zureik, 193–233. Minneapolis: University of Minnesota Press.

Mason, Paul. 2000. "Watching the Invisible: Televisual Portrayal of the British Prison 1980–1990." *International Journal of the Sociology of Law* 28: 33–44.

Mason, Paul. 2003. "The Screen Machine: Cinematic Representations of Prison." In *Criminal Visions: Media Representations of Crime and Justice,* ed. Paul Mason, 278–297. Devon, UK: Willan.

Mathiesen, Thomas. 1987. "The Eagle and the Sun: On Panoptical Systems and Mass Media in Modern Society." In *Transcarceration: Essays in the Sociology of Social Control,* ed. John Lowman, Robert Menzies, and Ted S. Palys, 59–76. Brookfield, VT: Gower.

Mathiesen, Thomas. 1990. *Prison on Trial: A Critical Assessment.* Belmont, CA: Sage.

Mathiesen, Thomas. 2001. "Television, Public Space and Prison Population." *Punishment & Society* 3, no. 1: 35–42.

Mawby, Rob. 2003. "Completing the 'Half-Formed Picture'? Media Images of Policing." In *Criminal Visions: Media Representations of Crime and Justice,* ed. Paul Mason, 214–237. Devon, UK: Willan.

Mawby, Rob, and Judith Brown. 1984. "Newspaper Images of the Victim: A British Study." *Victimology* 9, no. 1: 82–94.

Maxson, Cheryl, Karen Hennigan, and David Sloane. 2003. *Factors that Influence Public Opinion of the Police.* Washington, DC: National Institute of Justice.

Mazur, Allan. 1982. "Bomb Threats and the Mass Media: Evidence for a Theory of Suggestion." *American Sociological Review* 47: 407–411.

Meyers, Marian. 1994. "News of Battering." *Journal of Communication* 44: 47–63.

Meyers, Marian. 1996. *News Coverage of Violence against Women.* Thousand Oaks, CA: Sage.

Meyrowitz, Joshua. 1985. *No Sense of Place.* New York: Oxford University Press.

Miller, Gale, and James Holstein. 1993. *Constructionist Controversies: Issues in Social Problems Theory.* Hawthorne, NY: Aldine de Gruyter.

Morgan, Michael, and James Shanahan. 1997. "Two Decades of Cultivation Research: An Appraisal and Meta-Analysis." *Communication Yearbook* 20: 1–45.

Nasheri, Hedieh. 2002. *Crime and Justice in the Age of Court TV.* New York: LFB Scholarly Publishing LLC.

National Institute of Mental Health. 1982. *Television and Behaviour: Ten Years of Scientific Progress and Implications for the Eighties. Vol. 1. Summary Report.* Rockville, MD: U.S. Government Printing Service.

Newburn, Tim, and Stephanie Hayman. 2002. *Policing, Surveillance and Social Control: CCTV and Police Monitoring of Suspects.* Portland, OR: Willan.

Norris, Clive, and Gary Armstrong. 1999. *The Maximum Surveillance Society: The Rise of CCTV.* Oxford: Berg.

Norris, Clive, Jade Moran, and Gary Armstrong. 1998. *Surveillance, Closed Circuit Television and Social Control.* Aldershot, UK: Ashgate.

Nyberg, Amy. 1998. "Comic Books and Juvenile Delinquency: A Historical Perspective." In *Popular Culture, Crime, and Justice,* ed. Frankie Bailey and Donna Hale, 71–70. Belmont, CA: Wadsworth.

Oberdorfer, Don. 1971. *TET!* Baltimore, MD: Johns Hopkins University Press.

O'Keefe, Garrett, and Kathaleen Reid. 1990. "Media Public Information Campaigns and Criminal Justice Policy: Beyond McGruff." In *Media and Criminal Justice Policy,* ed. Ray Surette, 209–224. Springfield, IL: Thomas.

O'Keefe, Garrett, Dennis Rosenbaum, Paul Lavrakas, Kathaleen Reid, and Renee Botta. 1996. *Taking a Bite Out of Crime.* Thousand Oaks, CA: Sage.

Oliver, Mark. 1994. "Portrayals of Crime, Race, and Aggression in Reality Based Police Shows: A Content Analysis." *Journal of Broadcasting & Electronic Media* 38: 179–192.

Paletz, David, and Alex Schmid. 1992. *Terrorism and the Media.* Newbury Park, CA: Sage.

Papke, David. 1987. *Framing the Criminal.* Hamden, CT: Archon Books.

Parrish, Penny. 1993. "Police and the Media." *FBI Law Enforcement Bulletin* 62, no. 9: 24–25.

Patton, Phil. 1995. "Caught." *Wired* (January): 125–130.

Pease, Susan, and Craig Love. 1984. "The Copy-Cat Crime Phenomenon." In *Justice and the Media*, ed. Ray Surette, 199–211. Springfield, IL: Thomas.

Penfold, Ruth. 2004. "The Star's Image, Victimization and Celebrity Culture." *Punishment and Society* 6, no. 3: 289–302.

Perez-Pena, Richard. 1995. "'How-To' Film May Have Inspired Subway Attack." *Miami Herald* (November 27): A3.

Perlmutter, David. 2000. *Policing the Media: Street Cops and Public Perceptions of Law Enforcement.* Thousand Oaks, CA: Sage.

Peterson, Ruth, and L. L. Thurstone. 1933. *Motion Pictures and the Social Attitudes of Children.* New York: Macmillan.

Pfuhl, Edwin. 1992. "Crimestoppers: The Legitimation of Snitching." *Justice Quarterly* 9, no 3: 505–528.

Poland, James. 1988. *Understanding Terrorism.* Englewood Cliffs, NJ: Prentice Hall.

Poyntz, Stuart. 1997. "Homey, I Shot the Kids: Hollywood and the War on Drugs." *Emergency Librarian* 25, no. 2: 3–9.

Price, James, Elaine Merrill, and Michael Clause. 1992. "The Depiction of Guns on Prime Time Television." *Journal of School Health* 62, no. 1: 15–19.

Pritchard, David, and Karen Hughes. 1997. "Patterns of Deviance in Crime News." *Journal of Communication* 47, no 3: 49–67.

Protess, David, Fay Cook, Jack Doppelt, James Ettema, Magaret Gordon, Donna Leff, and Peter Miller. 1991. *The Journalism of Outrage: Investigative Reporting and Agenda Building in America.* New York: Guilford Press.

"Public Confidence in Selected Institutions, 1973–1996." 1996. *Sourcebook of Criminal Justice Statistics 1995*, Table 2.9. Washington, DC: Bureau of Justice Statistics.

Rafter, Nicole. 2000. *Shots in the Mirror: Crime Films and Society.* Oxford: Oxford University Press.

Rafter, Nicole. 2001. "American Criminal Trial Films: An Overview of Their Development, 1930–2000." *Journal of Law and Society* 28, no. 1: 9–24.

Rapping, Elayne. 2003. *Law and Justice as Seen on TV.* New York: New York University Press.

Reinarman, Craig. 1988. "The Social Construction of an Alcohol Problem: The Case of Mothers against Drunk Drivers and Social Control in the 1980s." *Theory and Society* 17: 91–120.

Reiner, Robert. 1981. "Keystone to Kojak: the Hollywood Cop." In *Cinema, Politics and Society in America,* ed. Philip Davies and Brian Neve, 196–220. New York: St. Martin's Press.

Reiner, Robert. 2000. *The Politics of the Police.* Oxford, UK: Oxford University Press.

Reiner, Robert. 2002. "Media Made Criminality: The Representation of Crime in the Mass Media." In *The Oxford Handbook of Criminology,* ed. Mike Maguire, Rod Morgan, and Robert Reiner, 376–416. Oxford, UK: Oxford University Press.

Reiner, Robert, Sonia Livingstone, and Jessica Allen. 2000. "No More Happy Endings?" In *Crime, Risk and Insecurity,* ed. Tim Hope and Richard Sparks, 107–125. London, UK: Routledge.

Reiner, Robert, Sonia Livingstone, and Jessica Allen. 2003. "From Law and Order to Lynch Mobs: Crime News since the Second World War." In *Criminal Visions: Media Representations of Crime and Justice,* ed. Paul Mason, 13–32. Devon, UK: Willan.

Roberts, Julian, and Anthony Doob. 1990. "News Media Influences on Public Views on Sentencing." *Law and Human Behavior* 14, no. 5: 451–468.

Roberts, Julian, and Loretta Stalans. 1997. *Public Opinion, Crime, and Criminal Justice.* Boulder, CO: Westview Press.

Robinson, Matthew. 2005. *Justice Blind?* Upper Saddle River, NJ: Pearson Prentice Hall.

Rogers, Everett, and James Dearing. 1988. "Agenda-Setting Research: Where Has It Been, Where Is It Going?" In *Communication Yearbook 11,* ed. James A. Anderson, 555–594. Thousand Oaks, CA.: Sage.

Rosenbaum, Dennis, Authur Lurigio, and Paul Lavrakas. 1986. *Crime Stoppers: A National Evaluation of Program Operations and Effects.* Evanston, IL: Center for Urban Affairs and Policy Research, Northwestern University.

Rosenbaum, Dennis, Authur Lurigio, and Paul Lavrakas. 1989. "Enhancing Citizen Participation and Solving Serious Crime: A National Evaluation of Crime Stoppers Programs." *Crime and Delinquency* 35: 401–420.

Roskos-Ewoldsen, David, Beverly Roskos-Ewoldsen, and Francesca Carpentier. 2002. "Media Priming: A Synthesis." In *Media Effects: Advances and Research,* ed. Jennings Bryant and Dolf Zillman, 97–120. Mahwah, NJ: Erlbaum.

Rushkoff, Douglas. 1994. "Media: It's the Real Thing." *NPQ* (Summer): 4–15.

Sacco, Vincent. 2005. *When Crime Waves.* Thousand Oaks, CA: Sage.

Sacco, Vincent, and Robert Silverman. 1981. "Selling Crime Prevention: The Evaluation of a Mass Media Campaign." *Canadian Journal of Criminology* 23: 191–201.

Sasson, Theodore. 1995. *Crime Talk.* Hawthorne, NY: Aldine de Gruyter.

Schank, Roger, and Robert Abelson. 1977. *Scripts, Plans, Goals, and Understanding.* Mahwah, NJ: Erlbaum.

Schechter, Harold. 2003. *The Serial Killer Files.* New York: Ballantine.

Schmid, Alex, and Janny de Graaf. 1982. *Violence as Communication.* Thousand Oaks, CA.: Sage.

Sechrest, Dale, William Liquori, and James Perry. 1990. "Using Video Technology in Police Patrol." In *The Media and Criminal Justice Policy,* ed. Ray Surette, 255–264. Springfield, IL: Thomas.

Shelly, Joseph, and Cindy Ashkins. 1981. "Crime, Crime News, and Crime Views." *Public Opinion Quarterly* 45: 492–506.

Sherwin, Richard. 2000. *When Law Goes Pop: The Vanishing Line between Law and Popular Culture.* Chicago, IL: University of Chicago Press.

Shichor, David, and Dale Sechrest. 1996. *Three Strikes and You're Out: Vengeance as Public Policy.* Thousand Oaks, CA: Sage.

Shipley, Wes, and Gray Cavender. 2001. "Murder and Mayhem at the Movies." *Journal of Criminal Justice and Popular Culture* 9, no. 1: 1–14.

Short, Emma, and Jason Ditton. 1996. *Does Closed Circuit Television Prevent Crime?* Monograph of The Scottish Office Central Research Unit, Edinburgh, Scotland.

Short, Emma, and Jason Ditton. 1998. "Seen and Now Heard." *British Journal of Criminology* 38, no. 3: 404–429.

Shuttleworth, Frank, and Mark May. 1933. *The Social Conduct and Attitudes of Movie Fans.* New York: Macmillan.

Simpson, Philip. 2000. *Psycho Paths: Tracking the Serial Killer through Contemporary American Film and Fiction.* Carbondale, IL: Southern Illinois University Press.

Snell, Clete, Charles Bailey, Anthony Carona, and Dalila Mebane. 2002. "School Crime Policy Changes: The Impact of Recent Highly-Publicized School Crimes." *American Journal of Criminal Justice* 26, no. 2: 280–285.

Sorenson, Susan, Julie Peterson Manz, and Richard Berk. 1998. "News Media Coverage and the Epidemiology of Homicide." *American Journal of Public Health* 88, no. 10: 1510–1514.

Sotirovic, Mira. 2001. "Affective and Cognitive Processes as Mediators of Media Influences on Crime-Policy Preferences." *Mass Communication & Society* 4 (3): 311–329.

*Sourcebook of Criminal Justice Statistics—2000.* 2002. U.S. Department of Justice, Office of Justice Programs. Washington, DC: U.S. Government Printing Office (May).

Sparks, Glenn, and Robert Ogles. 1990. "The Difference between Fear of Victimization and the Probability of Being Victimized: Implications for Cultivation." *Journal of Broadcasting and Electronic Media* 34, no. 3: 351–358.

Sparks, Glenn, and Cheri Sparks. 2002. "Effects of Media Violence." In *Media Effects: Advances in Theory and Research,* ed. Jennings Bryant and Dolf Zillman, 269–285. Mahwah, NJ: Erlbaum.

Spector, Malcolm, and John Kitsuse. 1987. *Constructing Social Problems.* Hawthorne, NY: Aldine de Gruyter.

Stark, Steven. 1987. "Perry Mason Meets Sonny Crockett: The History of Lawyers and the Police as Television Heroes." *University of Miami Law Review* 42: 229–283.

Stark, Steven. 1997. *Glued to the Set.* New York: Dell.

Stevens, John, and Hazel Garcia. 1980. *Communication History.* Thousand Oaks, CA: Sage.

Stewart, David, and Algis Mickunas. 1974. *Exploring Phenomenology.* Chicago: American Library Association.

Sumser, John. 1996. *Morality and Social Order in Television Crime Drama.* Jefferson, NC: McFarland.

Surette, Ray. 1986. "The Mass Media and Criminal Investigations: Crime Stoppers in Dade County, Florida." *Journal of Justice Issues* 1: 21–38.

Surette, Ray. 1989. "Media Trials." *Journal of Criminal Justice* 17: 293–308.

Surette, Ray. 1992. "Methodological Problems in Determining Media Effects on Criminal Justice: A Review and Suggestions for the Future." *Criminal Justice Policy Review* 6, no. 4: 291–310.

Surette, Ray. 1998. "Some Unpopular Thoughts about Popular Culture." In *Popular Culture, Crime and Justice,* ed. Frankie Bailey and Donna Hale, xiv–xxiv. Belmont, CA: Wadsworth.

Surette, Ray. 1999. "Media Echoes: Systemic Effects of News Coverage." *Justice Quarterly* 16: 601–631.

Surette, Ray. 2002. "Self Reported Copy Cat Crime among a Population of Serious Violent Juvenile Offenders." *Crime and Delinquency* 48, no 1: 46–69.

Surette, Ray. 2005. "The Thinking Eye: Pros and Cons of Second Generation CCTV Surveillance Systems." *Policing* 28, no. 1: 152–173.

Surette, Ray, and Greg Noble. 2005. "Working Paper: Media Oriented Terrorism," Orlando, FL: University of Central Florida, Department of Criminal Justice.

Surette, Ray, and Charles Otto. 2002. "A Test of a Crime and Justice Infotainment Measure." *Journal of Criminal Justice* 30, no. 5: 443–453.

Surette, Ray, and Clinton Terry. 1984. "Videotaped Misdemeanor First Appearances: Fairness from the Defendant's Perspective." In *Justice and the Media*, ed. Ray Surette, 305–320. Springfield, IL: Thomas.

Surette, Ray, and Clinton Terry. 1985. "Video in the Misdemeanor Court: The South Florida Experience." *Judicature* 69, no. 1: 13–19.

Tarde, Gabriel. 1912. *Penal Philosophy*. New York: Little Brown.

Thomas, William Isaac. 1908. "The Psychology of Yellow Journalism." *American Magazine* (March).

Thomas, William Isaac. 1951. *Social Behavior and Personality*. Chicago: University of Chicago Press.

Thompson, Carol, Robert Young, and Ronald Burns. 2000. "Representing Gangs in the News: Media Constructions of Criminal Gangs." *Sociological Spectrum* 20: 409–432.

Tilley, Nick. 1993. *Understanding Car Parks, Crime and CCTV: Evaluation Lessons from Safer Cities*. Police Research Group Crime Detection and Prevention Series, paper no 42. London: Home Office.

Todd, Drew. 2000. "The History of Crime Films." In *Shots in the Mirror*, ed. Nicole Rafter, 15–45. Oxford: Oxford University Press.

Toplin, Robert. 1975. *Unchallenged Violence: An American Ordeal*. Westport, CT: Greenwood Press.

"Trial by Media." 1984. *U.S. Press* 10 (30): 4.

Tucher, Andie. 1999–2000. "Framing the Criminal: Trade Secrets of the Crime Reporter." *New York Law School Review* 6, no. 3–4, 905–913.

Tuman, Joseph. 2003. *Communicating Terror: The Rhetorical Dimensions of Terrorism*. Thousand Oaks, CA: Sage.

Tunnel, Kenneth. 1998. "Reflections on Crime, Criminals, and Control in Newsmagazine Television Programs." In *Popular Culture, Crime, and Justice*, ed. Frankie Bailey and Donna Hale, 111–122. Belmont, CA: Wadsworth.

*United States v. Burr*, 25F, Cas 49 (C.C.D. Va. 1807) No. 14692g.

*United States v. Knott*, 368 US 276, 281–82 (1983).

Wardell, Jane. 2004. "4.2 Million Cameras Keep Eye on British." *Orlando Sentinel* (August 15): B2.

Warren, Samuel D., and Louis D. Brandeis. 1890. "The Right to Privacy." *Harvard Law Review* 4, no. 5 (December 15): 193–220.

Wasserman, Elizabeth. 1995. "No Big Deal: O. J. Just Another 'Trial of the Century.'" *Miami Herald* (July 18): 1A, 10A.

Weimann, Gabriel, and Conrad Winn. 1994. *The Theater of Terror: Mass Media and International Terrorism.* White Plains, NY: Longman.

Weinstein, Neil. 1987. "Cross-Hazard Consistencies: Conclusions about Self-Protective Behaviour." In *Taking Care: Understanding and Encouraging Self-Protective Behavior,* ed. Neil Weinstein, 325–336. New York: Cambridge University Press.

Weitzer, Ronald. 2002. "Incidents of Police Misconduct and Public Opinion." *Journal of Criminal Justice* 30: 397–408.

Weitzer, Ronald, and Charis Kubrin. 2004. "Breaking News: How Local TV News and Real-World Conditions Affect Fear of Crime." *Justice Quarterly* 21, no. 3: 497–520.

Welsh, Brandon, and David Farrington. 2002. *Crime Prevention Effects of Closed Circuit Television: A Systematic Review.* Home Office Research Study 252. London: Home Office.

Welsh, Brandon, and David Farrington. 2004. "Evidence-Based Crime Prevention: The Effectiveness of CCTV." *Crime Prevention and Community Safety* 6: 21–33.

Wilbanks, William. 1984. *Murder in Miami: An Analysis of Homicide Patterns and Trends in Dade County (Miami) Florida. 1917–1983.* New York: University Press of America.

Williams, Chris. 2003. "Police Surveillance and the Emergence of CCTV in the 1960s." In *CCTV,* ed. Martin Gill, 9–22. Leicester, UK: Perpetuity.

Wilson, Barbara, Dale Kunkel, Dan Linz, James Potter, Ed Donnerstein, Stacy Smith, Eva Blumenthal, and Timothy Gray. 1997. "Violence in Television Programming Overall: University of California, Santa Barbara Study, Part I." In *National Television Violence Study: Volume 1.* Newbury Park, CA: Sage.

Wilson, Christopher. 2000. *Cop Knowledge.* Chicago, IL: University of Chicago Press.

Wilson, David, and Sean O'Sullivan. 2004. *Images of Incarceration: Representations of Prison in Film and Television.* Winchester, UK: Waterside Press.

Wilson, James Q., and Richard Herrnstein. 1985. *Crime and Human Behavior.* New York: Simon & Schuster.

Wisehart, Marion Karl. [1922] 1968. "Newspapers and Criminal Justice." In *Criminal Justice in Cleveland,* ed. Roscoe Pound and Felix Frankfurter. Montclair, NJ: Patterson Smith.

Yagade, Aileen, and David Dozier. 1990. "The Media Agenda-Setting Effect of Concrete versus Abstract Issues." *Journalism Quarterly* (Spring): 3–11.

Young, Jock. 1999. *The Exclusive Society.* Thousand Oaks, CA: Sage.

Zaner, Laura. 1989. "The Screen Test: Has Hollywood Hurt Corrections' Image?" *Corrections Today* 51: 64–66, 94, 95, 98.

Zillman, Dolf, and Jacob Wakshlag. 1985. "Fear of Victimization and the Appeal of Crime Drama." In *Selective Exposure to Communication,* ed. Dolf Zillman and Jennings Bryant, 141–156. Hillsdale, NJ: Erlbaum.

# Index

Page numbers in bold denote pages where the terms are defined.

# Image Credits